THE POSSIBILITY OF AMAZEMENT

AWAKENING THE FIVE SPIRITUAL FACULTIES

NAGAPRIYA

Windhorse Publications
38 Newmarket Road
Cambridge CB5 8DT
info@windhorsepublications.com
windhorsepublications.com

For General Product Safety Regulation (EU) queries, the authorized representative for Windhorse Publications Ltd is:
Buddhistisches Tor Berlin
Buddhistische Gemeinschaft
Triratna (Berlin) E.V.
Grimmstrasse 11B-C
10967 Berlin-Kreuzberg
info@buddhistisches-tor-berlin.de

Cover design: Dhammarati
Cover image: Photograph of detail from *The Fighting Temeraire* by J.M.W. Turner, National Gallery, London, by Sailko
Typesetting by Tarajyoti

British Library Cataloguing in Publication Data:
A catalogue record for this book is available from the British Library.

ISBN 978-1-915342-69-0

In memory of my teacher, Urgyen Sangharakshita
With much gratitude for all that he shared

Praise for *The Possibility of Amazement: Awakening the Five Spiritual Faculties*

The model of the five spiritual faculties is surely one of the most helpful ways that the Buddha presented his teaching. I was fortunate to attend Sangharakshita's seminar on the faculties in 1978 – later published as *The Way to Wisdom* – and I have always found this teaching an ideal way to approach Dharma practice in its depth and its breadth. Now, firmly within the tradition of Dharma teaching established by Sangharakshita, Nagapriya has brought his own fresh and original mind to bear on the subject – prepare to be inspired, challenged, awakened, and above all amazed. – **Mahamati**, Chair of the Triratna Buddhist Order's College of Public Preceptors

Bringing a concept from one culture or historical period to another can be risky. Words that are prominent in the English language simply don't exist in Sanskrit. Idioms can get lost in translation. And yet, as the poet Borges put it, without translation a tale must always be identically twice told, 'where a word can only be translated by itself.' In *The Possibility of Amazement* Nagapriya takes on this challenge to deftly explain the five spiritual faculties in their Buddhist contexts. Along the way, the reader encounters Borges' poetry, the art of Van Gogh and Rothko, and the philosophies of Marion, Bachelard, and Chrétien. Throughout, Nagapriya's own imaginative life of faith comes into view as he persistently pursues fresh insight into the meaning of key teachings. – **Dr Timothy Stanley**, Associate Professor in the School of Humanities, Creative Industries and Social Sciences, the University of Newcastle, Australia

I loved reading *The Possibility of Amazement*. The vision of life and Buddhist practice that Nagapriya opens out to us in his book is a potent one. It is a vision filled with energy, with curiosity, and with heart. It overflows. His book invokes a vibrant space which shimmers with possibility, and yet at the same time is real, grounded, and true. – **Subhadassi**

Nagapriya invites us to recover our sense that the sacred is not apart from the world but reveals itself whenever we are awake to it. Here is Buddhism in all its glory! – **Subhadramati**, author of *Not About Being Good: A Practical Guide to Buddhist Ethics*

Contents

About the Author

Nagapriya was born in the UK in 1969. While studying for a philosophy degree in Leeds, he began practising with the Triratna Buddhist Community and was ordained as a Dharmachari in 1992. He later completed a master's in the history of religions at the University of Manchester. Since 2013, he has been based in Mexico, where he helped found the Centro Budista de Cuernavaca. He is also co-founder and director of Editorial Dharmamegha, a publishing venture dedicated to sharing Buddhist teachings in the Spanish-speaking world. In addition, he is part of a team training men from Latin America for ordination into the Triratna Buddhist Order. Since 2019, he has been a member of the College of Public Preceptors.

Nagapriya's other books include: *Exploring Karma and Rebirth* (Windhorse Publications, 2004), *Seeing Like a Buddha: The Four Noble Truths* (Triratna Inhouse Publications, 2020), and *The Promise of a Sacred World: Shinran's Teaching of Other Power* (Windhorse Publications, 2022).

Author's Acknowledgements

Many kind benefactors have enabled this book to appear. Above all, Urgyen Sangharakshita, whose interest in the five spiritual faculties and whose spectacular spiritual imagination inspired the present work. Ongoing thanks are due to my study companion Dayamati, who kindly reads all my early drafts and offers very helpful guidance – even when he says very little. He is an invaluable witness. My thanks go likewise to my dear friend Subhadassi for many insightful reflections and suggestions. Thanks also to Ratnaprabha for some helpful remarks and tweaks. I also thank Dr Tim Stanley for stimulating philosophical dialogue and encouragement. As always, clouds of gratitude to my preceptor Subhuti for his inspiring example and unstinting friendship.

Some parts of this book are based on talks, courses, workshops, and retreats that I have offered over the past two or three years, mainly here in Mexico. Thanks to all those who participated in those contexts and thereby contributed to the development of my thoughts. A couple of sections had their genesis as proposed articles for *Tricycle* magazine; I am grateful for the editorial interest and stimulation.

Many other friends and colleagues offered comments that sparked productive reveries, often without knowing it. You are too many to list here, but I am deeply grateful to all of you. Finally, huge thanks to Windhorse Publications, and especially to Jñanasiddhi, for her confidence in this project and for her reminder to unpack some of the denser phenomenological passages. Needless to say, any shortcomings are my responsibility.

Publisher's Acknowledgements

We would like to thank the individuals who supported this book through our 'Sponsor-a-book' campaign (www.windhorse publications.com/sponsor) and the Friends of Windhorse Publications initiative (www.windhorsepublications.com/friends).

Windhorse Publications wish to gratefully acknowledge a grant from Future Dharma and the Triratna European Chairs' Assembly Fund towards the production of this book.

FUTURE DHARMA

Triratna
European Chairs Assembly

Foreword

As Buddhism evolved into an organized discipline comprising sets of theories and practices, an often-used form of presentation was a list. There were lists of skilful and unskilful actions, healthy and unhealthy mentalities, virtues and vices; there were lists of types of contemplative practice, levels of depths of concentration, ways of manifesting friendship; there were even lists of lists.

Lists, as such, can be rather dry and lifeless. What breathes life into all these lists is commentaries, whether oral or written. Life, by its very nature, is change and adaptation. Every culture that embraced Buddhism, and every generation of followers of Buddhism within those cultures, found ways to make the lists it had received meaningful and relevant. It is in this sense that the lists have been the DNA of a living body of teachings rather than dead letters.

One such framework central to Buddhist thought is what this book calls the five spiritual faculties. In Sanskrit, this list was sometimes called the *panca balani*, or five strengths. It was also called the *panca indriyani*, a term so rich in connotations that it is impossible to translate with a single English word. Among the meanings of *indriya* is 'a power', 'a controlling principle', 'a faculty', 'a function', 'a directive force', 'a dynamic'. Calling the *panca indriyani* the five spiritual faculties does the term justice.

The Sanskrit words for the five items on this list are *shraddha, virya, smrti, samadhi,* and *prajna.* Each of these terms, like the term *indriya,* can be translated in more than one way. In this book, Nagapriya has rendered them 'trust', 'vigour', 'mindfulness', 'meditation', and 'wisdom'. People who have read other authors presenting Buddhist thought in English may have encountered *shraddha* translated as 'faith' or 'confidence', *virya* as 'heroic energy', and *samadhi* as 'concentration'. The term *smrti* is nearly always translated as 'mindfulness', but the word literally means 'remembering'. Nagapriya's treatment of the term contains numerous insights into memory as a phenomenon, and, more importantly, as an indispensable feature of ethical conduct or moral hygiene.

Each culture and each generation that has embraced Buddhist theory and practice has found its own way of breathing life into this list of five faculties and other such lists. Nagapriya continues this tradition. His treatment reflects the breadth of his intellectual formation and the depth of his spiritual maturity, as well as his humility in using himself as an example of the challenges all human beings face in cultivating these five deceptively simple spiritual faculties.

Nagapriya's formal education was in philosophy, an interest he has maintained throughout his adult life by reading widely and reflecting deeply. Fortunately for us readers, he has a gift for making profound and sometimes abstruse ideas accessible and even enjoyable. The élan of good philosophy permeates his writing, as does an acute aesthetic sensibility – a fondness for poetry, literature, and the visual arts. His exploration of Buddhist teachings is equally broad: drawing on the Pali canon of Theravada Buddhism, the various sutras of Indian and Tibetan Mahayana, and East Asian Buddhism, including Zen and Pure Land. Indeed, his previous book, *The Promise of a Sacred World*, is a lively and thoughtful exploration of the writings of Shinran, the founder of the Jodo Shinshu school. The spirit of that book is continued and expanded in the present book, as is reflected in its title, *The Possibility of Amazement*.

Nagapriya's solid intellectual foundation is informed by his spiritual maturity as a practitioner of the Buddhist path, especially as presented in the Triratna Buddhist Order. In the present work, as in Nagapriya's previous writings, one finds a conviction that Buddhism has far more depth than is apparent in many modern Western presentations that portray it as little more than another pragmatic, secular, evidence-based system of humanistic self-improvement. While he is fully aware that many Buddhists and Buddhist sympathizers in the modern West have a reluctance to embrace teachings and practices that remind them of religions at the more narrow-minded, intolerant, and authoritarian end of the religious spectrum, Nagapriya extends an invitation to his readers to let themselves be amazed, awestruck, and enlivened by the often-overlooked possibility of becoming unstuck from the swamplands of despair, negativity, and cynicism that characterize so much of everyday Western society. It is an invitation well worth accepting.

Dayamati Richard Hayes

Preface

The teaching of the five spiritual faculties is one among many Buddhist formulas. Why, then, does it merit special attention? Each faculty radiates its own light, yet all interpenetrate, forming a sacred array – more a constellation than a ladder. My own teacher, Sangharakshita, was drawn to this pattern of awakened perception and returned to it on several occasions. In his magnum opus, *A Survey of Buddhism*, he structured his appraisal of Mahayana Buddhism around this model, interpreting each major school through the lens of a distinctive spiritual faculty. I believe he was attracted to this pattern because it reflects the way transformation unfolds – not as a linear ascent but as an ever-deepening enrichment of awareness. It offers a broad vision of Buddhist practice, one that values an integrated profile of spiritual qualities rather than prizing just a single one exclusively. More precisely, Sangharakshita insisted, the five spiritual faculties 'must be regarded as one whole, because you and your spiritual life must be regarded as one whole'.[1]

This book mines a number of overlapping seams – traditionally Buddhist, philosophical, poetic, autobiographical, and religious. While the teaching of the five spiritual faculties originates in early Buddhism, my elaboration also draws on insights and themes from a range of later developments – especially from Mahayana Buddhism, and specifically Pure Land perspectives, but also Vajrayana and Zen.

The five spiritual faculties can be understood as openings onto particular dimensions of awakened experience. Since they form a kind of mandala – an integrated whole in which each element interpenetrates the others – they do not follow a necessary sequence. One can enter the mandala at any point. This means that, rather than reading the chapters of this book sequentially, you could just as readily approach them in any order. If you are new to the five spiritual faculties, you may prefer to begin with Chapter 1 and then read the even-numbered chapters first.

The main body of the book devotes two chapters to each of the five spiritual faculties. Broadly, the first outlines the faculty as traditionally understood, often drawing on canonical Buddhist texts to trace its principal features. The second elaborates on particular aspects of the faculty in view, regularly borrowing from sources outside Buddhism to enrich key points. This division is not always rigid – the two kinds of chapters often speak to each other as they finesse particular themes.

An overriding concern of the present work – as it was in my previous book, *The Promise of a Sacred World* – is to develop a religious vocabulary through which to articulate Buddhist concerns. Even breathing that word 'religious' makes me a little uneasy, since I know it carries unhelpful baggage for many people. Still, in the Western reception of Buddhism, it has been far more common to frame it in terms of self-growth and secular psychology than to trust in explicitly religious language. Yet religion is concerned, above all, with coming into relation with the transcendent – however that may be understood – and with how that relation shapes the unfolding of our lives. The German theologian Friedrich Schleiermacher (1768–1834) believed 'true religion is sense and taste for the Infinite.'[2] It invites an amazed contemplation of the infinite. It concerns the ultimate purpose of human existence.

Many Westerners drawn to Buddhism are explicitly rejecting their religious inheritance, which is often Christian. It has become more common to justify Buddhism in the light of science than in that of revelation. As a consequence, this can give rise to a secularized, even blanched perception of Buddhism that strips it of all *glory*: its faith, its devotion, its myth, and its poetry.

It is revealing to notice what images, what metaphors, what styles of thinking repeatedly call our attention. If an image, in the broadest sense, calls us back, then it has something to give to us. In my recent exploration of Buddhist thought, I have focused especially on themes related to the transcendent – what some schools refer to as Other Power. Surprisingly, I have found a strong resonance with phenomenology, particularly in the work of several French philosophers, including Jean-Luc Marion and Gaston Bachelard.

'Phenomenology' is not a word everyone uses at the corner store, yet it points to a process that all of us are constantly engaged in: the interpretation of our always-unfolding experience. We often take this process for granted, assuming that it is given rather than chosen. Yet it is precisely when we step back to contemplate the wonders of consciousness that new possibilities of meaning and direction open up. To be a self-aware being is mysterious, astonishing, and ultimately sacramental. The habitual nature of life – and the clumsy narratives we fall into – means that we readily lose touch with the perpetual miracle that is conscious experience. It becomes 'no big deal', ceases to be a source of curiosity, and thus we overlook the ever-present opportunity for wonder and blessing. One way to understand this book, and the five spiritual faculties as a whole, is as an invitation to recover a sense of amazement. Consciousness itself is extraordinary, open, and bursting with possibilities that can never be exhausted. Mary Oliver evokes a spirit of humble, reverent amazement in her poem 'Mysteries, yes':

> Let me keep my distance, always, from those
> who think they have the answers.
> Let me keep company always with those who say
> 'Look!' and laugh in astonishment,
> and bow their heads.[3]

Every moment holds out the possibility of amazement. Every moment may lift itself to the dignity of a sacred disclosure, a revelation. What is amazing disrupts the flow of habit; it overwhelms our ready-made categories. In doing so, it opens up the possibility of a sacramental life. Infinite light is promised in any instant of awareness.

Instructions for living a life:

Pay attention.
Be astonished.
Tell about it.

Mary Oliver[4]

1

Awakening Our Spiritual Senses

> There are these five faculties. What five? The faculty of faith, the faculty of energy, the faculty of mindfulness, the faculty of concentration, the faculty of wisdom. These are the five faculties.
>
> One who has completed and fulfilled these five faculties is an arahant [...] one in whom these five faculties are completely and totally absent is 'an outsider', one who stands in the faction of worldlings.[5]

The Sacred Horizon

At the risk of sounding anti-Buddhist, I used to believe I could become enlightened – but now I know I can't. Let me explain. I first encountered Buddhism as a teenager. Drunk on enthusiasm, I embraced the ideal of Enlightenment as a heroic, personal quest. I imagined it as an extension – perhaps even an inflation – of myself: I would still be me, only vastly improved. I saw it as a goal within reach, a personal achievement that could be commemorated with a proudly worn pin. People might look at me with awe, and perhaps even a little envy. Imperious, I would live in glory.

Years later, that hubris collapsed. I came to see that my self-willed striving wasn't lifting me out of ignorance but dragging me still deeper into it. The more I struggled to break free, the more tightly the fetters bound me. But, in that despair, I discovered I wasn't alone. Centuries earlier, the Japanese master Shinran had confronted the same disillusionment: a painful admission of his inability to overcome his deep-rooted failings.[6] In one of his *wasan* (hymns), for example, he confesses:

> I am such that I do not know right and wrong
> And cannot distinguish false and true;
> I lack even small love and small compassion,
> And yet, for fame and profit, enjoy teaching others.[7]

Through Shinran, I encountered the teaching of Other Power, embodied in the transcendent Buddha Amitabha.

Enlightenment ceased to be a destination to reach, a summit to conquer, and became, instead, a sacred horizon, its light infusing meaning into my everyday routine. Dharma practice is no longer a means to an end but a continuous act of entrusting. It is a surrender to the impulse to go for refuge and an opening to a wise, compassionate summons that is always calling upon me. I no longer need to gird myself in heroic effort but awaken instead to subtle capacities – new senses. Even when floundering and in doubt, my ability to hear that summons shows how I remain attuned to it.

Buddhism draws on a glittering parade of images and metaphors to evoke the sublime possibilities of human potential. It speaks of Enlightenment or Awakening, of liberation, and of purification. One especially compelling image that vividly symbolizes our present spiritual condition comes from the *Larger Pure Land Sutra*. According to this scripture, those beings who lack the karmic conditions and trusting confidence to be born directly into Buddha Amitabha's Pure Land are instead enclosed within a sealed lotus bud.[8] For 500 years they remain trapped like this: unable to see the Buddha, hear the Dharma teachings, or commune with the Sangha (spiritual community). They are cut off from the three jewels, the most precious values of Buddhism.

At first glance, this might seem a harsh fate. Yet the image speaks less of punishment than of process. The closed lotus symbolizes the veils of delusion that still cloud our vision – our persistent alienation from the transcendent, our resistance to fully entrust ourselves to the truth. But, even in this contemplative darkness, something is stirring. The time within the lotus is not wasted. It is a sacred vigil of gestation and purification – an inward preparation – until the spiritual senses are mature enough to open at last to the light.

This transcendent drama evokes a world of expanded dimensions. It attests to a gradual, organic growth, a harmonious unfurling that serves as a captivating image for the teaching of the five spiritual faculties. Rather than a narrow, linear ascent, which might appear to leave the previous stages behind, this compelling model of Awakening affirms a balanced and integrated unfoldment – a sacred and bedazzling array.

The Limits of the Path

We depend on images and metaphors to convey truths that lie beyond the reach of literal expression, yet they can become so familiar, so habitual, that we forget that they are poetic invitations – ways of pointing towards what is mysterious, invisible, and unspeakable. Take, for instance, the image of the path (*marga*), one of Buddhism's central metaphors.[9] We find formulations of it everywhere: the eightfold path, the threefold path, the middle path or way, the path of purification, and the path of regular steps.

In one well-known early scripture, the Buddha likens his realization to the rediscovery of an ancient path in the forest, one that leads to a long-abandoned but magnificent city.[10] Just as someone might stumble upon and clear such a forgotten trail, the Buddha declares that he has found an ancient route once travelled by fully awakened buddhas of the past. He can now guide others along this path. That path, he says, is the noble eightfold path, and the city at its end is none other than nirvana, the ultimate destination of the Buddhist journey.

Thinking of practice in terms of a path can be very helpful. It gives us a sense of direction, of movement, even a sense of progress. But, like any metaphor, it has its limits. If we focus too much on the destination, we can miss out on the beauty of the journey itself – the vivid scenery, the unrepeatable moments, the connections we make along the way. Moreover, the goal of a self-willed path can resemble a receding horizon: always visible, yet never quite within reach. If we imagine Awakening as a point we are supposed to arrive at, we may end up feeling frustrated or inadequate, perpetually measuring ourselves against an imagined future state. In such moments, practice can lose its vitality and become burdensome.

Sometimes we rush ahead, skipping steps and fooling ourselves that we're further along than we truly are. At other times, we sprint for a while, only to burn out or lose momentum. Sangharakshita called this dynamic 'the path of irregular steps' – a pattern of practice marked by bursts of effort rather than steady, consistent progress.[11] The idea of *regular steps* can be helpful here, suggesting a more grounded and sustainable rhythm. Yet this metaphor, too, can mislead if taken to mean that Awakening unfolds according to a fixed sequence. In reality, the eightfold path – like the threefold path of ethics, meditation, and wisdom – can also be understood not as a linear progression, but as a set of interrelated qualities, each supporting the others. These aren't milestones to be passed and left behind, but expanding dimensions of practice.

A preoccupation with 'progress' can readily provoke *spiritual bypassing* – an unhealthy tendency to convince ourselves that we've moved beyond uncomfortable emotions, limiting habits, or unmet needs, rather than turning towards them with honesty and patience. In doing so, we may subtly distort our experience, reassuring ourselves that our efforts are bearing fruit even when deeper issues remain unresolved. We may, for example, use our apparent progress to offset feelings of inadequacy. If we use spiritual practice to avoid facing unresolved emotional issues, psychological wounds, and unfinished developmental work, it merely reinforces internal division, and results in us not being fully present.

The language of progress can also draw us into unhelpful comparison. We may begin to measure ourselves against others – seeing ourselves as ahead or behind, superior or inferior. This mindset easily gives rise to arrogance or discouragement, subtly reinforcing the very ego we are attempting to loosen, and generating further suffering rather than alleviating it.

There are no shortcuts on the journey of self-transformation. At times, the process is messy, even undignified, as hidden or long-avoided aspects of ourselves emerge. Yet genuine growth requires this willingness to face – and ultimately to integrate – the darkness within, as well as the light.

The Parable of the White Path

The metaphor of the path emphasizes the efforts of the individual as agent and initiator, implying that liberation is achieved primarily through willpower. Pure Land Buddhism offers a different understanding, vividly dramatized in the Parable of the White Path.[12]

In this story, a solitary traveller fleeing bandits and wild beasts encounters two vast rivers – one of fire, another of water. Between them lies a narrow white path, barely wide enough to pass. Desperate and trapped, the traveller hears a voice from the bank behind him (the historical buddha, Shakyamuni) urging him forward, and a voice from the far bank (the transcendent buddha, Amitabha or Amida) beckoning him to safety. Though the bandits menace him and doubt rises within him, the traveller entrusts himself to the path and takes the first steps. Eventually, he reaches the far bank, where he is greeted with relief and joy.

This parable offers a contrast to the daring ideal of self-powered Enlightenment. The traveller is no invincible hero, but an ordinary human being, prone to fear and doubt. His movement forward comes not from certainty or boldness, but from trust – responding to a call that meets him in his moment of need. The Pure Land promises itself as a transformation of consciousness, an opening onto an infinite range. Borrowing from John Caputo, we might say it bursts towards us as 'something for which no horizon of possibility or foreseeability is able to prepare us, something that contradicts our mundane expectations'.[13]

The Metaphor of the Senses

The five spiritual faculties are a model of transformation inspired by the metaphor of enhanced senses. Our common-sense perspective holds that our senses are not only reliable but comprehensive. We assume that our senses embrace the entire spectrum of what can be seen, heard, felt, smelled, and tasted. But we also know that dogs can smell many things that we cannot; some reports suggest that their sense of smell is up to 100,000 times stronger than ours.[14] We know that most birds can see ultraviolet light, but we cannot. It was once thought that there were only five senses, but neurobiologists now estimate there could be more than thirty.[15] For instance, nearly all life forms – including humans – have a circadian sense, an internal timekeeper, which functions even when deprived of light and dark. The swamp-dwelling star-nosed mole has twenty-two tiny tentacles on its spectacular snout, which means it can taste prey underwater using air bubbles. It boasts the most sensitive touch organ of any mammal yet recorded. Octopuses are masters of proprioception (the sixth sense of self-movement and body-position awareness). Other animals, including sharks and platypuses, possess electroreception:

the capacity to perceive electrical stimuli, which helps them to detect and locate prey. We do not. Despite our common-sense assumption, then, we know that there are more refined examples of the senses we do possess, and modes of sensing that are not available to us.

We place immense value on our outer senses, and are typically completely immersed in them. Buddhism, however, gives privileged attention to the mind, which it regards as a further kind of sense organ. While not dismissing the outer senses, Buddhism focuses far more on exploring the contents and possibilities of the inner senses that the mind confers. These inner senses are often poorly developed, which means we often don't really know what we think, feel, or believe. We fail to see the connections between our views, emotions, and actions, and often can't distinguish between raw feeling and the stories we tell ourselves. This results in a great deal of suffering.

Moreover, we are often not attuned to value, specifically, we are not receptive to the transcendent – to that which summons us beyond ourselves, our ultimate concern. Buddhism affirms the possibility of an expanded life horizon, which it calls Enlightenment or Awakening. The very notion of Awakening suggests that we are dozing, not fully attentive to what is happening. When we finally wake up, when we pay full attention, everything suddenly becomes more vivid, present, intense, and even more real. Awakening is primarily concerned with activating the latent capacities of the mind.

We tend to assume that perception is uniform – that our way of perceiving is the only way. Consequently, when we think of others, and of other creatures, we project our own perceptual framework onto them, imagining that they experience the world just as we do. If we imagine an enlightened being, we likely assume they perceive in much the same way, albeit in more vivid colour, intensity, and clarity. Rarely do we consider the possibility that they may awaken to additional senses that enable entirely new modes of perception.

'Spiritual Superpowers': The Higher Modes of Knowledge (*Abhijnas*)

The idea of becoming a spiritual superhero can be quite seductive. There is something alluring about the prospect that, through deep practice, we might gain powers or abilities beyond the ordinary – such as reading minds, walking through walls, or even travelling to distant realms. The belief that we might cultivate special capacities that others lack can give us a sense of power and greater agency. Many an Indian mystic has built a following by supposedly producing ash from his palms or turning water into ghee. Early Buddhism does not entirely dismiss such possibilities. In fact, it speaks of *abhijnas*, or 'higher knowledges', which are extraordinary abilities that may arise from deep meditation. In broad strokes, these higher knowledges signify an expansion of awareness beyond the limits of ordinary perception and are traditionally listed as six:

1. **Psychic power** (*iddhi-vidha*): abilities such as walking on water or appearing in multiple places simultaneously
2. **Clairaudience** (*dibba-sota*): the capacity to hear distant or subtle sounds, including those from celestial realms

3. **Telepathy** (*ceto-pariya-jnana*): knowing the thoughts and mental states of others
4. **Recollection of past lives** (*pubbe-nivasanussati-jnana*): a deep memory of one's previous births
5. **Divine sight** (*dibba-cakkhu*): the ability to see the arising and passing away of beings according to their karma
6. **Knowledge of the ending of the taints** (*asavakkhaya-jnana*): direct insight that cuts through delusion and leads to complete liberation.

It is important to place these supernormal powers in the context of the Buddhist vision of liberation. While the first five may seem spectacular, they are not the goal of the path. At best, they are by-products – indications that the mind is becoming more subtle and sensitive. At worst, they may become traps, reinforcing the very egocentric tendencies that the path seeks to attenuate. They may even result in delusions of grandeur. There is a Zen story that puts these powers into perspective. Master Huangbo (died 850) is travelling with a fellow monk when they come to a swollen river. The master pauses. He invites the other monk to cross. Gathering up his robes, the monk proceeds to stroll across the water as though treading on firm ground. 'You self-perfected fellow!' Huangbo barks. 'If I had known you would concoct wonders, I would have broken your legs!' The admonished monk sighs in admiration: Huangbo cuts through the display, reminding him that spiritual practice concerns transformation, not marvels.[16]

The sixth *abhijna*, by contrast, points to what truly matters. It signifies a mind that has seen through greed, hatred, and delusion – a mind no longer bound by the patterns that cause suffering. This, and this alone, is the knowledge that liberates.

While tales of supernormal powers may captivate the imagination, Buddhism teaches that the true miracle lies not in walking on water or soaring through the air, but in the purification of heart and mind, in the arising of the bodhicitta, the profound shift from self-centredness to wisdom and compassion. This is the power truly worth cultivating.

Awakening New Senses: The Five Spiritual Faculties

The five spiritual faculties offer a model of transformation that complements the image of the path. A faculty may be defined as an inherent physical or mental capacity or power. In fact, the five spiritual faculties are sometimes referred to as the five spiritual *powers*. A faculty is also an aptitude or talent for something. Really, we are speaking of expanded possibilities of feeling, connecting, even sensing; possibilities that transcend our ordinary mode of functioning, giving us greater access to reality, to meaning, and to what is of ultimate value. The five spiritual faculties are modes of attunement to the transcendent.

In Sanskrit and Pali, the five spiritual faculties are known as *indriya*s, literally meaning 'that which belongs to Indra'. According to Indian mythology, Indra is the chief of the gods. Each *indriya*, by association, fulfils the role of a ruler within its particular domain. Thus, the *indriya*s may be understood as 'governing or controlling principles'.[17]

The five regular senses (or six, including the mind) are also known as *indriya*s, since much of human life as we ordinarily live it is shaped and directed by these faculties. Most of the time, they determine how we think, feel, and act. This is especially noticeable when we wake in the morning. While we sleep, our senses are mostly quiet, but, as soon as we awaken, they stir into life. The senses look for things to latch on to: we might make a cup of coffee, reach for our smartphone, or even decide to laze in bed a bit longer. All day long, the senses reach out to the world, responding to what we see, hear, smell, taste, touch, and think, and, because this happens so constantly, we begin to identify ourselves with them – believing we are merely our body and mind reacting to the world. We become intoxicated by sensory input. Most of the time, we live on this rudimentary level, simply following the impulses the senses provide.

The fact that the *indriya*s signify not just the ordinary five physical senses but also the five spiritual faculties is no coincidence. It suggests that the spiritual faculties are as central to the inner life as the physical senses are to everyday experience. The two sets of *indriya*s serve an equivalent role: just as the five senses inform how we engage with the physical world, the five spiritual faculties guide and shape our spiritual journey – they orient us towards Awakening.

While our physical senses are relatively well developed, our spiritual faculties tend to be more nascent: like seeds that have yet to grow. One way to understand the process of Awakening is as one of cultivating and refining these five spiritual senses, which are:

- *Shraddha* – faith, trust, or conviction in the three jewels
- *Prajna* – wisdom or intuitive understanding

- *Virya* – vigour, energy, or courageous persistence
- *Samadhi* – meditation, mental focus, and creative imagination
- *Smrti* – mindfulness or recollection.[18]

We find accounts of the five spiritual faculties throughout the Pali canon. Here is one example:

> Bhikkhus, there are these five faculties. What five? The faculty of faith [...] the faculty of wisdom.
>
> And what, bhikkhus, is the faculty of faith? Here, bhikkhus, the noble disciple is a person of faith, one who places faith in the enlightenment of the Tathagata thus: 'The Blessed One is an arahant, perfectly enlightened, accomplished in knowledge and conduct, fortunate, knower of the world, unsurpassed leader of persons to be tamed, teacher of devas and humans, the Enlightened One, the Blessed One.'
>
> And what, bhikkhus, is the faculty of energy? Here, bhikkhus, the noble disciple dwells with energy aroused for the abandoning of unwholesome states and the acquisition of wholesome states; he is strong, firm in exertion, not shirking the responsibility of cultivating wholesome states. This is called the faculty of energy.
>
> And what, bhikkhus, is the faculty of mindfulness? Here, bhikkhus, the noble disciple is mindful, possessing supreme mindfulness and discretion, one who remembers and recollects what was done and said long ago. This is called the faculty of mindfulness.

> And what, bhikkhus, is the faculty of concentration? Here, bhikkhus, the noble disciple gains concentration, gains one-pointedness of mind, having made release the object. This is called the faculty of concentration.
>
> And what, bhikkhus, is the faculty of wisdom? Here, bhikkhus, the noble disciple is wise; he possesses wisdom directed to arising and passing away, which is noble and penetrative, leading to the complete destruction of suffering. This is called the faculty of wisdom.
>
> These, bhikkhus, are the five faculties.[19]

We might say that these five qualities are archetypes or figures of religious consciousness. In *A Survey of Buddhism*, Sangharakshita highlights the five spiritual faculties as 'one of the earliest and most important classifications of the Buddha's teachings'.[20] He applies this formative model to make sense of developments in later Buddhism now known as Mahayana: Pure Land traditions align with *shraddha*, Madhyamaka with *prajna*, Tantra with *virya*, and Zen with *samadhi*. He stresses that these schools are not really separate – studying just one in isolation is insufficient. 'They are a whole and must be studied and followed as a whole', he says.[21] Mindfulness, he adds, 'is represented by the spirit of tolerance which is diffused through all the schools and which holds them together as "moments" in the Mahayana-concept'.[22] For Sangharakshita, the five spiritual faculties are vital not only in the life of the individual Buddhist but also in the flourishing of any healthy Buddhist tradition.[23]

The importance of the five spiritual faculties is underscored by the fact that they appear twice in the compendium of lists known as the *bodhipaksya-dharmas* – the thirty-seven principles that support the path to Enlightenment.[24] This list, which aims to encompass all the core teachings of early Buddhism, includes them once as the five faculties and again as the five powers (*balas*). When, through consistent practice, these faculties are strengthened to the point where they can no longer be overrun by the passions, they become *balas* – powers or inner forces.

The Five Spiritual Faculties and Integration

The five spiritual faculties, traditionally known as the 'controlling' faculties, can be presented and analyzed in various ways. Each one masters a specific opposite: trust or conviction overcomes doubt and indecision; vigour or energy overcomes laziness and inertia; mindfulness overcomes inattentiveness; concentration or meditation overcomes agitation and dispersion; and wisdom overcomes ignorance. Thus, each faculty functions as an antidote to a particular spiritual obstacle.

Secondly, some texts present the five spiritual faculties as a sequence in which trust, vigour, mindfulness, and concentration culminate in wisdom as their 'chief':

> The lion, king of beasts, is said to be supreme among animals in strength, speed, and courage. In the same way, the faculty of wisdom is foremost among the qualities that lead to awakening.[25]

In a similar vein, using the analogy of a house, the Buddha teaches that the stability and functioning of the other four faculties depend upon wisdom. Just as the rafters of a roof remain unsteady until the central ridge is set in place, so too do trust, vigour, mindfulness, and concentration remain incomplete until noble wisdom has fully arisen. Only when supported by wisdom can these faculties come into proper alignment and so reach full maturity.[26]

A third way of understanding the five spiritual faculties highlights their balance and mutual support.[27] The faculties don't function in isolation – their efficacy lies in their dynamic interplay. Especially significant are the complementary relationships between trust and wisdom, and between energy and meditation.

When trust is strong but wisdom underdeveloped, it may result in a naïve or uncritical confidence – a kind of spiritual enthusiasm untempered by discernment, even a dogmatic blindness. Conversely, if wisdom is cultivated without trust, it may harden into cynicism or mere cleverness – a sharp intellect devoid of imagination and sensitivity to the transcendent. Such a person, the texts warn, is as difficult to help as a patient harmed by their own cure.[28] But when conviction and wisdom are held in balance, they foster receptivity, clarity, and a robust intuition of higher values.

A similar dynamic operates between energy and meditation. Without sufficient energy, meditation can tend towards complacency – a self-satisfied stillness devoid of self-scrutiny and transformative force. Conversely, energy without the stabilizing influence of meditation readily tips into restlessness or agitation.

It's not that we can genuinely possess 'too much' trust, wisdom, concentration, or vigour; rather, these qualities have 'shadows', and so our faculties may develop in distorted ways.

For this reason, mindfulness acts as the regulating faculty, the integrating thread that holds the others together. It serves as a guardian, protecting against the overexuberance of faith, the overdrive of energy, and even the dry superiority of ungrounded wisdom, while also guarding against the somnolent inertia that may accompany meditative calm. In every instance, mindfulness keeps the mind attuned – anchored in the present while remaining open to transformation. As Buddhaghosa beautifully puts it, mindfulness 'is as desirable in all instances as a seasoning of salt in all sauces, as a prime minister in all the king's business'.[29]

The five spiritual faculties evoke the image of a mandala, symbolizing the integration of our inner capacities in service of our highest purpose. At its centre lies mindfulness, with the remaining faculties – faith, energy, concentration, and wisdom – arranged in harmonious orbit around it. In cultivating them all, our whole being becomes unified at ever deeper and higher levels. Just as our five physical senses combine to create a coherent perceptual moment, so too do the spiritual faculties enable us to discern what is transcendent and to live in the light of its revelation. Sangharakshita argues that collectively the five spiritual faculties constitute 'a complete harmonious unfoldment of all the aspects of the individual human being'.[30] In this sense, we could also say that each of the faculties implies, or even contains, the others. At the same time, each brings into focus a particular aspect of an enlightened mode of perception.

Even so, the five faculties need not be active in equal measure at all times. Just as particular senses become more acute in certain circumstances, the requirements of different situations naturally call forth specific faculties. In devotional practice, for instance, the faculty of trust assumes a guiding role. During periods of sustained stillness, such as a solitary retreat, *samadhi* comes quietly to the fore. When we turn to study and reflection, wisdom becomes our leading edge. And when we engage with the resistances and challenges of daily life, vigour carries us forward. It's not a matter of engineering situations to cultivate a single faculty, but one of learning to call forth what each moment asks of us. In this way, our Dharma practice remains dynamic, responsive, and attuned to the ever-shifting conditions of existence.

The Five Spiritual Faculties as Infused

Initially, we may understand the five spiritual faculties as cultivated through individual, self-willed effort and disciplined practice. But it is also possible to understand them as *gifted*, as bestowed, and even as a form of blessing or grace. These two modalities can be compared with the notion of acquired and infused virtues as elaborated in scholastic Christianity.[31] The natural or cardinal virtues – namely prudence, justice, temperance, and fortitude – are typically understood to be *acquired*. They are ethical tendencies we embody by means of systematic cultivation – or, in Buddhist terms, through consistently skilful action. We can describe this as a self-power model. The supernatural or theological virtues – that is, faith, hope, and charity – in contrast, are not dependent on self-willed goodness but rather are gifted or *infused* by means of grace. This exemplifies an Other Power model. Once the infused virtues permeate our being, they come to supersede the acquired virtues, as they are oriented not to the pursuit of mundane happiness and fulfilment but rather towards the transcendent – in Buddhist terms, towards Enlightenment.

What might it mean to conceive of the five spiritual faculties as *infused*? It means understanding them as arising not from the egocentric will, but from a higher source – one that cuts through and dissolves self-centred tendencies, disclosing itself through us. This perspective recalls Shinran's conception of practice as a gift, granted through a transference of merit (*eko*, 回向) – the compassionate activity of Amida Buddha working within us. The spiritual faculties themselves – the very means by which we discern what is truly real – are not self-generated but bestowed. Even the capacity for insight is not a personal accomplishment, but a gift received. From this perspective, these faculties cannot be claimed or appropriated by the ordinary self; rather, they work to dismantle it, giving rise to a stream of intention no longer driven by selfish concern.

We can relate this shift in register to the concepts of *karma-niyama* and *Dharma-niyama* – the mundane and transcendental dimensions of conditionality.[32] From a limited, everyday perspective, we may believe that the five spiritual faculties arise solely from our own efforts. Yet, as these faculties deepen and mature, we begin to see that not all efficacy springs from the ego. Some actions unfold in alignment with a greater, selfless current – an impulse that transcends the personal will and flows from a suprapersonal source.

We might therefore propose that the five spiritual faculties operate on two levels. There is a *mundane* mode, shaped by personal striving, and a *transcendental* mode whose provenance lies beyond the constraints of self-centred will, whereby the faculties arise as blessing.

Conclusion: A World of Expanded Sense

Whether understood as self-cultivated or infused by Other Power, the five spiritual faculties offer both a metaphor and a model for Awakening – pointing to an expanded mode of perception, as if we were awakening to new senses. While we may never acquire magnetoreception or electrolocation like certain animals, we can develop more subtle inner faculties: refined sensibilities that allow us to discern and respond to transcendent values.

These spiritual senses open onto a world of greater richness, depth, and meaning – one no longer filtered through self-preoccupied desire, utilitarian calculation, aversion, and distorted views. As these faculties awaken, they begin to guide our lives in ways that our ordinary senses cannot, orienting us towards what is ultimately valuable.

Let's return to the image of the being enclosed within a lotus bud. When the petals open, the splendour of the Pure Land bursts forth – a realm of such profound harmony and beauty that it awakens entirely new emotions, new ways of relating, and new dimensions of meaning. From this perspective, Awakening isn't about acquiring superpowers to shape the world to our will. Instead, it's about attuning to more subtle modes of perception and responsiveness. Just as our physical senses instinctively reach out to interpret the material world, so the spiritual faculties, when cultivated, open us towards the sacred – disclosing what transcends the narrow demands of self. Awakening, then, consists in the activation and refinement of more subtle modes of knowing that reveal a world of expanded sense – a deepening into a realm illumined by meaning, value, reverence, and blessing.

2

Faithful to My First Astonishments: Trust

I don't trust the truth of memories
because what leaves us
departs forever
There's only one current of this sacred river
but I still want to remain faithful
to my first astonishments[33]

Beyond the Fog

When, aged nineteen, I first walked through the doors of a Buddhist centre, I was desperate. I didn't know what I was looking for or what I might find. I knew only that I was suffering, confused, and directionless. I was grappling with mental-health issues bordering on psychosis. One of my lecturers had noticed my withdrawn and disorderly state, and recommended that I see the university doctor, who immediately admitted me to hospital for psychiatric evaluation. I found myself lying on a hospital trolley at Leeds Royal Infirmary thinking: *What am I doing here? Where is this going?* Nowhere good, I knew that much. It dawned on me that I was at a dangerous crossroads, about to succumb to a darkness from which I might never see the light again. A voice from within surfaced, whispering: *Don't do it. This isn't the only way*. Somehow, I found the words to say I didn't want to be there. I was scared of where this was going. I wanted to leave.

The hospital had no power to detain me, so I was discharged under the condition that I would continue to visit the doctor regularly. At my next appointment, seeing my bedraggled state, the doctor was keen to prescribe medication. I told him I believed *meditation* would help pull me from my psychotic daze. At the time, I had very slim grounds for this conviction – having meditated for just a few weeks – but he couldn't insist.

What made me think that Buddhism could help me? I had already given up on Christianity as a possible path. While I had met some good and kind Christians, there was something about the fundamental myth of Christianity, and its monotheistic orientation, that didn't speak to me. It felt distant, even foreign. Although embedded in the culture I grew up in, it was not something I could fully resonate with or participate in. So why would a tradition with roots in the East be any different? Surely it would feel even more remote, even more foreign.

Yet, like many on their first encounter with the Dharma, something in me stirred – a flash of recognition, a spark of attraction, a faint sense of familiarity. Perhaps this was my first glimpse of *shraddha* – faith or trust – emerging quietly in the midst of confusion. It wasn't spectacular or exultant. There was no angel, no blinding light. Nothing so dramatic. And yet, something shifted, perhaps even decisively. Even so, I drifted in and out of the existential fog in which I had been immersed, but slowly it began to clear. It wasn't easy, but something kept calling me back. I didn't even get on well with my first Buddhist teacher. In my fragile, paranoid state,

I found him authoritarian and harsh. Still, I was drawn back again and again, summoned by something I could not name, but that would now carry me forward.

The Call

One way I've come to understand this process is in terms of hearing and responding to a call. Around the time of this first contact with Buddhism, I was also reading about Hinduism, particularly the god Krishna. Krishna plays the flute, and his music steals the attention of the *gopis*, the milkmaids, who symbolize the human heart. They are entranced and delighted by the beauty of his music, instinctively moving towards him. Through his flute, Krishna calls beings towards the divine. Krishna playing his flute symbolizes the transcendent breaking in on us, summoning us towards its beauty, glory, and mystery.

For philosopher Jean-Louis Chrétien, the 'call' is fundamentally a *recall* – a novel and 'unheard-of' summons that 'must call us back, convert us, and turn us toward *what we have in fact always/already seen*'.[34] This unsettling recall disrupts our inner poise, drawing us out of complacency. At its core, humanity is defined by *responsiveness*, and the Dharma life consists in responding to this call.

In Caravaggio's painting *The Calling of St Matthew* (*c.*1599–1600), the call remains unspoken, yet may be inferred by the hesitant gesture that signals the apostle's response: 'Who, me?' Our reaction to this summons consists in an unconditional offering of ourselves. This vividly portrays our existential situation. As Chrétien puts it: 'wherever we are, we are always already called and requested, and our first utterance, like our first glance, is already an answer to the request wherein it emerges.'[35] The call thus beckons us to self-recollection and towards a transcendent relation. It seizes us, awakening us to consciousness; before its claim we cannot expect to remain unchanged.

A Receptivity to the Light Streaming Down

Despite some contemporary moves to secularize Buddhism and recast it as a form of 'mind science', *shraddha* – trust or confidence – remains one of its foundational attitudes. Unlike empirical science, which depends on controlled experiments and testable hypotheses, Buddhist practice rests on a deep commitment to a particular vision of reality. This vision sees human beings as caught in a cycle of craving and aversion, and therefore of suffering (samsara), while affirming that liberation is possible through the path the Buddha revealed.

Buddhism considers trust a primordial faculty, an intuitive and sincere response to the ideal of Enlightenment as embodied in the three jewels: the Buddha, the Dharma, and the Sangha. Though often translated as 'faith', *shraddha* doesn't mean blind belief. Instead, it signifies a grounded trust in the possibility of awakening and the deep conviction that all beings possess the potential to become buddhas. This quality brings joy, serenity, and stability, and, most importantly, it's a faculty that can be developed and refined.

It is common to relegate 'faith' to a mere shadow of knowledge – a simulacrum. However, as Subhuti puts it, 'faith is a kind of "knowing"'.[36] The conviction to which genuine faith gives rise is rooted in the nature of things. Faith is thus not a weak approximation but a foreshadowing, an anticipation of wisdom. It consists in a kind of recognition that we have come into relation with an embodiment of our highest values. We might even say that faith is the emotional or affective *complement* of wisdom.[37] In following the indications of faith, we therefore honour and deepen our affinity with transcendent realities.

Trust or *shraddha* is not abstract; it necessarily points towards an object. For Buddhists, this object is embodied in the three jewels. First, we trust that the Buddha was awakened. As the Buddha died a long time ago, this cannot be verified empirically. So how do we come to trust in the Buddha's Enlightenment? In part, this arises through exposure to the second of the three jewels, the Dharma. While in its absolute aspect the Dharma is the transcendental truth to which the Buddha awakened, it also comprises the formulas, metaphors, and stories that the Buddha expounded to communicate that truth. Furthermore, we can come to trust in the Buddha through his impact on the Sangha – notably the remarkable lives of Buddhists throughout history. More immediately, we may observe the transformative effect of the teachings on our spiritual friends, especially those with more experience of the path. As we see the profound impact of the three jewels on their lives, we may begin to trust that our own lives can be transformed in the same way.

From the outside, faith may seem like something exultant, exuberant, a kind of hallelujah fervour. It might even suggest a teary vision of emotional ecstasy and profound connection. Yet faith doesn't usually manifest according to Hollywood clichés.

It is most often much quieter, gradual, even unobtrusive. Nevertheless, it shows itself in the orientation of our lives, in where we direct our energy, in what we give up and what we commit ourselves to. Indeed, my preceptor, Subhuti, points out that in many cases we will experience trust as 'a subterranean power, not necessarily ecstatic, and perhaps barely manifesting in conscious feelings at all, but nevertheless a real force, a feeling deeper than we can feel'.[38]

While faith may at times manifest in strong feelings of devotion, devotion isn't always accompanied by faith. Although it can be beautiful and pleasurable, devotion is not necessarily connected with insight into reality, or with the desire to change oneself in accordance with that insight. Devotional moods are not the sole measure of faith, and may even betray a kind of intoxication. Sometimes a newcomer arrives at a Buddhist centre for the very first time and seems immediately to be filled with inspiration, devotion, and enthusiasm. They proclaim that they have found their path and will attend every week without fail. Yet they never come back. A momentary thrill of devotion is not faith.

Instead, faith or trust may reveal itself in subtler movements of recognition and connection. To return to *The Calling of St Matthew*, the future apostle is caught by surprise when called, and his tentative response reveals a recognition mingled with doubt: not only 'Who, me?', but also 'Why me?' And even, 'Is this really happening?' Yet he *is* capable of responding. His faith is alive in his very capacity to discern the call.

Buddhist trust is an unconditional openness to the mystery of existence. Sangharakshita has characterized it in terms of an *affinity* between ourselves and the Buddha: 'the response of what is ultimate in us to what is ultimate in the universe'.[39] It is a kind of sacred resonance – a sensitivity and responsiveness to our ultimate concerns. In other words, faith is the capacity or faculty by which we attune to what is ultimate. As Paul Tillich puts it: 'Faith is the state of being ultimately concerned.'[40] In an evocative image, Sangharakshita proposes that faith is 'a receptivity to the light streaming down'.[41]

What Trust Makes Visible

What unseen regions, then, does the faculty of trust make visible? What extended sensing does it bestow upon us? Trusting opens a dimension of being that would otherwise remain sealed off. It enables a tentative relation with what is forever mysterious, boundless, and transcendent. Through trust, we become attuned to a scale of value – discerning what is most worthy of our reverent attention. In this way, it helps us orient our lives according to a sacred hierarchy. At the same time, trust enables the transcendent to break in on us, reorienting our priorities and saturating our perception with beauty, clarity, and serenity. As faith strengthens and deepens, it purifies the mind of afflictive, unskilful states. It illuminates our self-interested and narcissistic tendencies, revealing the painful patterns of our habitual reactions. In the light of faith, we feel drawn towards more wholesome, beneficial attitudes and begin to embody them.

Trust grants access to what can never be fully captured or received. It enables us to reach towards the transcendent, which cannot be calculated or framed as an object of scrutiny.

Awakening trust is more like opening a blind and allowing light to flood in. But then, perhaps all experience is like this; rather than a once-and-for-all apprehension of reality, there is an ever-deepening receptivity to its unfolding.

I recall the first time I saw a *kesa* – the Japanese-style, abbreviated robe worn by members of the Triratna Buddhist Order. It's little more than a strip of white cloth draped around the neck, fastened by a tassel near the navel. But, the moment I saw it, something in me woke up. It was like looking into a mirror. I knew, instantly: I wanted to be that person; I *would be* that person; in some sense, I already was that person. There was no room for doubt. I knew even then that I could expect no material rewards – no money, no fame, no power. So where did this impulse come from? I felt an irresistible attraction, as though the sacred dimension were calling to me through this quiet symbol of commitment and aspiration. It began to weigh upon me, settle upon me; it had summoned me.[42] My future now lay open before me:

> I hold the reel in my hand –
> I have tied the thread to the threshold.[43]

I had already been grasped by my ultimate concern – and it wouldn't abandon me. The unseen, the sacred, had crossed into visibility.

Cultivating Trust

Faith is an innate capacity of the mind. We might think of it as a faculty of responsiveness that opens access to higher values and truths to which the everyday mind is largely insensible. It follows that we need to identify, value, and 'educate' this capacity so that faith becomes a guiding factor in our lives. We can cultivate and strengthen trust through deliberate action. Traditionally, we nurture trust in the three jewels through devotional activities like chanting and puja, but contemplative practices, Dharma study, and spiritual friendship also play a vital role in deepening this subtle faculty.

Devotional practices foster receptivity to higher influences, but this receptivity is not passive. Through ritual acts centred on the Buddha – such as bowing, prostrating, chanting, and making offerings – we cultivate a sense of attraction, openness, and affinity to the qualities of the enlightened mind. The Buddha embodies the transcendent potential within every human being; by venerating and remembering the Blessed One, we connect with that potential and begin to realize it.

On a Buddhist shrine, the Buddha is honoured as a distinguished guest. Within this sacred domain, it is customary to offer three traditional gifts: candles, symbolizing the light of Enlightenment; flowers, representing impermanence; and incense, which evokes the purity of a life guided by the Dharma. These simple gestures express reverence and gratitude while also enacting the virtue of generosity (*dana*). In doing so, they embody our appreciation of, and receptivity towards, what is of ultimate value.

My first puja offered a vivid – if initially disorienting – taste of this. While I understood almost nothing of what was happening, I nevertheless felt somehow lifted into another dimension. I was granted a glimpse of beauty that seemed to come from beyond and that enveloped, permeated, and cleansed me. New emotions stirred in me; new modes of sensing awakened. I ended the ceremony in a daze, especially due to the final part: the transference of merit, which evokes the bodhisattva ideal – the aspiration to place oneself at the service of all beings. One verse that we recited spoke of renouncing everything:

> My personality throughout my existences,
> My possessions,
> And my merit in all three ways,
> I give up without regard for myself
> For the benefit of all beings.[44]

This left me dumbfounded, convinced I'd formally relinquished all my worldly goods. What was I to do now? It slowly dawned on me that a literal interpretation might be missing the point.

Devotional practices deepen trust not through restless novelty, but through faithful repetition. As these sacred patterns are enacted again and again, and we become intimately familiar with them, they begin to permeate deep into the body and mind, stabilizing our attention and transforming our depths. Reflecting on the loss of ritual in modernity, Byung-Chul Han observes: 'Rituals are characterized by repetition. Repetition differs from routine in its capacity to create intensity.'[45] Each repetition thus becomes a *reaffirmation* – a reenactment of sacred encounter.

The Shadow of Trust

To have trust is to be deeply engaged with the mystery of our existence, to open ourselves to its unfolding meaning. But what if that trust is misplaced? What if it leads not to Awakening but to betrayal? Trust isn't always healthy, and there are times when it is wise to suspend it or never offer it at all.

Trust doesn't operate in isolation. Like the five senses working together to form perception, our capacity for trust evolves in relation to the other spiritual faculties. *Prajna*, which means 'wisdom' or 'direct insight into reality', serves as the cognitive counterpart to *shraddha*. It's not a more advanced faculty, but a necessary parallel – essential for offsetting potential distortions in how trust is developed and where it is applied.

The shadow of trust assumes various guises. It faces far enemies like outright doubt and corrosive cynicism. But its near enemies are more insidious: overconfidence, rigid certainty, and, not least, blind credulity and gullibility.

Debilitating Doubt and Liberating Doubt

I'm someone who doubts a lot – myself, others, whether I've chosen the right path, the right friends, or even the right country to live in. You get the picture. When I meet people who seem certain about everything, I can feel a bit inadequate. They seem so sure of themselves, so confident, so... smug. And I wonder, why do I have to doubt so much? But I've also noticed something else: people who radiate certainty are often less willing to admit when they're wrong. Their assurance leaves little room for curiosity or humility. One well-known study found that 93 per cent of drivers rated themselves as above average. It's a trivial example, perhaps, but hints at a larger pattern: confidence is prized, doubt is not.

Culturally, doubt is often seen as weakness, while certainty is equated with strength. We're told to believe in ourselves, to affirm that anything is possible, that we can achieve whatever we set our minds to. That's the promise of the self-help gospel. A success guru who told us to cherish our doubt would win few followers.

There are certainly unhelpful, insincere, and even paralyzing modes of doubt. Doubt and indecision (*vicikiccha*) is one of the five hindrances to meditative concentration. It is a kind of resistance, a reluctance to fully engage. It has the nature of wavering and reveals a lack of integration and clarity of purpose. This kind of doubt is a dithering, a refusal to commit. Sangharakshita has glossed this form of doubt as 'vagueness', which he regards as a form of dishonesty.[46] Rather than commit ourselves, we prefer to keep our options open. Moreover, this unhelpful doubt often arises from giving unwise attention to the very matters that provoke it.[47] Indeed, sceptical doubt is one of the three fetters that, once broken, launch us decisively into the stream of the Dharma.

The early scriptures record the story of Tissa, a follower of the Buddha who is paralyzed by doubt:

> My body seems as if it has been drugged, I have become disoriented, the teachings are no longer clear to me. Sloth and torpor persist, obsessing my mind. I am leading the holy life dissatisfied, and I have doubt about the teachings.[48]

Perhaps you know the feeling? I certainly do. The Buddha responds to Tissa's doubt not by admonishing him to have faith but by instructing him in deeper reflection on the nature of reality. In particular, he instructs Tissa in relation to the renunciation of attachment to the ordinary senses. In other words, the Buddha introduces a wisdom teaching. In this case, rather than wisdom being a counterbalance to faith, it becomes the basis for it. Not only that, we can note the interconnection between clarity, trust, and engagement (*virya*), which here form a virtuous spiral. Tissa's greater clarity results in deeper trust, which motivates him to overcome his resistance and so engage more deeply with the Dharma life. This underscores how the faculties do not function in isolation but are interconnected and mutually reinforcing.

And yet, doubt can also be a sign of engagement, curiosity, and depth. It suggests that we're paying attention, that we care enough to question, to wonder. Doubt holds space for nuance; it can lead us beyond easy answers and phony commitment into greater understanding and authentic connection. It indicates depth and rigour. In reflecting on doubt in relation to Christian faith, Tillich writes:

> If doubt appears, it should not be considered as the negation of faith, but as an element which was always and will always be present in the act of faith. [...] Serious doubt is confirmation of faith. It indicates the seriousness of the concern, its unconditional character.[49]

For Tillich, doubt doesn't undermine faith – it affirms it. It shows that we are genuinely concerned. Doubt, in this sense, shows the serious and persistent nature of our concern, of our care.

Investigative Doubt

An early scripture encourages a kind of doubt that is not sceptical but curious, investigative, and receptive.[50] Someone who does not yet have trust in the Buddha is invited to examine the matter carefully. The enquirer begins by observing the Buddha's behaviour to see whether it reflects skilful or unskilful mental states. If it appears skilful, he then enquires whether this is a recent occurrence or a well-established trend. The enquirer also investigates whether the Buddha has become intoxicated by fame, and if his ethical behaviour is a response to fear or a free choice, and if he avoids sensual pleasures due to repression or genuine release from craving. He should then question the Buddha directly to determine if his responses bear out the enquirer's initial observations.

If so, the text says, the enquirer may then approach the Buddha as a teacher and listen to his Dharma. Through direct knowledge, the enquirer comes to a conclusion about the teachings, and so places his trust in the Buddha. When trust in the Buddha arises from such a meticulous investigation, the scripture describes it as 'planted, rooted, and established [...] supported by reasons, rooted in vision, firm'.[51]

In this case, trust is strengthened by increased awareness of its object. Through seeing more clearly the virtues of the Buddha, we come to trust in his Awakening and so in our capacity to emulate his example.

In Zen Buddhism, doubt is far from an obstacle. Instead, it becomes integral to the method of liberation, jolting us out of habitual complacency. But this is no ordinary doubt rooted in hesitation or indecision; it is rather 'Great Doubt' (*daigidan*), in which the whole body becomes a mass of doubt. According to an old saying, 'Great Doubt, Great Awakening; small doubt, small awakening; no doubt, no awakening.' Wrestling with such doubt has been likened to swallowing a red-hot iron ball that one can neither gulp down nor spit out.[52] Great Doubt sears through our settled habits, burning away delusions and false certainties. It propels the practitioner towards greater intensity of engagement. Without it, Zen practice risks becoming superficial or mechanical. Doubt in this sense isn't something to be 'solved'; it dissolves in contemplation of the mystery.

The Dangers of Certainty and Fanaticism

Bertrand Russell once wrote:

> The value of philosophy is, in fact, to be sought largely in its very uncertainty [...] it removes the somewhat arrogant dogmatism of those who have never travelled into the region of liberating doubt, and it keeps alive our sense of wonder by showing familiar things in an unfamiliar aspect.[53]

Seen from this perspective, the true enemy of trust isn't doubt, but certainty – especially when it hardens into overconfidence or fanaticism. Certainty shuts down enquiry. It leaves no room for curiosity. It assumes there is nothing more to learn. Worse still, certainty often begins to assert itself over other people, attempting to impose its version of truth. In its most extreme forms, it becomes fanaticism: a mindset in which all sensitivity to one's own limitations has vanished.

But the vehemence of our conviction is not always a sign of its reliability. Often, it reveals its fragility. If we find ourselves rigidly defending our allegiances – or worse, seeking to silence those who dissent – we should ask whether our trust has slid into dogmatism.

One of the clearest and most devastating examples of misplaced certainty shows up in the ultimately tragic story of the People's Temple, a Christian movement founded by Jim Jones in the United States in 1955. Over time, Jones' undeniable charisma gave way to authoritarianism. By the late 1970s, the Temple had relocated to Guyana, where Jones and his followers founded an intentional community named Jonestown. When a US Congressman travelled there to investigate reports of abuse, he, three journalists, and a defecting member of the cult were all murdered. To avoid facing repercussions, Jones ordered his followers to imbibe a cyanide-laced drink. Over 900 people died in this mass suicide, including many children – and Jones himself.

This tragedy wasn't just the product of a deranged leader; it stemmed from unchallenged certainty and misplaced trust: a man utterly convinced of his righteousness, and a community that had surrendered its capacity to doubt. It remains a chilling reminder that conviction, untempered by humility, and credulity, uninformed by critical awareness, can prove deadly.

The Gift of Trust

While it is usual to view trust as something we cultivate and refine through our own efforts (*jiriki*), within the Japanese Pure

Land tradition Shinran came to a radically different understanding. For him, a trusting and enduring connection with the transcendent – what he called *shinjin* – is not something we decide upon, but an unconditional gift. How, then, does it arise? We might say that *shinjin* is *infused*. It awakens through the grace of Other Power (*tariki*). It is the cosmic Amida Buddha who bestows upon us an intimate connection with the awakened mind – or, more subtly, *shinjin* consists in the realization that such an affinity has always already existed. This awakening gives rise not only to a deep and serene confidence, but also to a sense of gratitude and indebtedness, since we have done nothing to merit this intimate connection with what bears transcendent value.

Shinran taught that *shinjin* takes form through the invocation of the *nembutsu* (*namu amida butsu*), which is essentially calling on Amida Buddha and, in this way, fulfilling our connection with the Awakening mind. The two aspects – inner and outer – are inseparable: it is not that we first attain *shinjin* and then recite the *nembutsu*, nor that we recite the *nembutsu* in order to generate *shinjin*. Rather, they arise together as complementary expressions of Amida's working through us. We might say that *shinjin* is the inward, subjective assurance of being grasped by Amida – never to be abandoned – while the *nembutsu* is its outward, objective enactment.

The arising of *shinjin* is not an event that unfolds within linear time, but rather reveals itself when that ordinary time is ruptured – when our self-centred habits give way to a new mode of being. This amounts to a kind of spiritual rebirth or conversion, where our self-serving effort is superseded by Other Power – a compassionate influence that seems to break in on us from beyond. It does not originate within the calculating, striving self, nor can it be appropriated by it. Instead, it transcends that tightly enclosed self to reveal the boundless compassion embodied by Amida.

Shinjin isn't the outcome of an act of will or a decision; rather, we discover ourselves as already in relation to a sacred horizon. Through *shinjin*, our subjectivity becomes aligned with – indeed, identified with – Amida Buddha, the awakened mind. And yet, at the same time, we remain mired in our everyday foolishness. *Shinjin* does not relieve us from our delusion; it heightens our sensitivity to it, even as it assures us of our ultimate liberation. Shinran says, 'Even though I am also in Amida's grasp, I cannot see because of the blind passions that obstruct my eyes. *Nevertheless*, great compassion is tireless and always illumines me.'[54] In *shinjin*, the moment of final Awakening is brought forward, so to speak – guaranteed, and thus anticipated – as we awaken to the joyful recognition that we are always already 'truly settled'.

Shinjin, the *nembutsu*, our birth in the Pure Land, and our eventual Enlightenment are all founded on the mythic narrative of Amida Buddha and his progress towards Awakening. More specifically, they rest on Amida's unfathomable transference of merit (*eko*). The exclusive source of spiritual value and liberation is this immense merit, gathered over incalculable lifetimes of practice. Its transfer to us is guaranteed by the *Larger Scripture*, which confirms that Amida fulfilled a set of cosmic vows directed towards the benefit of the entire cosmos. Amida's transfer of merit is essentially the transmission, to all beings without exception, of the impulse towards Awakening. This endows beings with the necessary impetus to call on Amida and thus be reborn in the Pure Land. As Shinran puts it,

> whether with regard to practice or to *shinjin*, there is nothing whatever that has not been fulfilled through Amida Tathagata's directing of virtue to beings out of his pure Vow-mind.[55]

Paul Tillich points to a similar dynamic in elaborating his notion of existential faith within the context of Christian thought:

> in relation to the ultimate we are always receiving and never giving. We are never able to bridge the infinite distance between the infinite and the finite from the side of the finite.[56]

At the same time, the arising of *shinjin* leads us into a kind of double or contradictory awareness: on one hand, we experience joy as we recognize our essential identity with Amida; on the other, we feel still more keenly the gravity of our delusion, which in turn prompts an ethical reformation. Ironically, although Shinran presents *shinjin* as the 'easy path', he also makes it clear that 'the genuine difficulty is realizing true and real *shinjin*'.[57] This is because letting go of the dour calculations of self-power – relinquishing the ego-cherishing attitude – is profoundly challenging for us.

The arising of *shinjin* might also be understood in the light of an 'event', especially as characterized by the philosopher John Caputo:

> Think of a fortuitous visitation by something that we did not invite, the arrival of something unexpected, unforeseeable,

> unprogrammable, uncontrollable, and even unwarranted. We did not do anything to produce, earn, or deserve it.[58]

An event in this sense is something exceptional that disrupts habitual awareness and has an invigorating and transformative impact upon us. It happens *to us*, unsettling – and even overwhelming – our ego-subjectivity. In the words of Jean-Luc Marion, an event

> neither arises out of our initiative, nor responds to our expectation, nor can ever be reproduced, but [...] above all gives itself to us from its own self, to the point that it affects us, changes us, almost produces us.[59]

An event is thus characterized by its *excess*, in the sense that it overtakes us, breaking free of the ego's moorings. It is not our own doing; it is not solicited by the calculations of the ego-driven will, which resists it, but is rather something visited upon us.

In this light, *shinjin* as an event is a bedazzling gift – an unforeseen blessing that cannot be compelled or mastered by our habitual categories of perception and will. It does not camouflage a lack of understanding, but instead opens up a new mode of sensing. Marion proposes that faith is not a mere consolation for what we cannot see; rather, it provides the 'strength to bear the glare' of a reality that is too intense for the ordinary ego to endure. It is not that we lack evidence, but that we are overwhelmed by its abundance. Thus faith is the capacity that 'renders the gaze apt to see the excess of the preeminent saturated phenomenon, the Revelation'.[60] Accordingly, the advent of *shinjin* endows us with the confidence that we will close the breach between ourselves and the transcendent. It thus gives a sense of preceding ourselves. We have before having.[61]

While *shinjin* marks a permanent shift in subjectivity – one that brings with it reassurance and joy – it can never be regarded as a prior fact or a personal accomplishment to be flaunted like a trophy. *Shinjin* is not a property of the self, but a transformed mode of perception – or better, of *relation*. In the light of this new mode of relation, reality is transfigured into an infinite iconostasis. In Shinran's words:

> When a foolish being of delusion and defilement
> awakens *shinjin*,
> He realizes that birth-and-death is itself nirvana;
> Without fail he reaches the land of immeasurable light
> And universally guides sentient beings to
> enlightenment.[62]

It is not that *shinjin* has arisen once and for all, but that it is *always* arising – ever fresh, ever renewed. The present moment becomes a locus of sacred revelation as perception now gleams with a liberative glory. The distance between present and future collapses, for Awakening is no longer deferred – it is already assured.

Shinjin is the deep confidence that we have been gifted the *chintamani* – the wish-fulfilling jewel that grants our deepest aspiration: the realization of our own liberation and the release of all beings from suffering. It entails relinquishing the naïve pretence that we are the sole architects of our awakening. True freedom becomes possible only when we let go of ego-clinging, abandon the conceit of self-generated effort, and entrust ourselves to influences that seem to flow towards us from a transcendent beyond.

3

So Much to Admire

I know, you never intended to be in this world.
But you're in it all the same.

So why not get started immediately.
I mean, belonging to it.
There is so much to admire, to weep over.[63]

Not long ago, I visited the Harvard Art Museum, which is home to a spectacular self-portrait by Van Gogh.[64] The painting lights up the entire room. As I approached, it captured my attention and seemed to steal the glory from the other paintings that hang there (some of which are masterpieces in their own right by Cézanne, Monet, and Picasso). Van Gogh had originally painted it as a gift for Paul Gauguin who, after their friendship soured, promptly sold it for 300 francs. The painter's face is set against an ethereal, Veronese green backdrop. It radiates light, fervour, and a fierce human singularity. It imposed itself upon me as an uncapturable phenomenon, like an icon opening onto a spiritual dimension. The painting reveals the clarity and intensity of Van Gogh's perception; it transfigures the ordinary into the extraordinary and so humbles us with the weight of its inordinate evidence. In flooding us with existential transparency, it thwarts any attempt to frame it, calling forth a reverential gaze.

Having explored some of the primary aspects of trust – including its shadow – in the previous chapter, we turn now to its affective heart: the capacity for reverence. This vital human response enables us to attune to what is truly excellent, to that which uplifts us, and draws us towards what is transcendental – something that we can never fully assimilate or appropriate. Reverence ennobles our modest daily routine, sacralizes the moment, and organizes our world according to a scale of values. Reverence defines our sacred horizon. Without it, we are merely reproductive organisms, genetic transmitters, survival machines. Reverence bubbles up from within like a subterranean spring whenever it encounters the sublime, or even just an intimation of it, purifying and cleansing our perception and ennobling our sense of relation. Yet it is so often stifled, mistrusted, and even derided. It may be dismissed as naïve, unduly humble, a glorification of submission. Recognizing, honouring, and refining our primordial capacity for reverence is integral to the Buddhist life; indeed, it is essential to any attempt to connect with the transcendent or sublime. Without reverence, there is no intuition of higher value; there is no glory. Yet, this virtue is seldom valued in today's deconsecrated world.

We may reverence pop stars, politicians, influencers, and models. While these figures may incarnate our highest values to some limited degree, they mostly cannot support the dignity and scope of our reverence. They will inevitably disappoint, even coarsen, our reverential disposition. This may lead us to feel depressed, cynical, and less willing to trust in our reverential impulse in future. Reverence is no luxury but a necessity for any meaningful human flourishing. If there is no reverence, then there can be no hierarchy of value; perhaps there is no value at all – there are just competing choices that cannot be ranked according to merit but merely selected out of whim or habit. There is no call and no response.

The transcendent can never be discerned by the consuming gaze, which inevitably reduces, flattens, and brutalizes it. Such a gaze trivializes what is uncontainable by squashing its traces into digestible forms. It relegates icons to mere signs. In contrast, reverence aligns itself with the glory of the sacred, allowing its effulgence and grandeur to unfold. It is a mode of perception that makes the sacred manifest – what is transcendent, what opens out into vastness, what is filled with wonder and awe – bringing into awareness that which is supremely and gloriously valuable. Reverence not only renders the sacred perceptible but also shapes our response to it. Through reverence, we offer ourselves in service to the ideal; we become vessels through which the sacred finds expression. In such a state, the sacred is not perceived as an object but is already given as the very context within which perception, meaning, and value arise to astonish and bless us.

My Awakening to Reverence

When I crossed the threshold of a Buddhist centre for the very first time, I soon became aware of the customary ritual acts of bowing before the Buddha, offering incense, and performing puja or 'supreme worship'. At first, bowing before a statue was both awkward and compelling. While I was estranged from my reverential sensibility, I nevertheless felt summoned. In part, the estrangement was a hangover from having attended church as a child; far from discerning a sacred presence there, I had instead been haunted by the *absence* of the sacred. The church carried a lingering scent of elsewhere, but there was no bridge, no opening, no trace that led to any elsewhere. The way was blocked. I felt clumsy, self-conscious; my gestures of reverence felt bogus, directionless.

Soon after I became a regular at the Leeds Buddhist Centre, I was gifted my first buddha image by Becky, a fellow philosophy student. It was a small, brass figure in the style of the hunched Kamakura Buddha. Following the example of some of my new Buddhist friends, I took the opportunity to create my first personal shrine in my bedroom. I draped a satin cloth over a cardboard box and arranged the Buddha at the centre of several other valued items now long forgotten. I practised bowing before this image, although I admit that I felt a bit phony. While I cherished and reverenced this image as a manifestation of the sacred, I had only the haziest intuition of what that sacred signified and how it would remake my life horizon.

A couple of years later, as part of my preparation for ordination into the Triratna Buddhist Order, I took up the 'going for refuge and prostration practice'. This devotional exercise consists in visualizing a 'refuge tree' – a symbolic representation of sacred values and lineage – and then physically prostrating before the imagined scene. Later, through the medium of light, one absorbs the blessings from all the revered figures on the tree. Ideally, one completes 100,000 prostrations, though I think I still haven't reached that number. In undertaking this practice, I was following centuries of tradition within Tibetan Buddhism, since the going for refuge and prostration practice is one of its *mula yoga*s or 'root practices'.[65] In the first instance, I performed it daily for around two years, mostly with my roommates Arthapriya and Priyavadita. But, far from feeling reverence, I often felt resistance, irritation, and even boredom. Yet the practice worked on me – worked underground – gradually redirecting my volition, steering me towards an encounter with the three jewels, and shaping my response to them.

Much later, in 2016, I was on an ordination retreat near Alicante, Spain, during which I was blessed to ordain three men into the Triratna Buddhist Order. As part of the retreat's ritual structure, after reciting the standard 'Salutation to the three jewels', we performed the *panchang pranam*, the 'five-point salutation', which is a kind of prostration in which one kneels on the floor and touches the forehead and palms to the ground three times. This is the standard way to show reverence and respect in India – even to parents or teachers – but it goes quite a bit beyond a simple bow. I resolved to take this up as a practice, not just during the retreat itself but as part of my daily routine. When I carry out the *panchang pranam*, at times I feel clumsy, self-conscious, and even contrived. I ask myself: do I really mean this? What am I bowing to anyway? Isn't this just a kind of performance – a show to make others think that I am reverent? Yet I keep doing it. It feels as though a stubborn resistance is slowly breaking down, melting away; a certain distance is closing, and my capacity to connect with what is worthy of reverence is closer to hand. My cynicism is starved of its power, worn down by the persistence of this reverent gesture. It wears away my pride, my clinging to self-power, and, in moments, I render myself. It has given me a language with which to intuit the transcendent.

What Calls for Reverence?

Who, or what, truly calls for reverence? Reverence is not something to be fabricated, simulated, or extracted through obligation or force. That which merits reverence calls to us, and we respond – or not. It claims us, renders us, embraces us. Reverence draws us into a posture in which we are summoned by what is transcendent. It paves the way for a kind of 'counter-intentionality' – or supra-intentionality – in which the Other Power, the buddha mind, reaches towards us, prevails upon us, and gifts us back to ourselves in a more authentic state. Through reverence, we are reconstituted as a faithful, loving self. This dynamic is beautifully illustrated in the myth of the transcendent Buddha Amitabha, who vowed to open the path for all beings to be reborn in the Pure Land and thereby attain full awakening. Through reverent entrusting (*shinjin*), we are 'grasped never to be abandoned', to use Shinran's constant refrain when speaking of Amitabha's incalculable grace.

Through reverence, the counter-intentionality of Amitabha's grace is roused and so begins to work upon and transform us. Shinran puts it like this:

> In entrusting ourselves to the Tathagata's Primal Vow and saying the Name once, necessarily, without seeking it, *we are made to receive the supreme virtues, and without knowing it, we acquire the great and vast benefit.*[66]

In this case, the vehicle of reverent entrusting is Amitabha's name, enshrined in the mantric formula *namu amida butsu*, which enables the transfer of virtue to us from a transcendent source. As this source of blessing impinges upon us, it lifts us out of the pettiness of our ordinary calculations and restores to us the glory of our sacred horizon. Within the scope of this horizon, 'Everywhere the Buddha sends light inconceivable and unhindered, breaking the immense night-dark of ignorance.'[67]

As we answer the call of Other Power, our heart opens in gratitude, wonder, and repentance. We enter into a state of being blessed; we are sacralized:

> When persons awaken *shinjin* and utter the Name,
> Amida's [Amitabha's] light embraces and protects them,
> And in this life they acquire immeasurable virtue.
> This light, boundless and inconceivable, never ceases a moment,
> Nor does it differentiate by time, or place, or any circumstance.[68]

The Education of Reverence

Reverence is a natural human response to what draws us towards our highest possibilities. It is a faculty that permits us to discern the sacred, yet it is often underdeveloped and so open to manipulation. If it is to answer our ultimate concern, it must be nurtured and refined. The film *The Remains of the Day* shows how a healthy impulse towards reverence can be appropriated in the service of evil. Stevens is the butler of Lord

Darlington, a seeming paragon of English dignity and tradition. Stevens serves his master unfailingly in the belief that he is honouring the proper order of things; he reverences the class hierarchy in the conviction that his master is noble. But this naïveté is shattered when Stevens discovers that Darlington is in fact a Nazi sympathizer. His life of service has been wasted on an improper focus of devoted attention. This realization nearly destroys Stevens. Such bitter disappointments may lead us not only to mistrust our reverential response but even to repress it.

While the practice of reverent service may weaken our egocentric pride, and so permit an openness to a higher will, it nevertheless requires discernment. Our reverent sensibility may be awakened and then refined through contact with nature, art, and the transcendent.

Reverence for Nature

Our latent sense of reverence often awakens in response to the mystery, power, and awe of the natural world: the bewildering array of animal life, volcanoes, Japanese cherry blossoms, and the vastness of the cosmos itself. It is an attunement to the enchantment of existence – the majesty, the abundance, the excess that impinges upon us. As Wendell Berry writes:

> We must recover the sense of the majesty of creation, and the ability to be worshipful in its presence. For I do not doubt that it is only on the condition of humility and reverence before the world that our species will be able to remain in it.[69]

This inherent reverence – this capacity for wonder – is evoked in Ted Hughes' poem 'Full Moon and Little Frieda'. After describing the return of a herd of cows to their sheds after a day's grazing, Hughes witnesses the moon as a kind of hierophany through the eyes of his young daughter Frieda. 'Moon! Moon!', she cries with excitement. Hughes then observes:

> The moon has stepped back like an artist
> gazing amazed at a work
> That points at him amazed.[70]

The natural world reveals itself as a kind of miracle. Awareness itself is a miracle, and recognizing its sacramental power solicits reverence. As Mary Oliver puts it:

> I don't know exactly what a prayer is.
> I do know how to pay attention, how to fall down
> into the grass, how to kneel down in the grass,
> how to be idle and blessed, how to stroll through the
> fields.[71]

Reverence for Art

Creating an artwork (a poem, a painting, or any other form of art) can amount to an act of reverence that also evokes a reverent response in others. Writing of Cézanne's paintings, Rilke commented that 'one feels their presence drawing together into a colossal reality'.[72] Similarly, in his analysis of the meaning of a painting, Marion argues that the painting is not *what* is visible; rather, it is that which 'makes visible' something that is not explicitly shown. An artwork opens up new possibilities of perception – constantly new visibles – and so can never be seen once and for all; it continues to surprise and surpass our categories of capture. In this way, it enlarges our consciousness. At its highest, art makes manifest what must always remain in some sense invisible: interiority. In doing so, it establishes a compelling region of visibility. A great artwork can never be exhaustively grasped, never controlled or mastered; rather, it is always in the process of revealing itself, calling us back to it, insisting that we yield before it.

Let's consider a haiku by the Japanese master Bashō (1644–94):

how glorious
young green leaves
flash in the sun.[73]

In just seventeen syllables (in Japanese), we are transported into a world of vivid particulars; a palpable scene is summoned and actualized. It is as though Bashō enables us to see with new eyes, eyes that have greater perceptual intensity and power than we can normally call upon. He removes veils that obstruct us from encountering the depths of the instant more fully.

We are confronted by a similar experience in the paintings of Giorgio Morandi (1890–1964), who was renowned for his capacity to solicit the depth, serenity, and beauty inherent within everyday items. At first glance, a Morandi painting may seem unremarkable – even boring – a drab representation of utilitarian objects: a collection of bottles, vases, or a bowl of fruit. But Morandi arranges these objects into meditative compositions that exude a quiet profundity. This depth steals our gaze, pervades us, and elevates our perception to a greater level of stillness and intensity in which the objects become utterly and irresistibly visible. His use of a restrained palette – dominated by earthy tones and muted greys – deepens the sense of calm and contemplation that permeate his paintings. Morandi's still-life compositions transcend their ordinariness by engendering a sacramental awareness in which objects begin to disclose their more subtle properties. His meticulous attention to form, light, and shadow transfigures functional, daily items into visual poetry that evokes a timeless stillness. A painter like Morandi opens up an exceptional field of visibility that transforms the way we see, fulfilling Rilke's claim that 'Suddenly one has the right eyes.'[74] Morandi's ostensibly modest paintings invite us to awaken to the subtle beauty and abundance inherent within the instant. They elicit an absolute attention, which is a mode of reverence, even of love.

Reverence for the Transcendent

Jean-Luc Marion defines the reverential gaze by contrasting it with the predatory, consuming gaze of the voyeur. The reverential gaze entails going beyond mere spectacle and becoming receptive to what comes towards us, what gives itself. This entails a radical softening – even a reversal – of our habitual pattern of subject and object. The ego's impulse to capture or master the perceived is suspended, at least momentarily, allowing our subjectivity to be redefined, even reconstituted, by the object rather than the reverse. This reversal of agency is enacted in the veneration of an icon, in which, as Marion writes, 'it is a matter not so much of seeing a spectacle as of seeing another gaze that sustains mine, confronts it, and eventually overwhelms it'.[75]

Here, the perceived is no longer a passive object that submits to interpretive mastery, but an active subject that overturns our self-referential intentionality and floods us. Marion continues:

> it is precisely because the icon is not given for itself, but rather *undoes its own prestige*, that it perhaps demands veneration – veneration that it does not seize but rather lets pass through it to the invisible prototype.[76]

Thus the icon does not draw veneration towards itself but transfers it to what Marion calls its 'prototype' (τύπος). It does not seek to capture our gaze – and thereby condemn us to idolatry – but rather redirects that gaze beyond itself. Its purpose, therefore, is its own self-effacement: it functions as a transparent medium, a sacred window.

Reverence, properly speaking, is a response not to what is visible and manifest but to the transcendent, which by its nature remains ungraspable and invisible. As Marion puts it, 'Only the one who prays can thus climb from the visible to the invisible [...] only the one who prays crosses the icon.'[77] Reverence is thus the spiritual posture that renders us permeable to the transcendent – allowing it to call upon us, to pervade us, and, ultimately, to transform us.

Reverence in Buddhism

We have an innate capacity for admiration, an impulse to look upwards. We intuitively respond to what calls us to service, what seems worthy, noble, and exalted. This is a capacity we should treasure and refine rather than dismiss or repress, since it expresses our urge to reach towards what is of infinite value, or even to allow what is of infinite value to reach towards us.

Newcomers are sometimes surprised to see Buddhists engaging in acts of reverence, as they don't regard Buddhism as a 'religion' and may associate such acts with blind belief, and perhaps even with subservience. What are we reverencing and why?

Most obviously, we are reverencing the Buddha: the pathfinder, the exemplar, and the guide who shows the way. The Buddha incarnates the maximum possibilities of human existence: the possibility of Enlightenment. What the Buddha attained, we too can attain; we can become buddhas. Reverence is the means by which we come into relationship with this possibility and begin to close the gap between it and our present consciousness.

Reverence is integral to the Buddhist life. It affords a language with which to intuit the sacred. While we might assume that the more enlightened a being becomes, the less need there is to express reverence, the opposite is actually true. This is confirmed in various scriptures where the more 'advanced' spiritual beings are characterized by a greater impulse and capacity for reverence. For instance, in the *Larger Pure Land Sutra*, the great bodhisattva Dharmakara – who would become Amitabha Buddha – vows that, in his

Pure Land, beings reborn there will be able to honour all buddhas everywhere and at all times, travelling freely across innumerable worlds to make offerings to them.[78]

The Buddha himself stressed the importance of reverence, valuing its ritual embodiment in devotional acts. A pivotal discourse in the Pali canon reveals how central reverence is in the Buddhist cosmovision. In the *Garava Sutta*, we meet the Buddha still absorbing the momentous insights of his spiritual Awakening. As he reflects on what he has seen and understood, the Buddha muses: 'One experiences suffering if dwelling without reverence or deference.'[79] The word translated here as 'suffering' is *dukkha*, which is sometimes translated as 'dissatisfaction' or even 'lack'. The term translated as 'reverence' is *garava*, which can also mean 'admiration', 'amazement', and 'delight' – the delight we take in the existence of others who are more elevated or superior to ourselves in creative ability or spiritual attainment. It bears comparison with other important terms such as *vandana* ('salutation') and *puja* ('worship'). These attitudes express skilful emotion connected with coming into relation with what is worthy, what is magnificent, embodying our sensitivity to values beyond the mundane self.

The term translated above as 'deference' is *patissa*, which comes from a root connected with listening or hearing. It signifies paying careful attention to someone's counsel, most notably within the teacher–disciple relationship.

According to the Buddha, to live without reverence and deference is to invite suffering. Why is this so? In part, this suffering arises because living without reverence implies recognizing nothing beyond ourselves – no point of reference higher than our own egocentric will. We ourselves are, so to speak, as good as it gets: nothing more refined, sublime, or transcendent is admissible. What a terrifying thought! Such a view of the world may satisfy an extreme narcissist, but, for the great majority of humanity, it is profoundly insufficient. Sangharakshita puts it like this: 'To live without looking up to anyone represents an impoverishment of one's emotional life and, indeed, an impairment of one's very humanity.'[80]

We *need* something to look up to, a transcendent orientation, a point of reference that raises us up and inspires us to actualize our deepest aspirations. Without this, we risk feeling not just empty but even depressed. We know that we are not, at least not yet, the most noble beings possible. We know that it is possible to develop admirable qualities and carry out noble actions that we don't yet exemplify. Thus *garava* and *patissa* are words that underline our fundamental capacity to recognize and respond to more complete and refined manifestations of our highest ideals.

It is sometimes said that people conform to devotional and non-devotional 'types', such as the classic distinction between the 'faith follower' and the 'doctrine follower'. This logic might seem to suggest that devotion is rather a question of preference or personal character, yet Sangharakshita writes that

> Any attempt to minimize the importance of devotion in the spiritual life, or to limit it to a particular personality type, is a betrayal of the Buddha's teaching and does less than justice to human nature.[81]

This bold statement underlines that Buddhism can never be reduced to a package of personal growth strategies; it is, rather, born of a response to the transcendent – to that which evokes reverence. Devotion is not merely a personality preference, but an integral dimension of the human being – more precisely, it is an essential quality of any being who aspires towards Awakening. If we conceive of ourselves as 'beyond' reverence, we may begin to feel superior to the devotional types, to look down upon them, even to dismiss them as simple, primitive, and unschooled.

Elsewhere Sangharakshita asserts:

> You stand a better chance of making progress if you start off as a devotee than if you start off with an intellectual approach. At least the devotee does something; he has some energy and so understanding will develop. But if you start off with a one-sidedly intellectual approach, you may get more and more engaged intellectually, but be unable to develop any corresponding emotion. The non-intellectual devotee is in a stronger position in the long run.[82]

Thus, when lived with integrity, a Dharma life will embody the principle of reverence or devotion. This doesn't necessarily mean that we're constantly performing pujas or prostrating ourselves in the direction of Bodh Gaya (though these practices may indeed be valuable ways to express our reverence). Instead, reverence may be expressed in simple, everyday actions: cleaning the shrine room, making tea for a respected friend, offering a small gift to a distinguished visitor. Our whole practice – including the very act of meditation – becomes a quiet offering of attention and presence.

Indeed, our entire life may become an offering put at the service of others. Within the Mahayana imagination, this outlook is enacted in symbolic form. *The Lotus Sutra*, for instance, recounts the story of a bodhisattva who drinks gallons of perfume and then sets himself alight.[83] He burns for some 12,000 years, exuding a sublime fragrance throughout the universe – all as the ultimate act of reverence towards the buddhas.

The Buddha as Transcendental Object or Phenomenon

As human beings, we need heroes – figures whose exemplary actions and qualities solicit our devotion and inspire us to emulate them. Our hero (or heroine), in some sense, hints at the transcendental, even *anticipates* it.

Sangharakshita has stressed the importance of having a 'transcendental object' – usually the Buddha or a bodhisattva – to evoke our ideal and serve as the focus of our Dharma life. The Buddha exemplifies both the path *to* Awakening and the principle *of* Awakening. Thus, the Buddha is our 'hero' and serves as a transcendental object – a focus upon which we may project our most sacred values. Alternatively, one could say we become the 'screen' by means of which the transcendental object reveals our ultimate values to us. This process enables us to begin a conscious fusion with the transcendental object – or, perhaps, to permit it to fuse with us. This fusion means that, as we actualize these ideals in practice, we integrate existentially with our most sacred values.

Mandala of Reverence

We might carry out a spiritual inventory of reverence. How and towards what is reverence expressed in our own lives? This will enable us to see our most prized values with greater clarity. We might usefully ask ourselves: are we reverencing something mundane, an improper focus for our most sacred praise (what Tillich calls idolatry)? Or are we reverencing something that raises us up to itself, that inspires us towards self-transcendence, that properly corresponds to our ultimate concern? In the words of Henry Corbin:

> Idolatry consists in immobilizing oneself before an idol because one sees it as opaque, because one is incapable of discerning in it the hidden invitation that it offers to go beyond it. Hence, the opposite of idolatry [...] would rather consist in rendering the idol transparent to the light invested in it. In short, it means transmuting the idol into an icon.[84]

We might even create a kind of mandala of reverence. A mandala, we could say, is a map of value. What we place in the centre tells us what we truly value, or, in other words, what we go for refuge to. Through such an exercise, we may discover that the values we have chosen to prioritize are rather mundane ones. We may differentiate between false or limited refuges and the ultimate, true refuge. For Buddhism, the most complete refuge is the three jewels, which function as our transcendental object. Consequently, if the three jewels are not at the centre of our mandala of reverence, we are engaged in a form of 'idolatry' – that is to say, settling on a limited refuge.

To that extent, we remain alienated from our ultimate concern and thus from the true significance of our lives.

Through devotional acts and attitudes directed towards the three jewels, we can restore and even celebrate our connection with our ultimate concern and so allow that ultimate concern to bless our existence. To go for refuge to the Buddha means to comport ourselves towards the Buddha as a focus of devotion, inspiration, and aspiration. It means to convert the Buddha image into an icon. It means to commit ourselves to minimizing, and even closing, the breach between our mind and the mind of the Buddha. Ultimately, this means to *become* the Buddha. Through reverence, I permit the transcendent to reconstitute me – to work upon me by means of its counter-intentionality. I give way to the weight of its glory, which fills me with blessing.

4

Carrying Dung in the Rain: Wisdom

> The dawn is the forerunner and precursor of the sunrise. In the same way, right view is the forerunner and precursor of skilful qualities.[85]

Wisdom (*prajna*) and faith (*shraddha*) form a complementary pair; not only do they reinforce one another, they also keep each other in check. Rather than being discrete faculties, they are interwoven aspects of our spiritual perception. As Buddhaghosa observes, when faith outstrips wisdom, we are prone to believe blindly, lacking discernment. Conversely, when wisdom dominates and faith is lacking, we may grow overly sceptical, even cunning – like someone made ill by the very medicine meant to heal them. When these two are held in balance, we are able to trust, yet only when there are firm grounds for doing so.[86] When wisdom arises, it dispels ignorance, illuminates the mind, and reveals the noble truths. The Dharma eye opens. With this expanded vision, we see clearly the three marks of existence: the impermanence, unsatisfactoriness, and lack of inherent existence that characterize all things. To use a classic analogy, it's like bringing a lamp into a darkened room – the darkness vanishes, and previously hidden shapes come into view.

In this chapter, we take up the topic of views (*drishti*) – how they inform our perception of reality and so influence our conduct. Some views impede the path towards wisdom, while others lead us towards it. Uncovering and dissolving unhelpful views enable us to adopt perspectives that harmonize rather than conflict with the nature of reality, thereby opening up new possibilities of perception. Crucially, wrong or limiting views are not so much propositions we affirm, but lenses through which we perceive the world. For this reason, they are difficult to recognize, especially when those around us think the same way.

We tend to assume we see the world just as it is. In truth, however, the world arises already shaped by our needs, interests, and expectations, not to mention the mediation of our senses. We're far from being surveillance cameras impartially registering their surroundings. As Anaïs Nin wrote, 'We don't see things as they are, we see them as we are.'[87] Our perception is embodied – woven through flesh and feeling – and deeply influenced by culture, memory, and history. We actively select, categorize, and construct. Indeed, without this selectivity, the sheer volume of sensory input would be overwhelming. Yet *how* we interpret the world is no small matter. Our views have profound ethical and existential implications, shaping not only how we act, but also what we care about – our ultimate concerns. Moreover, wrong views are a principal cause of our suffering and, often, lead us to inflict suffering on others.

If we accept that our suffering arises from how we interpret experience, then liberation depends on learning to see – and even to *be* – in a fundamentally different way. To do this, we must first make visible the views in which we are entangled, coax them into the light, and recognize how they limit us and thus give rise to suffering. We also need to cultivate new ways of perceiving and interpreting. Crucially, we must ensure these new perspectives actually reduce suffering, rather than simply replacing one regime of affliction with another.

From Wrong View to Right View

Views matter. They can inspire acts of generosity, courage, and compassion – or just as easily give rise to prejudice, cowardice, and cruelty. A single view can fuel the bloodlust to destroy an entire people or awaken the nobility to save one. Views can cripple or liberate us; they can ennoble or degrade us. The stakes are high, which is perhaps why Buddhism places such profound importance on views. The following example vividly illustrates their power.

Dr Bhimrao Ambedkar was born into a marginalized Dalit (formerly labelled 'untouchable') community in India – a group oppressed by the brutal degradations of the caste system. The prevailing view in his society was that caste-based inequality was natural and religiously sanctioned. Rejecting this oppressive worldview, Ambedkar was driven by an unshakeable belief in the fundamental equality and dignity of all human beings, which led him to denounce the evils of caste and strive for social justice. Ultimately, he was moved to reject Hinduism altogether as intrinsically contaminated by the poison of caste, and took the momentous decision to embrace Buddhism. Millions of his followers did likewise in the hope of bringing about their own uplift and a more just society.

The first stirrings of wisdom begin with the cultivation of right view (*samma-ditthi*). Early Buddhist texts analyze right view on two levels: the mundane (as the necessary foundation) and the transcendental (which amounts to true wisdom or Awakening). Crucially, embracing right view also requires the discernment to recognize and then abandon wrong views, which are often hidden and deeply rooted.

We might ask ourselves: how seriously do we take the views that we uphold? How much do we examine their consequences for our way of thinking, relating, and acting? Very often, we are not aware of the views that drive our behaviour, since we assume that they are facts and not convictions. This can lead us into a sense of superiority over others and often into conflict with them.

As the starting point of the noble eightfold path, right view is often described as its 'forerunner' – without it, progress cannot even begin.[88] Right view isn't about accumulating conventional knowledge or assenting to prescribed beliefs; it's more akin to taking up a set of directions and following them towards a destination – nirvana. One way to approach views is through considering three overlapping dimensions: their content, their function, and our relationship to them.

Content: A Thicket of Views

In terms of content, wrong views can be grouped into three broad categories. First, views that deny that actions have consequences – more specifically, a rejection of karma and its results. Second, views that are limiting or distorted beliefs about the nature of the self. Third, speculative, metaphysical beliefs that offer no practical value and serve only to distract from the path to liberation.

Ethical nihilism and the rejection of karma

In a conceptual and ethical sense, right view begins with affirming the principle of karma – that our volitional actions of body, speech, and mind shape our happiness and suffering, now and in the future. This view provides the ethical grounding for the path, and is expressed through the ten skilful courses of action, or ten precepts: refraining from harm, cultivating generosity, speaking truthfully, and so on.[89] In this context, right view stands in direct contrast to nihilistic perspectives that erase moral agency and the consequences of action, thereby eliminating ethical responsibility.

In the *Tittha Sutta*, the Buddha identifies three philosophical positions as instances of wrong view because they undermine moral responsibility.[90] Each attributes all experience – whether pleasurable, painful, or neutral – exclusively to one of the following causes:

1. **Past deeds (*karmic determinism*)** – the belief that all experiences are solely the result of past actions
2. **Divine creation (*theological determinism*)** – the belief that everything arises from the will of a creator god
3. **Randomness (*acausality*)** – the belief that experiences occur without any intelligible cause.

The Buddha points out that, if everything is predetermined by past karma, is ordained by divine will, or is entirely causeless, then there are no grounds for striving towards the good or avoiding evil. These views, each in its own way, negate the principle of karma and thereby remove any incentive to act skilfully. There's no moral jeopardy, nor recompense – no reason to pursue the good or avoid the harmful. Since all is determined or random, there are no grounds for moral accountability; killing, stealing, or lying would carry no moral consequence. As a result, those who hold such views become passive, indifferent, and ethically disoriented, unable to distinguish what should be cultivated from what should be avoided. Such points of view are dangerous because they fundamentally undermine moral agency and obstruct the path of spiritual development.

Ethically nihilistic views like the ones described above may seem remote, perhaps even ridiculous, yet a diluted form of the same outlook surfaces in the complaint that we are hapless victims of an unjust society. According to this view, people are basically good and are provoked into doing bad things only by the distortions of society. Therefore, we must all rage against the machine. If only we were to usher in a new social structure, everything would be better. But, while any society will be plagued by many ills, and these ills will always be a conditioning factor in our conduct, we also have agency in how we respond to societal conditioning and to the broader circumstances of our lives. Even if we didn't create our situation, we can still take responsibility for how we meet it. To blame society for all evils absolves us from ethical responsibility and, moreover, disempowers us. If our affliction is caused purely by society, then, until society changes, there is nothing we can do to improve our lot. We are perpetual victims. If true, this would indeed be a bleak situation.

I too have sometimes fallen into this self-limiting outlook. Since my early childhood, I have clung to the view that I have been hard done by, that life hasn't treated me fairly. Recently, a dear friend suggested that, far from being disadvantaged, I have a lot of merit. 'Merit' is the notion that we have carried out many skilful actions in the past (even in previous lives) and, for that reason, have invited beneficial circumstances for our life in general and our path to Awakening in particular. My instinctive response was to fall back on my habitual view that I have been hard done by. My childhood was unhappy. I had very little positive influence from adults, and many of my hopes and aspirations have been frustrated. Far from having a lot of merit, I often feel like a victim, that I have been dealt an unfair hand. Honestly, at times I even succumb to resentment.

But something about my friend's comment resonated. Suddenly, I started to think of all the people who have helped me, and still do, and began to feel that, far from being hard done by, I am blessed. I began to notice how often I receive gifts, seeing that, instead of being a victim of the world's indifference, I am a recipient of persistent benevolence. Of course, sometimes people act unfairly with me, some people are rather ungracious, but this is the exception rather than the norm. Above all, I realized that my narrative determined what I paid attention to – and therefore what I could perceive. My victim narrative was determining my lifeworld, my *Umwelt*, to borrow a German term.

This was recently brought into stark relief when I heard the life stories of a couple of Indian friends who were brought up in the hell of untouchability. One recounted how, as a child, she had to sleep in shrouds that, during the day, were used to carry corpses to the funeral pyre. When she and her family worked for caste Hindus, their employers would fling the coins of payment on the ground for her to pick up from the dirt. This assault on human dignity beggars belief. Yet she spoke about these matters without a trace of self-pity, having overcome these humiliating circumstances to live a noble and compassionate existence. Her circumstances did not determine her responses; she was able to see the value of the Buddhist teachings and adopt them as her pathway to freedom.

Another crippling variant of wrong view I sometimes fall into is what might be called the Cassandra complex. In Aeschylus' *Agamemnon*, the seer Cassandra predicts the king's murder by his wife Clytemnestra, only to be ignored. In a fit of bloodlust, Clytemnestra and her lover Aegisthus slaughter not only Agamemnon but Cassandra too. I readily succumb to the self-pitying view that no one listens to me, that what I say doesn't matter because it has no real impact. This way of thinking not only feeds my self-commiseration but also discourages me from speaking up when I ought to for the benefit of others. In the grip of this demon, I feel paralyzed, convinced that my efforts are meaningless, that reaching out to others makes no difference. When we believe our words and actions are inconsequential, we disempower ourselves and forfeit the chance to positively shape our own lives and to bless the lives of others. In effect, we erode the efficacy of karma – and, with it, the possibility of compassion.

In contrast to these wrong views, which merely serve to undermine ethical agency, another early scripture affirms that one who possesses right view 'understands the unskilful and its root, and the skilful and its root'.[91] Right view is thus defined primarily in ethical terms: a view matters because of how it motivates us to act. The unskilful is identified with the ten unwholesome actions, which arise from the roots of greed, hatred, and delusion. The skilful, conversely, is the opposite: the ten wholesome actions grounded in generosity, benevolence, and clarity of mind. The same scripture further elaborates right view in terms of various formulations of conditionality, or dependent arising – most notably the teaching of the four noble truths (see below).

Distorted views of the self

The second group of wrong views concerns limiting conceptions of the individual or self. Like the first group, these views obstruct the development of calm and insight, lead away from skilful action, and reinforce craving (*tanha*) and ignorance (*avijja*). A common misconception is that simply denying the existence of a self constitutes right view. This, however, is not the case. A view asserting 'there is no self' can be as deeply rooted in attachment and clinging as one that asserts 'there is a self.' Both constitute dogmatic postures and, as such, are obstacles to liberation. Taken to an extreme, the denial of the self might seem to justify the rejection of ethical accountability. After all, who can be held responsible?

The nature or basis of the self is central to an early text called *The Questions of King Milinda*. The king meets a monk and asks his name. 'I am Nagasena,' replies the monk, 'but that is just a conventional notion, there is no permanent individual who corresponds to that name.' Confused, the king retorts that, if it is true that there is no permanent self, then there is neither murderer nor crime, as no one is truly murdered.[92]

In response, Nagasena questions the king regarding the nature of a chariot, asking whether it corresponds to any individual part, the collection of parts, or something entirely beyond them. When the king negates each possibility, he is forced to acknowledge that 'chariot' names no independent thing, but arises only as a way of speaking about the assembled parts. The chariot remains real and functional – it can still be ridden – yet it possesses no inherent, independent identity. Just so with the human being. Nagasena shows that the self, like the chariot, exists only *conventionally* – able to act and bear responsibility, yet without any fixed, lasting essence.

This insight points to the most basic form of clinging to self, known in Buddhist tradition as 'identity view' (*sakkaya-ditthi*). Some sources regard this as the root from which all other wrong views sprout.[93] It arises when we identify ourselves with a reduced range of experience – for example, the body through vanity, our beliefs through dogmatism, or particular emotional states such as anger, depression, or even happiness. According to classic Buddhist analysis, we read a self into one or more of the five aggregates (*skandhas*): form, feeling, perception, mental formations, and consciousness. This is like conflating the chariot with its axle or wheels.

Such views are not merely intellectual beliefs; they betray a deeply ingrained tendency to grasp at a sense of enduring identity. Under the sway of identity view, we distort experience, mistaking what is impermanent and contingent for something lasting and essential. Faced with the torrent of thoughts and the flow of sensations, we seek some grounding, some stable reference. Everything feels insubstantial, fleeting, and insufficient. To compensate, we fix ourselves as a kind of habit – a defensive contraction that limits our possibilities. We create an image of ourselves that is not fully real, investing a great deal of energy to sustain and protect it. This is an exhausting project that generates a constant strain.

Speculative views

The third group of wrong views concerns speculative theories about the ultimate nature of reality. The early scriptures make it clear that such views should not occupy our attention, as they give rise to new defilements and reinforce existing ones – particularly sensual desire, the craving for continued existence, and ignorance.[94] Moreover, they distract us from what really matters. Instead, the mind should be directed towards reflections that give rise to skilful mental states and help weaken and abandon defilements already present.

In one well-known dialogue, the ascetic Vacchagotta poses a series of ten metaphysical questions to the Buddha, asking about the nature of the universe, the self, the relationship between mind and body, and the fate of the enlightened after death. The Buddha declines to answer, describing each of these as 'a thicket of views, a wilderness of views, a contortion of views, a vacillation of views, a fetter of views'.[95] He adds that such views are 'beset by suffering, by vexation, by despair, and by fever' and consequently do 'not lead to disenchantment, to dispassion, to cessation, to peace, to direct knowledge, to enlightenment, to Nibbana'.[96]

This thicket of ten speculative views – known as the 'undeclared questions' (*avyakata*) – is set aside because such questions are not conducive to liberation. According to the Buddha, engaging with them 'does not belong to the fundamentals of the holy life'. He illustrates this with a striking analogy.[97] Suppose, he says, that a man is wounded by a poisoned arrow. Instead of urging the surgeon to extract the shaft, the man insists on knowing the archer's caste, name, and appearance, as well as the materials used to make the bow and arrow. Just as this man would die before his curiosity could be satisfied, those who refuse to embark on the path until the cosmos is fully explained will die with the 'poison' of suffering still working within them. The Buddha makes clear that he has abandoned all speculative views,[98] not by replacing them with other metaphysical doctrines, but by realizing their futility through liberating insight.

Function: The Raft

Reflecting on the views discussed above, it becomes clear that the function of right view is not to describe reality in some conclusive and triumphant turn of phrase. Instead, such views are meant to support transformation. The Buddha wasn't interested in formulating a complete theory of the universe: he was motivated to help people let go of unnecessary suffering.

A view is valuable not because it's philosophically persuasive, but because it helps reduce craving, confusion, and attachment. It moves us towards greater clarity, freedom, and peace. If a view leads to more suffering – through clinging, pride, or conflict – then, from a Buddhist perspective, it no longer serves us and should be let go. This explains why the Buddha often stayed silent when asked speculative or metaphysical questions – they didn't lead anywhere useful.

The famous parable of the raft illustrates the Buddha's understanding of the function of views in relation to liberation.[99] Imagine a traveller encountering a dangerous flood. Finding no bridge or ferry, the traveller builds a raft from branches, leaves, and grass to safely cross to the far shore. Once across, the traveller wonders whether to carry the raft onwards. The Buddha asks if this would be sensible. His disciples reply that it would not; since the raft has served its purpose, it should be left behind.

The Buddha then equates this raft to his teachings, explaining that they are a tool for 'crossing over' – that is, for achieving liberation – not something to cling to for their own sake. In this light, right view is valuable not in itself, but for the crucial role it plays in freeing the mind from suffering. It serves a specific purpose, and, beyond that, it holds no independent meaning or value.

So the real question is not 'Is this view true?', but rather 'What does this view *do*?' Does it lead to more peace or more tension? More openness or more rigidity? More freedom – or more grasping? The notion of non-self or not-self, for example, is not so much a theory to be affirmed than a contemplative instruction: 'This is not mine, I am not this, this is not my self.' Far from being a metaphysical proposition, this method becomes a means of undoing attachment and so opening ourselves to greater possibilities.

Covered in Filth: Our Relation to Views

We might ask: what does it actually mean to hold a view, and how do we know when we are under its sway? To hold a view is not merely to give verbal assent to it, but to act as though it were true. It follows that we may espouse views that we don't truly believe, in the sense that these views fail to shape our conduct. Conversely, we may hold beliefs that we outwardly disavow, yet that nonetheless show themselves in our actions, speech, and patterns of thought. Adding to this complexity, we may cling to views at various levels of depth, sometimes even maintaining contradictory ones that surface at different times.

It's also worth reflecting more generally on why we hold on to views so tightly. Why do we defend them, argue over them, even fight about them? Often, it's not just the content of the view, but what it represents – our identity, our need for certainty, our fear of being wrong. Views often serve to rationalize desire, and so even an ostensibly right view can harden into dogma when grasped rigidly. When this happens, a view becomes another object of clinging, and therefore another source of suffering.

There's a parable found in the early scriptures that captures this situation with remarkable insight and humour. It centres on a debate between the monk Kassapa and Prince Payasi, a determined sceptic.[100] Payasi denies the reality of karma and rebirth, asserting that actions carry no moral consequences, and that ethical precepts are ultimately pointless. Kassapa responds through a series of analogies that gently expose the prince's flawed reasoning, showing that his views, far from being liberating, are themselves a source of suffering.

Yet Payasi stubbornly resists. Even as the force of Kassapa's arguments begins to strike home, the prince doggedly defends his position – not because it makes sense, but because he fears being judged a fool.

Kassapa then offers a parable. While travelling between villages, a pig keeper comes across some dry dung and decides it will make excellent feed for his pigs. He spreads out a cloth, gathers the dung, and carries it home on his head, as was customary. Partway through his journey, however, he's caught in an unseasonal downpour. The dung softens into sludge, oozes down his scalp, soaks his clothes, and drips from his fingertips. Onlookers cry out, 'You must be mad! Why are you covered in filth?' Defiant, the man insists, 'You're the crazy ones. This dung will make fine food for my pigs!' Kassapa tells Payasi: you are like this man. Even when your views have turned foul – when they no longer serve any useful purpose – you stubbornly cling to them.

Wrong views are afflictions. They harm us, yet, like Payasi, we still cling to them. Moreover, they are not always easy to let go of, for they are rarely mere intellectual postures. Often, they behave more like demons: lurking in the deep, surfacing when we are least prepared, and dragging us back into the darkness. Even when we think we have finally pinned one down, it may wriggle free and torment us once more.

Consequently, adopting right view is not just about exchanging one set of positions for another, like changing a shirt. It also requires understanding what drives us to insist on a view in the first place, and loosening our grip on views altogether. Even ostensibly right views can be misused – for instance, to bolster the self or to defeat others in debate and lord it over them. Importantly, any view held with attachment becomes a wrong view. Right view, then, is not fundamentally a type of knowledge, but rather a way of seeing that is free from attachment.

Right view is commonly defined through the four noble truths. Contemplating these truths leads to decisive insight and, ultimately, freedom from attachment to all views.

The Four Noble Truths

The Buddha set out on the path towards awakening upon realizing that suffering is universal and inevitable. No matter how stable or secure we feel, pain and difficulty will eventually confront us. This emphasis on suffering leads some people to dismiss Buddhism as pessimistic, even life-denying. But directing attention to the imperfections, frictions, and even hardships of human existence has a noble goal: to transcend this predicament and ultimately achieve Awakening, or nirvana.

This transformative vision is encapsulated in the four noble truths – a simple yet profound formula that serves as a fundamental statement of right view and the primary application of conditionality. According to tradition, the Buddha expounded this sacred prescription in his very first teaching, and its insights remain powerfully relevant today.[101] The four noble truths are formulated as follows:

1. Suffering or dissatisfaction
2. The cause of suffering (craving or attachment)
3. The end of suffering (nirvana)
4. The path that leads to the end of suffering (the noble eightfold path).

The four noble truths show why Buddhism focuses on suffering, and how nirvana serves as its remedy. They provide a framework for reflection and action to reduce our own suffering and avoid causing suffering for others. Paying careful attention to suffering helps us foster greater sensitivity to ourselves and all other beings.

1. Suffering

Suffering is endemic to human existence. This doesn't mean that every part of life is painful or bleak; it highlights that suffering is a fundamental constraint of our condition – something none of us can ultimately avoid. At the same time, we should never lose sight of the fact that life also contains beauty, joy, and love. Still, even in the midst of life's wonders, we're bound to hit a pothole in the road.

When I visit friends in Mexico City, we often go for breakfast at Frutos Prohibidos,[102] a small café in the Roma neighbourhood, a *colonia* now world-renowned thanks to Alfonso Cuarón's nostalgic film about his childhood. As I sit enjoying my favourite chilaquiles, a slow, sad carousel of marginalized passersby circles the tables, hoping for a sale or a *moneda* (coin). Among them are *ambulantes* (street vendors), shoe cleaners, and beggars – most bedraggled, some elderly, some just children already resigned to their lives of dispossession. I find myself reflecting on the privileges I enjoy while others live right on the edge of survival. Then I look up. Just a few doors down, there's a line of shiny, affluent young people waiting to be admitted to an exclusive restaurant. And in that moment, a strange unease arises. I catch myself wondering – *has life somehow passed me by?*

To grasp the implications of the first noble truth, we can recognize suffering on three levels. First, there's everyday suffering: pain, illness, death, and other common hardships. This kind of suffering is inevitable, yet we often try to escape it – which almost always makes things worse. Second, there's suffering that arises from change. Even when we experience pleasure, it inevitably fades. This not only causes anxiety but also leaves us with a sense of loss. Third, there's existential suffering – a subtle yet pervasive lack that seems to underlie everything. It points to a deeper truth: ordinary pleasures and worldly experiences, however vivid, never fully satisfy our deepest needs and longings. To address this kind of suffering, we need a spiritual path. We need to respond to the call of our ultimate concern.

If we pay attention, suffering may open a crack in our habitual world, allowing the transcendent to shine through. Suffering thus invites us to relinquish our reliance on limited forms of refuge and to turn instead towards what is truly sustaining: the three jewels. The first noble truth, then, does not reject life; rather, it calls upon us to contemplate the underlying disquiet we carry within, urging us towards what is more deeply meaningful.

2. The cause of suffering: craving or attachment

How does suffering arise? While it seems to spring from life itself, striking us suddenly and without invitation, the Buddha explains that, fundamentally, it arises from compulsive craving or attachment. For instance, if we desperately want something to remain unchanged – be it a relationship or our physical body – we resist the onward rush of life. But change happens regardless; we cannot stop it. Things break, the people we love change, our bodies age. When our desires conflict with this reality, we suffer. Instead of relinquishing our desires, we often cling on even harder, yet life continues to slip through our fingers.

Craving is a neurotic, out-of-control compulsion – a bottomless longing that devours its object. In Buddhist cosmology, this compulsive desire is embodied in the *pretas*, or hungry ghosts, who are in a state of perpetual torment. Trapped in a cycle of insatiable desire from which they can never free themselves, *pretas* are self-condemned to interminable frustration. They possess huge bellies but tiny mouths; everything they drink turns to liquid fire, and everything they eat spoils into excrement. While this situation may sound grotesque, we should remember that the *pretas* mirror the way we ourselves so often experience the world.

We often project the cause of our suffering onto a particular situation or person. We then change the situation, or distance ourselves from people, mistakenly believing that we will find freedom from suffering. But this doesn't work, because, fundamentally, suffering arises from our own mind. An early scripture speaks of the 'two arrows of suffering'.[103] The first arrow represents unavoidable events: physical pain, disappointment, or loss – it strikes regardless. But the second arrow is our reaction to that pain: 'Poor me... Why me?... I don't want this... It's not fair...', and so on. This is the second arrow, by which we pierce *ourselves*. According to the Buddha, we can learn not to react in this way and so open up greater possibilities for freedom and joy.

3. The end of suffering: nirvana

Nirvana is characterized as a state of freedom from suffering, and as one of knowledge, peace, purity, joy, and compassion. While each of these conceptions discloses an aspect of the infinite expanse that is nirvana, they remain analogies. The peace of nirvana, for instance, is something far deeper and more intense than the peace felt when contemplating the sunset. While such experiences may foreshadow nirvana, it remains transcendent – always beyond.

Similarly, nirvana is evoked through metaphors, images, and elaborate visionary scenes. It is compared, for example, to a cool cave offering relief from oppressive heat, or a tranquil island refuge in the midst of a devastating flood.

While early Buddhism characterized nirvana as a personal awakening that profoundly transforms our individual outlook, some later traditions – especially strands of Mahayana Buddhism – imagined it in more concrete, spatial terms: as an ideal world, even an ideal community or sangha. This is suggested through analogies of infinite light, space, and time. This approach crystallized in the notion of the Pure Land, a perfect realm in which to realize the truths of Buddhism. These visionary realms are described through lavish imagery: jewel trees, jewel lakes, and birds that sing the melody of impermanence. Above all, the Pure Land is characterized by infinite space and scintillating light, evoking an atmosphere of brilliance, vastness, and sacred splendour. Such imagery expands our imaginative horizon so that we may intuit a reality beyond the ordinary senses – not precisely another world, but an expanded dimension in which everything is illuminated. When imagination stirs, we may see everything as a revelation of the true nature of things: we see with the Dharma eye.

In Mahayana Buddhism, nirvana is no longer restricted to a personal quest for liberation from suffering; it becomes instead a cosmic myth in which all beings participate. The sacred life of the individual Buddhist – the bodhisattva, the 'Awakening being' – unfolds within an infinite dimension: a realm of innumerable buddhas, incalculable worlds, and immeasurable time. The bodhisattva does not crave escape from the rounds of birth and death but, moved by compassion, aspires to be reborn again and again in order to guide all beings towards Awakening.

4. The path to the end of suffering: the noble eightfold path

The path to the end of suffering – nirvana – is evoked through many images and models. Alongside the five spiritual faculties, another classic formulation is the noble eightfold path. As will be clear, there is considerable overlap between the two models:

1. **Right view** means developing a vision of existence that accords with reality and supports spiritual development.
2. **Right aspiration** means purifying our motivations, so that our engagement with the Dharma is sincere and consistent.
3. **Right speech** calls for ethical communication – truthful, kind, beneficial, and harmonious – guided by Buddhist values.
4. **Right action** entails living ethically, applying the precepts to our choices and behaviours in daily life.
5. **Right livelihood** extends this ethical sensitivity to how we earn our living, ensuring it supports rather than undermines our highest values.
6. **Right effort** involves working with the mind to eradicate unskilful mental states, prevent their further arising, and develop and maintain skilful ones.
7. **Right mindfulness** is the cultivation of awareness of oneself, others, the environment, and ultimately reality.

8. **Right meditation** (or right concentration) consists in the integration of the mind through meditative absorption, laying the foundation for insight into the true nature of things.[104]

While these elements are sometimes presented as sequential steps, they can also be understood as qualities to be cultivated simultaneously – just like the five spiritual faculties. Taken as a whole, the eightfold path amounts to a comprehensive programme for self-transformation.

Perfect Wisdom and Insight

Buddhist scriptures distinguish two levels of right view – mundane and transcendental.[105] The second level is what we might properly call wisdom, but even mundane right view isn't a matter of merely adopting certain propositions. Rather, these propositions are taken up in order to reshape our actions so that we act consistently in a non-selfish way. Ultimately, right view fosters a new mode of relation with reality – an expanded field of perception purified of greed, hatred, and delusion.

While abandoning wrong views and, especially, gaining supramundane right view are often associated with meditation practice, the Pali canon more commonly shows people achieving decisive insight through seeing the Buddha, listening to one of his talks, or engaging in a Dharma dialogue either with the Buddha himself or with one of his disciples. A classic example is Upali, who initially approaches the Buddha in the arrogant expectation of worsting him in debate.[106] After a vigorous exchange of views, Upali eagerly embraces the Buddha as his teacher. The Buddha then instructs him in the four noble truths and, 'just as a clean cloth with all marks removed would take dye evenly', so too, while Upali listens – spellbound – the spotless, immaculate vision of the Dharma arises in him and he understands directly: 'All that is subject to arising is subject to cessation.' The text continues:

> Upali saw the Dhamma, attained the Dhamma, understood the Dhamma, fathomed the Dhamma; he crossed beyond doubt, did away with perplexity, gained intrepidity, and became independent in the teacher's dispensation.[107]

Once the Dharma has been fathomed in this way, and one has crossed beyond doubt, even the raft that is right view is no longer needed, since one now sees directly into the nature of things.

The Shadows of Wisdom

Like all the spiritual faculties, wisdom has both near and far enemies. Its most obvious and persistent adversary is ignorance – not so much a deficit of information as a stubborn resistance to reality itself, a wilful refusal to face things as they are. According to Buddhism, this is our basic existential condition, so it is no surprise that ignorance can be deeply entrenched. It manifests as a kind of closed-mindedness, a refusal to open to deeper possibilities, which may appear threatening. Sometimes we catch a glimpse of reality, but its implications unsettle us; frightened, we retreat into the false security of ignorance, though it never truly consoles. We may take refuge in knowledge, hoarding information to make ourselves feel more solid and assured. Yet knowledge is not wisdom. Knowledge catalogues and classifies, circling the outer surfaces of things, whereas wisdom penetrates to their interior. Knowledge is extensive; wisdom is intensive. Knowledge is acquisitive; wisdom is transformative.

A subtler enemy of wisdom is literalism, often accompanied by dogmatism. Literalism obstructs the religious imagination because it collapses the vital distance between symbol and meaning – the very interval where reverence awakens. By insisting that words, images, or doctrines refer only to what they explicitly declare, it denies the depth-dimension of experience. The sacred becomes what can be measured or proved, rather than what may be evoked through wonder and participation.

When we cling to the surface meaning of teachings or symbols, we fashion conceptual idols. We mistake the finger for the moon, and the Dharma – meant to liberate – hardens into a system of beliefs to accept and defend. Such a mentality underlies many forms of fundamentalism, religious and otherwise. It is born of fear, a defensive recoil from the complexity of life, and ends in servitude to dogma.

Moving beyond literalism means not abandoning reason, but recovering symbolic perception: seeing the world not as a busy exchange of facts, but as a living field of significance through which reality radiates. In this sense, wisdom is as much an awakening of imagination as it is a refinement of understanding.

5

What Cannot Be Exhaustively Seen

> The perfection of wisdom gives light [...] brings light to the blind, she brings light so that all fear and distress may be forsaken. She has gained the five eyes, and she shows the path to all beings. She herself is an organ of vision.[108]

In the first instance, wisdom might seem to imply a cool, distanced contemplation of reality: a sage meditating on a mountaintop or a scholar poring over ancient texts. But, in this chapter, we'll explore how wisdom evokes wonder, openness, and loving attention. Within Buddhism, the path to wisdom is often described as a progression through three stages: listening, reflection, and transformation. While these stages can unfold sequentially, insight may arise at any point – through absorbing new ideas, through the rigorous work of examining our assumptions, or through deep contemplation on the nature of reality.

Wisdom is not about stockpiling knowledge or chasing peak experiences. It is not about arriving at a tidy, finished answer. Rather, it is an ongoing process of discovery – a form of embodied meaning-making that draws us into deeper relationship with ourselves, with others, and with the world. We are called not to abandon our interpretive capacities, but rather to refine them, so that experience may begin to yield its inexhaustible richness. Wisdom, then, is not a cold mirror that merely reflects – it is a creative capacity. It is imaginative, relational, and alive.

1. Listening

I confess to a habit of compiling lists of books that I hope to read. When I come across a survey that proclaims 'The hundred greatest books in English', or 'The hundred greatest books of the twentieth century', I immediately want to check off how many of them I have read. If there are big gaps, I create a list of priorities, imagining how smug and erudite I will feel when I have read them all (I never do). But, when reading a classic work, I sometimes get bored – I never finished *Moby Dick*, for example, nor *Don Quijote*, not to speak of *Ulysses* – and so fall into an attitude of 'getting through' the book in order to mount it on my trophy list. The book becomes an object of consumption rather than an opportunity to enlarge my consciousness. In moments, I come to my senses and realize that I have 'read' several pages but don't have the slightest idea what they were about. My attention drifts off, and my reading degenerates into a mechanical act, not at all connected to my imagination. Years later, I may have completely forgotten the content of *Madame Bovary*, *Crime and Punishment*, or some other eminent tale. Perhaps you have experienced something similar.

My struggles with 'trophy reading' hint at some of the complexities and pitfalls that surround the first level of wisdom: *hearing* or *listening*. This refers to the process of learning something for the first time – perhaps hearing a talk, reading a book, or even coming across a Buddhist quote online. At this level, we process the material to understand it in a basic way. This invites a number of key questions: why are we reading? What to read? And how to read?

Why are we reading?

In my example of reading classic novels, while I genuinely aspire to open myself to the sensibility and reflection of the author, I readily reduce the opportunity to a mode of consumption. The book becomes something merely 'added on' to my experience. Instead of recognizing that reading a book is an invitation to enlarge my imagination and transform my conduct, it becomes a quantitative, acquisitive enterprise. Given the dominance of a consumerist mentality, this is quite understandable. A book becomes an experience to be consumed – just like a meal or a visit to a theme park.

Within a Buddhist context, however, the purpose of reading is to inspire transformation. At an initial level, this involves becoming more aware of our limiting patterns of belief, as well as our hidden assumptions, and adopting frames of reference – right views – that lead in the direction of greater freedom. Our chosen text becomes a mirror through which we can see ourselves with greater clarity.

What to read?

There is so much to read. We truly now live in Borges' mythical library of Babel (a metaphorical universe containing all possible books). Given the overwhelming volume of material available, our first dilemma is what to read. For now, we will focus on Buddhist material. What should we expose ourselves to? There are so many possibilities that it can be paralyzing even to think about it. There is Tibetan Buddhism, Zen Buddhism, Theravada Buddhism, and so on. There are scriptures, traditional commentaries, and contemporary adaptations. As never before, the entire gamut of Buddhist inspiration is open to us. This situation is very different from that of the traditional Buddhist, who would not have been able to read – and certainly would not have had direct access to Buddhist scriptures. Their learning would have been mediated by a teacher, usually a monk. For lay people, this exposure was limited to special occasions such as festivals or funerals. For a monastic, it meant studying with an elder.

A likely outcome of encountering such a bewildering volume of material is confusion. Not all schools share the same assumptions; their differing foundational views can make it challenging to reconcile concepts across traditions. One of the first books I read on Buddhism was Lama Govinda's classic *Foundations of Tibetan Mysticism*. While I now recognize that Govinda was an inspired interpreter, at the time I barely understood a word.

Since the possibilities are vast, we need to be selective about what we choose to read or learn – not simply because of the danger of confusion, but also in view of time constraints. It may make sense to read a restricted number of texts several times, allowing for deeper engagement and absorption, rather than constantly looking for new things to read. I am reminded of the novel *Fahrenheit 451*, in which the outlaws memorize just one classic work. Of course, it is not just about mechanical memory but about becoming intimate with a text. Once we have read a few works, it may make sense to adopt one of these as a regular touchstone – such as the *Dhammapada* or Shantideva's *Bodhicharyavatara* – returning to it again and again. This anticipates the second level of wisdom: *reflecting*. I had a friend called Susiddhi who only ever offered workshops on the *Heart Sutra*. He reasoned that it made more sense to go deeply into one short but profound text rather than skim a large volume of material.

Sangharakshita emphasized the importance of reading the early texts and studying the earlier teachings in order to better understand the later ones – and not the other way around.[109] He suggested that we focus our attention on what he called 'basic Buddhism': the key teachings such as conditionality, the four noble truths, and the ethical precepts. He stressed that these early teachings are generally simpler and more direct, less burdened by metaphysical speculation, which he believed had crept into later developments.

How to read?

This first level of wisdom also involves training ourselves to listen effectively. If we're distracted – like a sieve that retains none of the water – we won't absorb anything we're trying to learn. We need to *prepare* the mind to pay attention. This requires the right timing, a suitable environment (one relatively free from disturbances), and a mind at least temporarily freed from distractions and worries. If our reading material is complex, we may drift away and seek diversion, perhaps in fantasy, social media, or calling a friend. For this reason, it is very helpful to read and study with others. This invites us into a more intensive, intimate relationship with a text.

Reading a Buddhist text is nothing like consulting a furniture-assembly manual. It requires a different quality of attention: curious, careful, receptive – even reverential. To 'listen well' means allowing the text or talk to personally impact us, spurring a change in how we think and, therefore, how we live. The Confucian thinker Zhu Xi (1130–1200) emphasized three key aspects of a rigorous approach to reading: carefulness (*xixin*), patience (*naixin*), and modesty (*xuxin*). First, we should carefully read a passage over and over again to grasp its meaning, until the 'ideas seem to come from our own mind'.[110] Such reading enables us to understand and empathize with the thoughts and experiences of others. Second, we should read patiently, and 'concentrate fully, without thought of gain'.[111] We shouldn't hurry our reading. Instead of reading a lot, we should focus on just a short paragraph and read it repeatedly. It is best 'to read less but to *become intimately familiar* with what you read'.[112] Often we read 'ten separate pieces when it would be best to read one part in ten'.[113] We should extend the time we devote to reading but, at the same time, limit the *quantity* of material. Finally, we should approach reading with modesty, which means that we remain open to what the text has to teach us, without assuming that we already know, or that we know better. We should 'open the heart' (*xuxin*) to the text and so allow ourselves to be enlarged by its message.

The philosopher Byung-Chul Han warns against what he calls 'serial perception', which is a constant chasing after the new, which never really sticks in one's mind because it is disposable, momentary. Serial perception

> rushes from one piece of information to the next, from one experience to the next, from one sensation to the next, without ever coming to closure. [...] At the level of media consumption, this habit leads to binge watching, to comatose viewing.[114]

We can readily import this attitude into our own reading habits. Serial perception is 'extensive', concerned with quantity, rather than intensive, which focuses instead on quality and depth of relation.

As an antidote, Han emphasizes the value of *repetition*, and even learning by heart, as means of taking material more deeply into ourselves, so that it soaks into us, becoming part of our matter. 'Repetition stabilizes and deepens attention', he argues.[115] It creates an *intensity* of connection. Repetition is our daily bread.

2. Reflection

The second level of wisdom is *reflection*, in which we consider the consequences and implications of what we've read or learned. We also apply it to our own experience. A helpful exercise – though perhaps not a comfortable one – is to take stock of our views, assumptions, and perceptions, and ask: how many of these have emerged from my own, independent reflection? If we're honest, the answer is likely to be not many. Unless we are unusually independent-minded, most of what we 'know' comes not from direct insight but from what we've read, heard, or just absorbed from the cultural atmosphere we inhabit.

We live in an age of relentless information. Opinions and soundbites circulate constantly – on our screens, in conversation, in the media. Now, perhaps even more than ever, it's important to examine the prevalent narratives and ideologies that dominate the cultural space. Yet, in view of all this mental traffic, how often do we take the time to think something through – to interrogate an idea patiently, trace its roots, and explore its implications? Unless our livelihood depends on reflection, we may feel we can't afford the luxury of thinking deeply. But can we afford not to?

Ideologies promise certainty, but at great cost. They simplify the world into neat categories, offering ready-made answers where instead we should be asking deeper questions. Though often grounded in partial truths, ideologies distort reality by repressing nuance. They beguile us with a sense of certainty, clarity, and even righteousness, but, in doing so, they close down genuine enquiry and blind us to complexity.

Such rigid thought is antithetical to the spirit of *prajna*. Pursuing true wisdom requires the humility to recognize that we are fallible, that our views may be distorted, our information may be faulty, and the world is not susceptible to formulaic interpretations. Rather than box reality into ideological frameworks, we can train the mind to rest in openness, to observe carefully, and to enquire sincerely and persistently. We should never override our doubts and concerns, but see them as opportunities to reflect more deeply on an issue at stake. When we start to ignore such solicitations, we surrender our capacity for thought and abandon our individuality in favour of conformity or convenience.

Much of what passes for thinking is simply the recycling of

received opinion. Much of our thinking then is not our own; it has not been consciously chosen but rather unconsciously absorbed. Have we ever reflected on a question so attentively, so honestly, that something fresh and genuine revealed itself – however modest or provisional? If our understanding of the Dharma is to deepen, it must involve more than the passive reception of teachings. It requires an active, even courageous, engagement – a willingness to question, to doubt, and, eventually, to see for ourselves.

How do we reflect?

There is no shortcut to developing deeper reflection. We start by recognizing that it is worthwhile. If we practise reflection, we will get better at it, just as, if we exercise regularly, we will get fitter. Reflection depends in part on curiosity: noticing when something doesn't seem to add up, when it contradicts what we believe, or when we simply don't fully grasp an idea or its relevance. These are all clues that can provoke us into deeper thought.

Reflection often emerges from a 'disruptive mood', such as perplexity, wonder, surprise, and even anxiety. It may also arise in situations of disagreement. By disrupting our routine equilibrium, these moments allow us to step back, to question, and so to make sense of the world in new ways.

Often our minds are so busy processing material that there is no space to stand back and reflect. Therefore, we must actively create time for reflection, seeking moments when we are not preoccupied with other tasks. This might mean a quiet walk, or sitting peacefully in a chair, and consciously bringing a topic to mind to explore with questions.

We can also have conversations with others and listen to their reflections. Often this inspires us to think more deeply about any given subject. We shouldn't rush ahead to the next learning before this process has had time to unfold. We can even enter into 'conversation' with a text. We can ask: what is the claim here? What is the evidence? What is the argument? We could try rewriting an argument in our own words and review whether it makes sense.

Writing in general can support deeper reflection. It demands greater precision than dialogue and, through trying to put an idea down on paper, we can begin to see how confused we are or how poorly we have reflected on the issue at hand. Keeping a journal of our reflections could be one way to support this process.

When we come across an idea and find ourselves resisting it, we are faced with a golden opportunity to discover what we truly believe and feel. This creates the possibility to consciously reassess our views and decide whether we want to endorse them.

If a contrasting perspective provokes anger, this doesn't necessarily mean that we are wrong, but it does offer a means by which we can bring a view to the surface in order to examine its credentials. The same is also true if we find ourselves strongly attracted to a certain perspective. If we find ourselves affirming something vehemently, this will tell us something about what we truly think.

Soliciting our prejudices

Hans-Georg Gadamer proposed that all understanding relies on prejudices or 'fore-understandings'. He used 'prejudice' neutrally, referring to pre-judgements that can be favourable, negative, or neither. When engaging with anything – an idea, a text, a painting, even a platypus – we project a meaning based on our expectations or prior experiences. This means a crucial aspect of understanding is becoming aware of our own interpretive habits, as these can lead to limited and even harmful readings. Consequently, understanding any phenomenon really requires us to understand ourselves, bringing our own values and beliefs to light.

As we become conscious of our prejudices, the object of our understanding can 'assert its own truth against one's own fore-meanings'.[116] We 'try on' interpretations, and, if they work, they gain currency. Our understanding proceeds by anticipation, much like predictive text on a cellphone: we project an interpretation and then see whether it withstands scrutiny. If our projection is resisted, we revise our interpretation, and so the process begins anew. Prejudices, therefore, are not inherently bad; they are a necessary precondition for any understanding. Without them, we would have no basis to engage with anything new.

Understanding relies heavily on comparison and analogy: we grasp new concepts by relating them to what's already familiar. Consider the first European encounters with the platypus: it was initially dismissed as a composite of familiar animals that had been stitched together. Our understanding always builds upon existing referents of knowledge.

The real problem, then, isn't having prejudices, but being unwilling to review or abandon them even when experience outgrows them. This intellectual laziness can lead to rigidity, a kind of wilful blindness, hindering our growth. If an initial interpretation doesn't fit, we should drop it. This invites a process of continuous revision: a 'conversation' with ourselves, with a text, and with others, which Gadamer called the 'hermeneutic circle'. Understanding is therefore never finished, but always renewed.

According to Gadamer, prejudices become visible only when 'provoked'. Encountering difference is key to this provocation. When our existing frameworks fail to 'grip' a new experience, phenomenon, or person, we become aware of our ready-made thinking. Noting this moment of resistance is the starting point for reflection and so for new learning.

3. Transformation

The third level of wisdom is meditation or transformation, where what we've learned becomes so deeply absorbed that it shapes how we live, even the way we perceive. This raises the question: what does it mean to 'have wisdom'? More specifically, what does it mean to realize Enlightenment or nirvana? One of the difficulties in conceiving of Enlightenment is that we must always project it as an extension of the non-enlightened self whereas, properly speaking, it arises when that self is disrupted or even transcended.

Is nirvana an 'experience'?

> I've never really had a religious experience, in a religious place. Closest I've ever come to seeing or feeling God is listening to rap music. Rap music is my religion. Amen.[117]

So says Killer Mike. Perhaps you can relate to his sentiment, or perhaps not. In any case, it's worth asking how much stock we should place in 'experience', especially when evaluating progress in the Dharma. 'Experience' is a sacred tenet of postmodern, consumer culture. Shopping, for instance, is no longer a burdensome weekly chore, but rather an 'experience' to be savoured. Many people seek out extreme sports in search of peak experiences. Happiness is measured out in spoonfuls of experience. Yet, as Gadamer pointed out, experience is 'among the least clarified concepts which we have'.[118] We invoke it constantly, but rarely pause to consider what it truly means. Experience is private, subjective, and thus often beyond the reach of scrutiny, especially when divorced from tradition, community, and ethical norms. In today's climate, where subjective feeling is often valued above objective truth, shared commitments, and tradition, it's easy to assume that experience should be the guiding factor in Dharma life.

This mindset leads to a seductive narrative: 'I am an unenlightened worldling now, but, through intense practice – or perhaps a special method or teacher – I will one day have a sublime experience that changes everything.' Enlightenment, on this view, becomes a peak psychological event to be attained in the future. Once it arrives, life will be permanently better.

But there are serious problems with conceiving of Enlightenment as an experience to be looked forward to or retrospectively glorified. Here we will touch on three: experience is a reconstructed narrative; the consumerist seizure of spiritual experience; and the private character of all experience.

Experience is a reconstructed narrative

Experience itself isn't as stable or transparent as we might assume. What we usually call 'experience' is in fact a narrative reconstruction – a story we tell ourselves to make sense of what happened. This means we might look back on a particular moment and declare, 'That's when I gained nirvana.' Worse, we feel discouraged if we can't pinpoint even a hint of such a moment. Either way, the underlying assumption is flawed.

We tend to think of experience as if it were something stored – like a file in a drawer. Memory, especially episodic memory, seems to allow us to locate that file, take it out, examine it, and then return it, unchanged, to its original place. On this view, experience is fixed in the past, and, through mental time travel, we can revisit it at will.

In reality, we're constantly reimagining our past experiences. This happens because we're always reorganizing them in relation to our current self-understanding. Experience doesn't exist in some preserved past, like something in a jar on a shelf that we can return to and open. Rather, it's continuously remade through memory in the present – always renewed, and thus always different. Memories aren't photographs but creative retellings, shaped by what seems meaningful to us now. Mystical experiences are never pure – they are shaped by culture, language, doctrine, expectation, and history.[119] They are not simply revealed but *created* through interpretation. So insight, too, cannot truly have 'taken place' in the past; it reveals itself, if at all, as a dimension of awareness within the present.

What constitutes an insight is more than a momentary glimpse of reality. In retrospect, we may highlight a luminous instant as decisive, yet its true value lies in how it continues to work within and upon us – how it is absorbed, integrated, and applied, gradually reshaping the texture of our lives. Deeper insights tend to unfold over time, as the initial upwelling of understanding seeps into consciousness like water filling an underground cistern, until our whole being is quietly saturated and refreshed.

The consumerist seizure of spiritual experience

When nirvana is framed as an experience, spiritual life risks being reduced to a consumer transaction. We begin treating this profound orientation like a product – something to possess, to accumulate, to flaunt. In a thrill-seeking culture, even spiritual experiences risk becoming yet another source of craving and attachment. As Sangharakshita observes, we have 'a neurotic need for experience to alleviate our mundane boredom and frustration'.[120] This craving can readily contaminate Buddhist practice, prompting us to chase fleeting moments of insight to validate ourselves – or to avoid confronting ourselves. When insight is conceived as a commodity, subjective feeling is prized above the enduring quality of our relationships, or service to our family and community.

As Sangharakshita warns: 'Unconsciously we try to use Nirvana to settle problems which can only really be resolved through awareness.'[121] Far from inspiring deep transformation, the prospect of nirvana becomes a means of bolstering our fragile sense of self, compensating for a sense of lack. It becomes a projection of our mundane needs. Moreover, we convert nirvana into an object of hope, leading to a deferred life – a perpetual anticipation.

The private character of experience

The intrinsically private character of experience provides fertile ground for self-deception. No one else can confirm or deny what we have seen or felt. This can bypass the corrective influence of tradition, spiritual friends, and the wider community. We may come to cherish an image of ourselves as awakened when, in fact, we have merely grasped at a subtler image of self, and thereby reinforced our delusion. In this way, what begins as a moment of apparent breakthrough may end up entrenching self-clinging rather than dissolving it.

Rather than craving nirvana or lamenting its absence, what matters is our present capacity to respond wisely, compassionately, and with increasing freedom. This shift in perspective loosens the grip of grasping – and, with it, the persistent feeling of spiritual failure.

Enlightenment, then, isn't a subjective experience to be recalled, cherished, and paraded. It shows itself in how we live, how we respond, how we relate to others and to the world. It shines through the overall pattern of our life. Dōgen was especially sensitive to this: for him, Enlightenment can never become a past accomplishment, a trophy, but is an ever-present disclosure of truth – always fresh, always unfolding. He writes:

> If a human being, even for a single moment, manifests the Buddha's posture [...] the entire world of Dharma assumes the Buddha's posture and the whole of space becomes the state of realization.[122]

We don't need to chase after distant revelations, since the vital moment is always at hand. Nirvana is never a closed event but a living awareness, always unfolding as if for the first time. Wisdom is not a static repository of truths but an enhanced mode of perception that opens up new possibilities for meaning, value, and wonder.

Seeing Things as They Really Are

When visiting Mexico City, I love to ramble through the Roma neighbourhood, adopting the spirit of the *flâneur*, who has no particular purpose in mind. I'm usually there to visit our Triratna Buddhist Centre on the corner of Jalapa and Tabasco. Just a block away lies Álvaro Obregón, a handsome boulevard with a tree-lined median designed for pedestrians. At intervals along this strip, there are full-sized, bronze replicas of ancient Greek statues, including the *Discobolo*, or discus thrower, originally sculpted by Myron of Eleutherae (480–440 BCE). It is thrilling to speculate that Myron may have been crafting this image around the same time the Buddha sat beneath the bodhi tree, still absorbing his Awakening.

As I contemplate this bedazzling figure, which is naked but for a modesty-protecting leaf, my mind soars. Who was he? How far could he launch that discus? Did he win glory (*kleos*) through his athletic feats? The sculpture assails me as a joyous celebration of male flourishing, grace, and daring. It's as though the *Discobolo* summons me, inviting me into its world. The French philosopher Jean-Louis Chrétien describes beauty as something we don't merely observe, but which calls us to respond. It draws us out of our poise and disquiets us. The statue's aesthetic power isn't passive;

it comes to find me, it solicits my attention, draws me in, demanding a response.[123]

The artist, too, intrigues me. What inspired him to create this startling image of masculine embodiment? From generic form, the *Discobolo* bursts forth in his individual glory. It brings to mind Myron's contemporary, Pindar (*c*.518–*c*. 438 BCE), who celebrated athletic gallantry by means of epinicians, or victory odes:

> But one who gains some new success
> on wings of soaring manliness
> and splendid hope takes flight
> toward future deeds, for he has caught
> a passion beyond wealth. In no time, man's delight
> bursts into bloom, but just
> as fast collapses in the dust
> shaken by a breeze, a shift in thought.[124]

Now let's transport ourselves to ancient India. According to a traditional formula, when the Buddha awakened he 'saw things as they really are'. He saw through the veil of illusion, abandoned distorting views, and was freed from the suffering they caused. Famously, in the *Udana*, the Blessed One exhorts the seeker Bahiya to perceive in the seen only the seen, in the heard only the heard, and so on.[125] Guided by this cryptic instruction, Bahiya gains a decisive insight into reality. He becomes a noble one.

But what does it really mean to see – hear, or feel – things as they truly are? It might seem to imply the abandonment of all interpretive categories. But is such a thing even possible? And is this what Buddhist wisdom ultimately consists in?

Far from bypassing all interpretation, wisdom depends on the activation of the creative imagination. It calls forth a kind of 'iconizing awareness': a contemplative openness in which deeper meaning can disclose itself.

The promise of 'seeing things as they really are' assumes that our current perception is flawed – and that this distortion lies at the root of our most intractable problems. So what are we missing? The Buddha's guidance to Bahiya might seem to suggest that we should turn ourselves into human surveillance cameras – merely registering sensory input without applying any interpretation or narrative. Even if this were possible, it would yield a drastically reduced palette of experience, stripped of all the creative emotions that Buddhism encourages us to cultivate – such as goodwill (*metta*), compassion (*karuna*), and sympathetic joy (*mudita*). Abandoning all interpretation would render us confused, paralyzed, incapable of recognizing value, and so unable to fulfil any human purposes. A surveillance camera lacks the discernment to favour a Cézanne masterpiece over an absent-minded doodle. It has no scale of worth.

In addition, the promise of 'seeing things as they really are' can imply that our raw senses grant us full access to 'what is there'. But this is not how perception functions. First, sensory phenomena can never appear to us in their entirety. For example, if we look at the front cover of a book, we cannot simultaneously see its back. Even if we unfold the book to reveal both front and back, the interior remains out of view. Second, our biological apparatus limits our sensory capacities. Consider smell: a dog's olfactory sensitivity far exceeds our own, allowing it to detect scents from miles away – enabling it to find bombs or even smell cancer. We lack such canine superpowers and can never possess them. Third – and crucially – seeing requires a process of selection and focus. Without intentional looking, we are buffeted by the shapes, sounds, and colours to which we are exposed, overwhelmed by the scope and richness of sensory input. To truly 'see', we must direct our attention to something specific. For instance, if I am to see the *Discobolo*, I must single it out amid the surrounding stimuli – the blue sky, the traffic noise, the river of pedestrians. For our experience to cohere, perception must frame objects according to a particular intentionality.

Maurice Merleau-Ponty observed that the body is not merely an object in the world; it is our fundamental means of engaging with it. He described it as 'the latent horizon of our experience, itself ceaselessly present prior to all determining thought'.[126] Objects present themselves to us from particular perspectives – and never in totality – precisely because we see from a specific place rather than from everywhere at once.

To grasp what it might mean to 'see things as they really are', let's review the basic Buddhist account of reality – an account we are invited to dwell upon if we aspire to supramundane insight. The three *lakshana*s, or marks, guide us to contemplate experience through three notable features: suffering (*dukkha*), impermanence (*anitya*), and the absence of a fixed, underlying self or essence (*anatman*). It is through understanding that these characteristics suffuse our daily experience that we awaken to reality. Yet these features are not immediately given; their full significance emerges only through reflective contemplation. In other words, to truly 'see' the three *lakshana*s, we must engage and activate our creative imagination.

While some suffering may be directly observable, this is limited to basic manifestations of physical pain felt within our own bodies. Most of our suffering, as well as our ability to recognize it, arises from our imaginative capacities. We can rarely observe the suffering of others directly; instead, we infer it through imaginative identification. As for the other two *lakshanas*, our penetration into them arises, at least partly, from our capacity to imagine beyond present awareness. Understanding impermanence in its full extension, for instance, depends on our ability to conceive of duration – something we do not observe directly. It requires memory and projection to envision both past and future. Without these imaginative processes, impermanence would have no meaning.

To see things as they really are doesn't mean becoming a disinterested, emotionless register. Rather, it involves opening ourselves to an excess of meaning – a superabundance that continually overflows our interpretive categories. This provokes a reversal in perception such that, in the words of Jean-Luc Marion, we are 'no longer the transcendental *I* but the *witness*, constituted by what happens to us'.[127] Perception is liberated when no longer confined by the horizons we impose upon it. It surpasses all ready-made categories of expectation, all attempts at final classification, and so becomes a form of *revelation*.

Wisdom possesses an aesthetic, receptive dimension that allows experience to burst towards us, and so maximize our astonishment and wonder. This gives rise to a kind of sacramental perception, in which each act of looking is irrepeatable, always leaving something yet to be discovered. To see things as they really are is, in Marion's words, to recognize that 'what can be visible will never be a closed object, exhaustively seen'.[128] Experience calls us to remain open to its inexhaustible possibilities, unveiling ever greater depths of meaning and value. Such seeing also deepens our ethical awareness, attuning us more fully to the sufferings, needs, and aspirations of others. It entails a shift towards greater empathy and understanding of the inwardness of those around us.

Returning to the *Discobolo*, seeing him 'as he really is' involves more than registering materials shaped into body parts. It means opening oneself to the mystery of human embodiment, being momentarily transported to the lifeworld of ancient Greece, and absorbing the impact of Myron's unique aesthetic sensibility. While I may never know if Myron saw the world as the Buddha did, the *Discobolo* steals my admiration by 'drawing onto itself all the glory and confiscating it from everything else'.[129] This entire process unfolds through the activation and refinement of imagination. For wisdom, as a process of meaning-making, is inherently creative.[130]

6

In Victory There Lies Bliss: Vigour

> Keep watch over your mind. Lift yourself clear of the difficult road (of the mental defilements), as an elephant sunk in a bog (hauls himself out).[131]

On 6 December 1956, my late teacher Sangharakshita arrived in Nagpur, central India, to meet some of the city's newly converted Buddhists. Within minutes, he received the devastating news that Dr B.R. Ambedkar – the Dalit leader and architect of the Buddhist revival – had died the previous night in Delhi. Nagpur, the site of Ambedkar's own conversion just seven weeks earlier, had become the epicentre of a movement in which millions of Dalits renounced the caste oppression endemic to Hinduism and embraced Buddhism.

A condolence meeting was hastily organized, at which Sangharakshita was invited to speak. With no stage, and lit only by a couple of paraffin lamps, he perched on a rickshaw to address a crowd that had rapidly swelled to 100,000 mourners. He did what he could to console the stricken Ambedkarites, speaking for an hour and managing to lift the spirits of the grieving multitude.

Over the next four days, he addressed nearly thirty mass meetings, speaking to a total of around 200,000 people. Later, writing to a friend, he recalled:

> On the last day of my visit I gave no less than eleven lectures. The final meeting was held at 1:30 in the morning, when fifteen thousand people were converted to Buddhism. [...] My own spiritual experience during this period was most peculiar. I felt that I was not a person, but an impersonal force. At one stage I was working quite literally without any thought, just as one is in *samadhi*.[132]

The determination, compassion, and courage to respond so unreservedly to such monumental, collective grief is both humbling and deeply inspiring. It is hard to imagine such indefatigable energy – not a turning away, but a wholehearted turning towards suffering with boundless compassion and tireless resolve. In Buddhist terms, this was *virya*: not mere effort or perseverance, but a joyful, self-transcending energy that arises from deep alignment with the Dharma. Sangharakshita's actions during those days of communal agony were driven not by ordinary will alone, but by a deeper current of spiritual inspiration – a heroic vitality grounded in love, clarity, and a profound sense of purpose. In that moment of shared sorrow, he became an instrument of the Dharma, his actions inspired by the spirit of the bodhisattva ideal.

Virya is translated in various ways, including 'energy', 'diligence', 'perseverance', 'vigour', 'zeal', 'exertion', 'strenuousness', and 'spiritual ardour'. In addition to being one of the five spiritual faculties, it features in several other important Buddhist patterns of transformation, such as the seven factors of Enlightenment (*bojjhanga*s), the six perfections (*paramita*s) of the bodhisattva path, and the eleven positive mental events of the Abhidharma tradition. In the early scriptures, *virya* is also closely associated with the four right efforts, linking it directly to the noble eightfold path.[133]

Above all, *virya* concerns the transformation of our motivation and conduct. It is an active, dynamic quality that is the counterbalance to *samadhi*, or meditation, which is a more contemplative faculty. Agitation tends to overwhelm those strong in *virya* but lacking in *samadhi*, while laziness creeps in among those inclined to meditation but deficient in spiritual ardour. When concentration and energy are balanced, however, neither laziness nor agitation prevails. This harmonious equilibrium gives rise to absorption (*jhana*) – deep meditative states that nourish and sustain progress on the path.

This balance is illustrated in the early scriptures by Sona, a disciple of the Buddha renowned for his prodigious energy.[134] Despite his reputation, Sona struggles with meditation: his mind remains fettered, and he is on the verge of abandoning the holy life in despair. So he seeks the Buddha's guidance. A former harpist, Sona is asked by the Buddha: 'If your harp strings were too tight or too slack, was the harp resonant and playable?' 'No', Sona replies. Only when the strings were tuned to an even tension, he confirms, did the instrument play properly. 'In the same way,' the Buddha explains, 'there must be a balance between energy and serenity.' By finding this crucial equilibrium, Sona attains liberation.

In the first instance, *virya* concerns the development and strengthening of an impulse – a directionality – that arises from within (self-power). But it can also be understood in terms of Other Power: opening to the influence of the bodhicitta, a supra-individual intentionality that informs our conduct but does not originate in the mundane will.

What Is *Virya*?

Gampopa defines *virya* as striving for what is good and wholesome.[135] It expresses a genuine delight in what is good, ethical, and even beautiful. One rejoices in virtue, feels naturally drawn towards it, and desires to cultivate it. *Virya*, then, has to do with channelling aspiration in a spiritual direction and avoiding whatever conditions weaken it. It directs the mind away from unskilful attitudes and towards skilful ones. *Virya*, we might say, is our spiritual drive, our spiritual impulse – it motivates us to sustain and deepen our connection with the transcendental. *Virya* is not simply 'energy' in a general sense because it is shaped by an ethical sensibility and a commitment to a spiritual goal. *Virya* is dedicated to the realization of this goal.

In contemporary culture, it is common to associate Buddhism with soft, glossy images like flowering lotuses, bronzed beauties meditating on the beach, or massage at a holistic spa called 'Zen'. But the path to Awakening requires determined, consistent effort. It requires heroic qualities. If we are to confront and break free of our limitations, we need to call up this kind of vigorous energy. We will have to endure challenges and even some hardships.

As part of his quest for Awakening, the Buddha confronted paralyzing doubt and profound, existential terror that called forth his moral courage, determination, and resilience. He deliberately sought out solitary places in the forest – often spots believed to be haunted by ghosts and spirits – where fear and panic were likely to arise.[136] And, indeed, those very feelings did invade his mind.

How did Siddhartha respond? If fear and terror arose while he was walking, he continued walking until he pacified such feelings. He didn't run away or try to suppress the discomfort. Likewise, if such feelings surfaced while he was sitting or lying down, he faced them directly, conquering them on the spot. In this way, he triumphed over fear.

Many of us experience fear and dread – panic, anxiety, or at least unease – especially in solitude, whether physical or emotional. But, wherever and however these experiences arise, it is vital to confront them with courage and resolution. The unknown provokes fear, change provokes fear, and too often we flee from it, seeking the familiar, seeking comfort or distraction. We therefore miss an opportunity to break free. But if we have the strength to face our inner demons – just as Siddhartha did – we too can overcome them.

The Defeat of Mara: *Mara-Vijaya*

This fierce inner struggle is vividly portrayed in accounts of the Buddha's life as a dramatic battle against Mara, the Evil One, who symbolizes all that obstructs the path to liberation. It is striking, and perhaps surprising, how military language is used to evoke this confrontation. In fact, one of the Buddha's alternative titles is the *Jina*: the Victorious One. His victory is precisely over all the forces that seek to obstruct Awakening, as symbolized by Mara.

A famous episode in Buddhist literature describes this conquest and is frequently portrayed in Buddhist art. The future Buddha is shown seated on a mound of *kusa* grass beneath the outstretched branches of a sacred fig tree – known ever since as the bodhi tree, or 'tree of Awakening', in his honour. Closing in on all sides are thousands of fearsome figures, grotesquely twisted and deformed. Some brandish enormous clubs, others spit fire, hurl boulders – even entire mountains – or shoot arrows. This is Mara's terrifying army, intent on breaking the Buddha's resolve and derailing his path to Awakening.

But the Buddha doesn't flinch. He remains still, exuding an aura of calm, golden light. As soon as any of the projectiles touch this aura, they transform into flowers and fall harmlessly at the Buddha's feet, as if in involuntary veneration.[137] Even when Mara summons his three daughters – Craving, Boredom, and Lust – and commands them to dance in the most seductive, alluring manner, the Buddha's determination is not shaken. He continues meditating in deep stillness.

Finally, Mara is defeated. His forces vanish, his daughters retreat in confusion, and the Buddha remains seated beneath the bodhi tree, calmly absorbed in meditation. And there, in that very posture, he attains Enlightenment.

There is a vivid account of this confrontation in the *Padhana Sutta* – a title that can be translated as 'Striving'. Mara approaches the Buddha and warns him that the path of effort is hard to begin and harder still to sustain. The Buddha replies in striking military terms:

> Sensual pleasures are your first army,
> the second is called discontent,
> hunger and thirst are the third,
> and the fourth is said to be craving.

Your fifth is dullness and drowsiness,
the sixth is said to be cowardice,
your seventh is doubt,
contempt and obstinacy are your eighth.

Profit, praise, and honor,
and misbegotten fame;
the extolling of oneself
while scorning others.

This is your army, [Mara],
the strike force of the Dark One.
Only a hero can defeat it,
but in victory there lies bliss.

Let me gird myself –
curse my life!
I'd rather die in battle
than live on in defeat.

Here some ascetics and brahmins
are swallowed up, not to be seen again.
And they do not know the path
traveled by those true to their vows.

Seeing Mara ready on his mount,
surrounded by his bannered forces,
I shall meet them in battle –
they'll never make me retreat!

That army of yours has never been beaten
by the world with all its gods.
Yet I shall smash it with wisdom,
like an unfired pot with a stone.

Having brought my thoughts under control,
and established mindfulness well,
I shall wander from country to country,
guiding many disciples.

Diligent and resolute,
following my instructions,
they will proceed despite your will,
to where there is no sorrow.[138]

In this scene, as Mara unleashes his full fury, the Buddha outfaces him. He gives Mara no attention – no energy. He defeats Mara not through aggression, but by remaining resolute in purpose, confident in his enlightened aspiration. The sutta captures the intensity of the Buddha's determination, his willingness to face every fear and obstacle with unshakeable courage and resolve.

Mara-vijaya, the victory over Mara, symbolizes the inner battle with everything that obstructs the spiritual path. One meaning of the word *jayati*, 'to conquer', is 'to surpass all others through one's own excellence'. It implies being 'the highest'. In that sense, the Buddha's victory was won not on Mara's terms but through the sheer brilliance of his moral and spiritual virtue.

The Victorious One: The *Jina*

The Buddha is not only the *Buddha*, the Awakened One – he is also the *Jina*, the Conqueror. This title, so resonant in the early Buddhist tradition, evokes not just Awakening, but a profound inner victory. The *Jina* is the one who has triumphed – not over others, but over himself, and over the forces that bind and blind the heart. Buddhists might therefore also be called *Jinists*: followers of the *Jina*, the Victorious One. To follow the Buddha is to take up arms – not guns and bombs, but the weapons of ethical discipline (*shila*), meditative absorption (*samadhi*), and liberating wisdom (*prajna*).

The Buddha once described his disciples as *ksatriya*s – spiritual warriors. They were engaged in a noble battle: striving not for land or power, but for integrity of life, clarity of mind, and freedom from delusion. To live the Dharma is to take up that same cause. It is not a passive life, nor a retreat into comfort. It's a dynamic, and at times even militant, path of transformation. We don't wait for Mara to sneak up on us but confront him directly, on the battlefield.

This perspective highlights that we shouldn't fall into a sentimental, romantic view of the Buddhist life. It requires discipline, courage, resilience, and even combativeness. We won't be true Buddhists – and certainly not true *Jinists*, true spiritual warriors – without burning with the fire of such intensity.

There is so much to overcome – both within ourselves and in the world. So much that calls out to be transformed in the golden light of the Dharma. If we want to share in the Buddha's Awakening, we must follow his courageous path. The demons he faced, we too must face. The freedom he won, we too can claim – not just for ourselves, but for the sake of all beings. Of course, it's not easy. And no sincere follower of the Buddha has claimed it would be. But a human being should not shrink from what is most difficult. A noble heart should rise to the challenge. We should not allow fear, doubt, or inertia to block our way.

Yes, at times the task seems overwhelming. But we are not alone. The Buddha offers us a model of courage, unshakeable resolve, and radiant hope. He shows us that transformation is possible. That Mara can be defeated. That liberation is real. So let us summon our strength for the spiritual battle. May we overcome our obstacles. May we defeat Mara. May we too become victorious.

We could do no better than to remember these fighting words from the *Dhammapada*:

> Perceiving the body to be (fragile) like a clay pot, (and) fortifying the mind as though it were a city, with the sword of wisdom make war on Mara. Free from attachment, keep watch over what has been won.[139]

A useful exercise is to ask ourselves: how does Mara appear in my own life? What are his weapons? And what must I do to disarm him?

The Courage to Begin Again

What does true courage look like? It isn't always a dramatic confrontation with our inner demons. Sometimes, true courage (*virya*) reveals itself in quiet, subtle acts like contrition, confession, or apology.

As we progress along the Buddhist path, we may begin to cling to a false self – a rather too polished image of ourselves. Others may even reinforce this impression, and slowly we succumb to our own hype. As the gap between our public image and our inner reality widens, it becomes harder to admit our flaws. We fear losing the respect and admiration we've acquired. So, rather than acknowledge our shortcomings, we hide them. Transparency feels dangerous – too much honesty might cost us the admiring gaze we've come to depend on. To disclose our failings – and risk losing the affirmation that sustains our self-image – demands real courage. To face and confess the darker aspects of ourselves calls on all our reserves of vigour and determination.

I have felt this tension firsthand. Not long ago, I was talking with a dear friend who expressed a view I strongly disagreed with. In responding, I became vehement. I desperately wanted her to see my side, and, when she didn't, my words became increasingly urgent, bordering on heated. The conversation ended on a distinctly awkward, unresolved note.

The next time we met, my friend, with remarkable humility and kindness, asked me not to express myself so forcefully. I felt humiliated – but I was also given a gift. I could have become defensive, but her graciousness allowed me to apologize, to thank her, and to commit to communicating more sensitively in future. What mattered in the end was not the disagreement itself, but how we resolved it. Thanks to my friend's generosity of spirit, I was able to let go of the need to be right, and to acknowledge that my response had fallen short of harmonious communication. In that moment of regret, the polished image cracked, and I was able to begin again.

Even the Buddha himself reached a certain point when he had to admit that he had wandered into a spiritual dead end. He had embarked on a programme of severe austerity. According to the scriptures, he survived on just a single grain of rice a day. His body withered; he came close to death.

Yet there were compensations: his reputation grew and people revered him. In those days, it was widely believed that liberation could be achieved through self-mortification – and the harsher the austerity, the better. Five ascetics became his disciples, vowing to remain by his side until, through sheer self-denial, he attained Enlightenment.

But Siddhartha did not find liberation through this path. Despite his monumental efforts, he remained as far from Awakening as before. And so, despite years of extreme asceticism, he just let it go. To the astonishment of his companions, he began eating solid food. Disillusioned, they walked away. He was no longer the man they believed him to be; to them, he had succumbed to weakness.

What looked like a defeat was, in fact, a hard-won victory. Siddhartha overcame a powerful inner resistance: the unwillingness to admit that he had gone astray. To acknowledge a mistake – to recognize that a path we've followed with great devotion is a dead end – is no easy thing. It wounds our pride. It unsettles our sense of identity.

When we've invested immense time, energy, and belief in a pursuit, it can be painful – even humiliating – to admit that it has led us nowhere. But Siddhartha was willing to do just that. He let go of pride, status, and the admiration of others.

He could easily have carried on: becoming ever more emaciated, ever more venerated, and gathering ever more disciples along the way. Instead, Siddhartha had the courage to risk unpopularity and ultimately rejection by the group. He had the humility to admit: *this is not the way*. He stepped away from what no longer served his purpose and, with renewed resolve, resumed his search.

How Is Vigour Cultivated and Strengthened?

Many people experience a deep sense of dissatisfaction with life. They encounter the Dharma and feel strongly drawn to it, yet their engagement lacks intensity and consistency. They hear the call, the spiritual impulse stirs within them, but other concerns crowd it out. How can we strengthen the impulse to move wholeheartedly towards the three jewels, and sustain that momentum over time?

One way to arouse and cultivate vigour is by deepening our sense of *urgency*. An early Buddhist text known as the *Subjects for Contemplation* offers a powerful set of reflections designed to stimulate just such urgency and commitment to the spiritual path.[140] We are exhorted to reflect over and again on the following five truths:

1. I am subject to illness, I haven't gone beyond illness.
2. I am subject to ageing, I haven't gone beyond ageing.
3. I am subject to death, I haven't gone beyond death.
4. I will be separated from all that is dear and agreeable to me.
5. I am the owner of my actions, heir to my actions; whatever I do, for good or ill, I will inherit.

The first three contemplations mirror the Buddha's transformative encounters with the realities of old age, sickness, and death – the 'three sights' that enabled him to recognize the flaws inherent in human life and to yearn for something beyond. He encountered this in the fourth sight: a holy man. These first three reflections target our *intoxication* with the self – our tendency to act as if we were immune to impermanence and suffering. In particular, they address our intoxication with health, youth, and even life itself. By bringing the reality of our contingent, embodied nature into clear view, these contemplations weaken our attachment to mundane purposes and goals, and open up the possibility for the noble search: the quest for liberation.

The fourth reflection directs our attention towards the inevitability of loss. By contemplating the reality of separation – from loved ones, possessions, and everything we hold dear – we weaken our craving and attachment to what is agreeable and coveted: all that stops us from going forth more fully and completely.

Finally, by contemplating our karma, we're inspired to amend our conduct and act more skilfully, knowing we don't want to experience the negative outcomes of unskilful behaviour.

As these five truths sink in personally, we move to a second, broader phase: contemplating their universal scope. We reflect that:

1. All beings are subject to old age; none is exempt.
2. All beings are subject to illness; none is exempt.
3. All beings are subject to death; none is exempt.
4. All beings will be parted from everyone and everything dear and agreeable.
5. All beings are subject to their karma.

Through this broader reflection, we realize that our predicament isn't unique: it's the universal human condition. This understanding fuels our resolve to embark on, pursue, and fulfil the path. It helps us break free from our spiritual fetters and uproot the deep-seated tendencies that bind us to habit. In this way, we break the painful cycle of rebecoming.

Receptivity and the Dynamics of Other Power

The notion of Other Power (*tariki*) symbolizes the potential for a transcendent volition to surge through us – a counter-intentionality that manifests as wisdom, compassion, and generosity. It is not something we can claim as our own, but rather something that acts upon us, overturning our habitual sense of initiative and autonomy. This volition is not a passive potential but an active urging – the momentum of the *Dharma-niyama* – that longs to reveal itself.

An Other Power perspective calls us to abandon reliance on our distorted notion of the self and its imagined capacities, and instead to entrust ourselves to the compassionate blessing of the Buddha Mind. At first glance, this may seem to undermine personal responsibility, especially since our pedestrian efforts are dismissed as mere calculation (*hakarai*). It might even seem to contradict our basic understanding of spiritual development as a self-directed process. Moreover, it seems to erase the role of vigour. But, as Sangharakshita writes:

> It is merely intended to assert the absolute discontinuity of the Transcendental and the mundane. The Real is not to be attained by means of a series of increments of the unreal. In the last resort, emancipation depends upon the irruption into the universe of a factor that confronts our ego-consciousness as the Other Power.[141]

Other Power then is itself a metaphor. The compassion of the buddhas, while transcending all categories of thought – including that of subject and object – appears to the ego-bound mind as an external force. But it is not literally 'outside' us. As Sangharakshita puts it, 'To surrender to the Other Power means to transcend the distinction between subject and object.'[142] Other Power is not so much in tension with self-power, but symbolizes its transcendence in a higher understanding of oneself and of reality itself. Thus Other Power is really beyond self and other, beyond the dualistic mind; it points to a transcendent mode of conditionality and thus indicates a source of motivation liberated from narrow self-interest.

Such a perspective depends upon cultivating a profound receptivity. However, far from being a form of passivity, receptivity is a very active state that is not easy to develop:

> To be receptive isn't easy. It requires a lot of hard work, because one's normal state is either to be active or to be passive [...] [T]o make yourself receptive, to get yourself into that sort of mental state, requires a great deal of hard work, because you need to remove all sorts of blockages.[143]

Practices such as puja, contemplation of the Buddha, and making offerings can help develop such receptivity. These acts clear away the stubborn resistances inherent in self-power so that the current of the *Dharma-niyama* may flow through us.

In a paradoxical remark, the mystic Simone Weil comments, 'There is an easiness in salvation which is more difficult to us than all our efforts.' She contrasts a more subtle, receptive approach to what she terms the 'muscular will', which, far from enabling liberation, becomes an obstacle to it, since it reinforces the limited self. She goes further and proposes:

> That we have to strive after goodness with an effort of our will is one of the lies invented by the mediocre part of ourselves in its fear of being destroyed. Such an effort does not threaten it in any way, it does not even disturb its comfort – not even when it entails a great deal of fatigue and suffering. For the mediocre part of ourselves is not afraid of fatigue and suffering; it is afraid of being killed.[144]

Opening up to Other Power, then, means consenting to a kind of spiritual death – a rupture in our habitual sense of identity (see also Chapter 8). If we look closely, we may notice how deeply attached we are to the illusion of control. We want to believe we are in charge of our destiny. Entrusting ourselves to a mystery that exceeds the ego's grasp feels risky, even threatening. And so we cling to self-power, as if it could secure our imagined autonomy. To borrow from Michael Taussig, in spiritual death we exchange 'standing above the fray' – a kind of God posture – 'for something that is more like swimming, more like nomads adrift in the sea'.[145] In an evocative poem about grace, Denise Levertov captures this attitude: 'As swimmers dare to lie face to the sky and water bears them'.[146]

I experienced something like this the day my teacher, Sangharakshita, died. Having travelled back from Mexico City the previous night, I woke up late. On discovering the sad news I panicked, feeling I lacked the inner resources to meet the gravity of the situation. Yet, within hours, members of the sangha had arrived, transforming the Cuernavaca Buddhist Centre with *cempasúchil* – the marigolds associated with the Day of the Dead – along with candles and images of Sangharakshita. The whole space now glowed with sacred light, infused with gratitude and love. Over the next two days, almost all members of the sangha came to honour him through a commemorative meditation or puja. I felt as though a strength I couldn't generate for myself was nonetheless carrying me – lifting me up, sustaining me. In our shared solemnity, I glimpsed what it might mean to be upheld by a larger current of grace. The sangha's presence became a living manifestation of that current: not something 'outside' me, but a compassionate field that *included* me yet transcended me.

Ordinarily, we think dualistically: self inside, other outside. We think in terms of effort (self-power) versus help from beyond (Other Power). But, rather than viewing Amitabha as an external power acting upon us, we might think of the Buddha *becoming us*. Liberation is not a passive acceptance of some external gift. Instead, we hear the Buddha resounding from the depths of our own being, calling us to awaken to who we truly are. The Buddha is not outside or apart from us, but born within us – signifying the arising of a new kind of self, a new kind of consciousness.

Other Power ultimately challenges the fiction of independence. It invites us to see that we are not autonomous islands but beings embedded in a vast web of interdependence. Our subjectivity is shaped and sustained by a multitude of conditions: historical, material, emotional, cultural. In realizing this, we can begin to let go of deeply rooted ego-stories. Moreover, we can begin to feel gratitude for the innumerable lives and conditions that make ours possible. In this sense,

Other Power is not a supernatural force that absolves us of all effort but a symbol of the transcendence of the limited self.

The Enemies of Vigour

Vigour has many enemies, both near and far. While laziness is the most obvious, it takes various and even surprising forms. Gampopa describes three primary types:

1. Indolence
2. Faintheartedness and despondency
3. The laziness of busyness.

The first of these, indolence, is laziness in the most obvious sense: lethargy, sloth, and a general lack of engagement. This kind of laziness betrays a lack of awareness of the consequences of not seizing the precious human opportunity. It also reflects complacency – a failure to appreciate that favourable conditions may not always continue. Moreover, according to Shantideva, it arises from 'apathy for the sufferings of cyclic existence'.[147] We wake up in the morning and, instead of preparing to meditate, we think: I feel a bit tired today, so maybe I will leave it until tomorrow. In such moments, Shantideva urges us to respond immediately and decisively, just as we would leap up without hesitation if a snake were to slide into our lap.[148]

The second form of laziness is faintheartedness, a state of despondency in which we think: 'How can dejected people like myself ever attain enlightenment, even if we try to do so?'[149] This attitude convinces us that our efforts are futile – so why bother? The ocean of suffering seems so vast; how could I possibly make a difference? We feel overwhelmed, believing the challenge is simply too great to even begin.

I regularly succumb to a subtle form of this, convincing myself that my presence doesn't matter. 'Whether I go to the class at my local Buddhist centre here in Cuernavaca or not,' I think, 'it will make no difference.' At times, this leads to despondency, making me feel my efforts have no real impact. What, then, is the point?

Another way this form of laziness manifests is through self-excuse – or, more starkly, the victim mentality. It rears its head whenever we cling to past traumas or present difficulties as a means of evading moral or spiritual effort. This manipulative posture constructs a clever, pseudo-moral fortress around itself: it justifies our refusal to take responsibility and renders itself almost impervious to critique. Left unchallenged, it corrodes our sense of agency and so undermines our capacity for transformation.

The third form of laziness is an active resistance to the skilful: 'an unwillingness to mobilize available energy towards a positive end'.[150] Gampopa describes this kind of laziness as an 'addiction to such evil and unwholesome practices as subduing enemies and hoarding money'.[151] In practice, it means pouring the vast majority of our energy into what is largely unimportant, while offering only the meagre remnants to what matters most. It often shows up as slipping into a life of ease and predictability, avoiding anything that might genuinely stretch us. We luxuriate in the comfort zone in all its cosy splendour: binge-watching Jackie Chan films and seeking counsel from a tub of Ben & Jerry's.

Vigour is not about directing energy at just anything; it is not simply enthusiasm without purpose. We live in a world that often glorifies constant activity, mistaking sheer effort for virtue, regardless of the aim. Rumi once wrote:

> There is one thing in this world which must never be forgotten. If you were to forget everything else, but did not forget that, then there would be no cause to worry; whereas if you performed and remembered and did not forget every single thing, but forget that one thing, then you would have done nothing whatsoever.[152]

What is that one thing? It is to remember the meaning of our existence, to fulfil the potential of human life. Being lazy means remaining caught up in activities not conducive to skilful mental states or spiritual development. This frenetic engagement prevents us from giving attention to what is most important, what touches on our ultimate values. We indulge in pursuits that don't serve our noblest interests. To overcome this form of laziness, we must prioritize what is of ultimate value above that which has lesser value.

When people ask what I've 'done' today, I often feel a twinge of guilt. It's as if admitting to 'nothing' is a failing, as if *any* activity, however banal or useless, would be more worthy than idleness. Yet genuine 'doing nothing' can be profoundly creative, since it lays the ground for deeper reflection and connection. Byung-Chul Han describes inactivity as an *intensity* and 'a radiance within human existence'.[153] If we lose the ability to be inactive, then we begin to degenerate into mere functional machines. He emphasizes the value of *waiting*, since it opens us to a reality that no amount of activity can reach.[154]

Sangharakshita observes that laziness sometimes results from a lack of vision.[155] It is a form of complacency – merely treading water. In such a state, there is an absence of what he calls 'divine discontent': an active awareness of the limitations of mundane existence that impels us to seek what lies beyond.

All these reflections highlight that, if we are not actively cultivating the skilful or immersing ourselves in creative inactivity, we are likely to succumb to a mode of laziness. Given its deceptive character, we must learn to recognize the many ways it manifests in our lives, often in seemingly respectable disguises.

For the bodhisattva, vigour becomes a joyful play – no longer effort or work in the usual sense. It would be remiss to conclude a discussion of the topic without invoking the most famous image of all:

> [E]ven at the conclusion of one task, one should plunge straight away into the next, as does a tusker, inflamed by the midday heat, immediately on coming to a pool.[156]

7

Liberating Psycho-Cosmic Energies

> Buddhism does not think of sentient beings in terms of separate forms of life, one absolutely discrete from another, so much as in terms of separate currents of psychical energy each of which can associate itself with any form. Energy is primary, form secondary. It is not that man wills, but rather that will 'mans'.[157]

The five elements – earth, water, fire, air, and space – are the primary categories through which we perceive and make sense of the world. At the same time, they offer a rich symbolic language for understanding and transforming our inner life. One way to view the path towards Awakening is as the progressive liberation of psycho-spiritual energy. Because this energy is often blocked, repressed, or dissipated, we need methods to release, direct, and refine it. The stupa serves as a powerful symbol of this inner process. According to the Tantric tradition, its structure embodies the five elements as successive stages in the unfolding and transformation of inner energies. Through contemplating the stupa, then, we may begin to activate, purify, and harmonize these energies within ourselves. In this way, we internalize the path to Awakening.

Engaging with the five elements in this way enables a process of deeper self-understanding – revealing both our strengths and our vulnerabilities – and provides us with a symbolic vocabulary through which we can articulate and intensify our spiritual development. This elemental language offers a vivid and compelling alternative to more analytical, psychological models. It speaks directly to the imagination, to our depths, to the non-conceptual part of us that is often harder to reach. According to Gaston Bachelard, the elements 'demand to be imagined in depth'.[158] Each element, he suggests, awakens a specific form of reverie that invites a distinct mode of relation with ourselves and with the world. This deep engagement awakens what he calls the 'material imagination', out of which images and understandings arise that are deeply informed by the properties of matter.

The five elements not only represent stages of transformation; they can also be seen as distinct modes of energy that must come into balance – much like the harmonious structure of a mandala. Through contemplation, we become intimate with the felt textures of the elements and, in doing so, we also come to know ourselves more fully. This understanding allows us to enact our spiritual potential in a holistic way.

The five elements are potent symbols open to multiple interpretations. Not only may a given element allow contradictory meanings, but distinct elements may also overlap in their symbolism. This is part of the richness of symbolic language: it is not neat and tidy, and thus invites continual reinterpretation.

A Brief Contemplation of the Five Elements

Begin by simply sitting with each of the elements as an image or something felt. You may want to associate each element with a bodily sensation – solidity for earth, flow for water, warmth for fire, movement for air, and openness for space. How is this element in my life? Is it balanced, blocked, or overactive? You needn't interpret the elements rigidly. Instead, allow them to serve as gateways: metaphors that draw you into deeper intimacy with experience as it arises.

Over time, this kind of elemental contemplation can help to identify where energies are stuck, coarse, or scattered – and how they might be released, refined, and brought into harmony.

Transforming Energy: The Guru Principle

'Energy' is a somewhat elusive term. We often say, 'I have no energy' or 'I feel really energetic', but what does this truly mean? After all, someone may seem highly energetic and yet channel that energy in destructive ways. Energy can be blocked, coarse, dissipated, or integrated.

In Tantric Buddhism, primal forces and raw energies are not rejected or destroyed, but rather converted and integrated into the path. This is the function of the tantric guru: through initiation, the guru activates the disciple's deeper energies. The 'guru principle' – especially as embodied in the figure of Padmasambhava – symbolizes the engagement and transformation of our deepest layers of being. The guru does not teach conceptually, but subdues demons. Such figures are not merely mythological; they represent powerful forces within the depths of the human mind. They dwell at the threshold where the individual psyche meets the collective unconscious. Though buried deep, these forces continue to shape and influence our conscious minds – until we begin to awaken to a level of superconscious awareness.

Untrained, these primordial forces can sabotage our progress. Consequently, we must subdue or, better, convert them – not by repression or brute force, but through their integration into conscious awareness. Far from cutting ourselves off from these forces, or disowning them, our aim is to draw them into the service of our highest purposes. In this way, our conscious personality is enriched and deepened. Thus our spiritual life begins to glow and pulse with the energy of the *dakini*s, and with the transformed forces of gods and demons now tamed and harnessed. It is this integration that gives spiritual practice its depth, radiance, and potency. This is the particular function of the guru principle.

What Is a Stupa?

The stupa (*chorten* in Tibetan) is perhaps the most ubiquitous and resonant symbol in Buddhism – historically, even more significant than the image of the Buddha. It is a multifaceted symbol of the universe, representing not only the external, material world, but also the internal world of the mind. In this sense, it encompasses successive levels of consciousness and, more precisely, the progressively higher stages in the transformation of psycho-spiritual energy. The stupa thus symbolizes the Buddha, Enlightenment, the universe, and human potential.

'Stupa' literally means 'mound' or 'heap', and its most basic meaning is that of a tomb or reliquary. It's believed that stupas may have originated from pre-Buddhist tumuli, known as *caitya*, used for burying revered holy men in a seated position. In early Buddhist inscriptions, *stupa* and *caitya* often appear interchangeable, although *caitya* (from Sanskrit *cita* or *ci*, meaning 'heaped up') has a broader meaning and does not define a specific architectural form.

During the aniconic phase of Buddhist development – before the Buddha was represented in human form – the stupa became a key symbol of the Buddha and other enlightened figures. It thus transcended the notion of a mere burial site, instead evoking the path to Enlightenment, which implies the death of ignorance. The stupa came to represent the Buddha's continued material and spiritual presence. As a result, stupas became centres of devotion, offering, and worship, often housing the relics of important monks. For instance, the great stupa of Sanchi in northern India is said to hold the remains of the Buddha's principal disciples, Shariputra and Maudgalyayana.

The symbolism of the five elements was incorporated into the stupa during the Vajrayana or Tantric phase of Buddhism in India. Tantra viewed the stupa as an architectural symbol of the entire material universe as it exists in space. Beyond its representation of the cosmos, the stupa also mirrors the human being, symbolizing our various aspects and energies

– especially our potential for Enlightenment. Transposing its symbolism from the material to the mental and spiritual planes, the stupa embodies the world of the mind, mapping successive levels of consciousness and the unfolding of psycho-spiritual transformation. It is thus a potent tantric symbol of both the path and the goal.

The elements are mysterious, elusive, ungraspable. In Sanskrit, the four material elements are known collectively as 'form' (*rupa*). They are also known as the *mahabhuta*s – great spirits – which speaks to their elusive nature.

The five elements may be understood as:

- Earth: stability, blocked or latent energy, potential
- Water: fluidity, reactivity, transparency, purification
- Fire: transformation, destruction, transcendence
- Air: expansion, weightlessness, freedom
- Space: openness, unbounded creativity, nonduality.

While we may respond to different elements in nature, we can learn a lot about ourselves by observing the element with which we especially identify.

Earth: The Resistant World

Earth is primarily characterized by *resistance*. The resistance of earthly matter is immediate and constant, exposing the limits of our will to impose itself on the world. It shows us the boundaries of our mastery; it doesn't yield easily to our bidding.

Earth symbolizes latent energy – energy that is potential rather than active, or even energy that is blocked and obstructed. Many of us are all too familiar with this state. Unprocessed emotional experiences, trauma, or chronic stress can lead to blockages in energy, which leave us cut off from creativity and imagination. We can also become bored and even alienated as a result of dull, repetitive tasks that hold no meaning for us.

You might sense a wellspring of energy buried deep within, yet it cannot find a way out; there's no open channel for expression. Over time, this blockage may not only persist but solidify into repression. The energy is pushed down, denied, and finally sealed off like fire trapped within a closed volcano. This can manifest as the repression of emotions, of desires, even of any sense of ambition or aspiration.

When this condition continues over years, the energy begins to congeal. It solidifies into a hard, cold mass – a psychic rigidity. The person experiencing this becomes increasingly unresponsive, uncommunicative, withdrawn, and emotionally numb. Something vital hardens and goes quiet. Life becomes routine. Occasionally, to break the monotony, there may be an outburst – an explosion of repressed force – scattering fragments in all directions. But, usually, things soon return to the same blocked state as before.

Earth is subject to gravity. Simone Weil posits gravity as the primary force of the created world – not only a principle of physical necessity but also a metaphor for the psychological and spiritual pull towards self-preservation, self-assertion, and separation from the transcendent. Gravity, then, is the law governing beings absorbed in self-concern, seeking solidity, stability, and control. As Weil writes,

> Every time that we raise the ego [...] as high as we raise it, we degrade ourselves to an infinite degree by confining ourselves to being no more than that.[159]

The more we assert the self, the more we become imprisoned by its gravitational force.

The only force capable of counteracting gravity is grace. Grace does not alter external events, but works from within – quietly, and only if we consent. It operates not by resisting or violating the law of gravity, but by subtly penetrating it, like water seeping through layers of rock. Weil speaks of a necessary 'decreation' – an undoing of the created self – not through sheer force of will, but through the blessing of grace. The impulse towards creative transformation arises not from the self, but from beyond it.

All human beings have a longing to grow – even to fly, we might say – but this impulse is often stunted, blunted, and blocked. An overpreoccupation with the physical body, with appearance, with mundane desires, keeps us tethered to earth.

This is the inner landscape the earth element reveals. It invites us to recognize both the stability and the stagnation that define our current state – and to begin the work of releasing what has long been trapped within. The power and potential inherent in the earth element is evoked in the Buddha's earth-touching gesture, when he calls upon the Earth Goddess to bear witness to his right to sit on the seat of Enlightenment.

Contemplating earth

As the first element to contemplate, earth is represented by the yellow cube and reflects the solid, grounding aspects of life. It symbolizes stability, determination, confidence, and potential, but it also has shadow aspects such as stagnation, repression of certain emotions, and self-centredness. Earth energy can be lumpy, turgid, and lacking in creativity.

The earth element invites us to explore the tension between will and resistance. It points to the limitations we face, the obstacles in our path, and the potential for overcoming them. In the practice of the stupa, we reflect on these aspects, allowing the earth element to ground us before moving on to transform stagnant or obstructed energy into purposeful action.

We can explore the earth element both as a property in the world – observing its physical characteristics like solidity, rootedness, and endurance – and as a quality of energy within ourselves. This dual approach helps us connect the external landscape of the elements with our inner psycho-spiritual state, and recognize how these cosmic energies manifest in our individual lives.

Water: The Liquid Reflection of Being

Water represents a freer, more fluid energy than earth, but it tends to oscillate between opposing poles. Always in motion, it symbolizes a restless, reactive energy that manifests as powerful emotions such as love and hatred. Yet water also embodies clarity, serenity, and purity. It hints at mysterious, deep-down things and vast expanses. Water is elusive, unfathomable. For this reason, in Buddhism, the ocean is commonly used as a symbol of wisdom.

Water is life. As rain, it softens and nourishes the parched earth. In Mesoamerican cosmology, rain is the cosmic semen that fertilizes the land, a sacred fluid through which life is conceived and sustained. Water enacts both forgetting and purification: a washing away, a cleansing, and a quiet renewal. It cleanses not only the body, but memory, identity, and time. It dissolves the fixed, the rigid, the hardened, allowing new forms to emerge.

As the liquid element, water reflects the mind's perpetual flux, its pliability and adaptability. Though fluid and yielding, water can also exert immense destructive power when it floods and overwhelms the land. Its nature, then, can be extreme, mirroring inner struggles, a lack of control, and an absence of boundaries. This recalls how, at times, we can feel engulfed by our emotions, swept from one extreme to another.

Water is also deeply linked to the unconscious mind and the realm of dreams, evoking subterranean powers and currents. Attesting to its oneiric quality, Bachelard writes: 'To contemplate water is to slip away, dissolve, and die.'[160] The unconscious is housed in liquid depths. Water is the material element of the unconscious, the medium of dreams: 'In our eyes it is *water* that dreams.'[161]

Water has long captivated painters, thanks to its elusive, symbolic properties and its evocation of hidden depths and emergent creation. The Spanish painter Joaquín Sorolla (1863–1923), for example, often places human activity at the sea's threshold, where earth and water meet in creative interplay. In *Swimmer, Jávea* (1905),[162] a woman in a white gown – dyed pale green by the sea – swims across the sun-blessed surface, as though she were part of it, as if born of the sea itself. Similarly, in *Washing the Horse* (1909),[163] a naked, glistening youth leads a powerful, gleaming grey horse away from the sea's edge, as though accepting a gift cast up by the fertile waters. This brings to mind Dido's jealous exclamation: 'This that the sea rejects is mine, I said.'[164]

Like a mirror, water reflects, gesturing towards a growing self-awareness. Paul Claudel beautifully captured this: 'Water is the gaze of the earth, its instrument for looking at time.'[165] Water returns our gaze, making us visible to ourselves, and so draws us into deeper self-reflection.

The potential of water is evoked in the subaqueous beings known as *naga*s – guardians of the treasure of perfect wisdom – who, in auspicious moments, may rise to the surface and offer up riches born of the unfathomable deep.

Contemplating water

The element water is symbolized by a scintillating white sphere, effortlessly balanced upon the yellow cube of earth. First, notice the wetness of your eyes and tongue. Swallow: experience the liquid nature throughout the body. In contemplating water, we open ourselves to its fluidity, movement, and transparency. This creates a vital channel for blocked energies to flow, initiating a process of integration with unconscious forces and profound purification. Consciousness is an infinite well of liquid depths.

How Can We Liberate and Conserve Our Energies?

Our energy is often blocked or misdirected. But how do these blockages manifest – and how might they be released? Sometimes our energy is frozen in a defensive posture, owing to fear or trauma. At other times, we experience a sense of disconnection: we turn away from unpleasant feelings or sensations (*vedana*), distancing ourselves from certain uncomfortable experiences or emotional currents. This leads to alienation. Moreover, we often waste or divide our energy, dissipating it through distraction, overstimulation, or neurotic activity. Energy may also be coarse and so not readily available for more refined purposes.

Yet this energy – however blocked, divided, or buried – can be liberated, refined, and conserved. Creative activities, such as writing or artwork, can help liberate and refine blocked energy. Another method is meaningful communication, which can enable us to contact a broader spectrum of our emotions and bring these into conscious life. Remembering our dreams can be an additional way to contact our deeper energies and impulses, and begin to draw them towards the surface of awareness.

To utilize, direct, and conserve our energy, we must stop wasting it and begin to unify its divided aspects. This involves cultivating mindfulness and positive emotions, abandoning self-destructive mental states, embracing silence, and reducing unnecessary stimulation. Meditation can be especially effective, offering a context where energy is unified, purified, and gradually transformed.

Fire: The Creative Ascent

Jean Cocteau was once asked what one thing he would carry away from a burning house. He replied, 'I would take the fire.'[166]

Fire is the creative spark, the catalytic force of life – it is heat and light. It embodies energy that moves upwards, that liberates. No longer locked away or lying dormant, this energy begins to stir, to surge, bubbling up from the depths. Where there is fire, there is joy, radiance, and inspiration. This is a state of continuous creativity, the realm of the true artist and the mystic – not in their everyday lives, but in those peak moments when they touch the transcendent, when the flame soars towards the heavens. In this inspired state, something is always being born, always unfolding. This release brings a profound sense of elevation: consciousness rises, lifting the whole being. With this upward movement, psychological conflicts begin to dissolve into smoke, leaving purified energy in their wake. Bachelard proposes that 'The flame illustrates every form of transcendence.'[167]

The fire element is warmth, enthusiasm, and passion. When balanced, fire is the force that transforms: it burns away doubt, dispels confusion, dissolves negativity, and restores direction when we have lost our way. Fire consumes our impurities and lifts us out of ourselves, beyond ourselves – towards the transcendent.

Fire is the light of awareness. It is the sun. It is the light that makes forms visible. Without this essential heat, life becomes flat, dull, and listless. It becomes difficult to connect with others, to sustain spiritual practice, and we easily give up when faced with hardship. It reminds us that, without inspiration, inner uplift is impossible.

Like all powerful energies, fire can also be destructive. Excess fire may manifest as aggression, impatience, anxiety, or impulsiveness, leading to volatility and conflict. Anger, like a stray spark, can ignite an entire forest. Without grounding from earth or cooling from water, fire causes constant agitation and a loss of centre. People dominated by fire react impulsively, flaring up in choleric words or gestures before there is time to pause and reflect.

And yet, fire is also the energy of spiritual transformation. It invites a vital question: how do we activate our energy? In many traditions, the answer is clear: through initiation. Initiation marks the moment something awakens within us – when the fire is lit not only to burn, but to illuminate and transfigure.

The wrathful deities of Tantric Buddhism embody this process of transformation, especially the bodhisattva of energy known as Vajrapani. Naked, his cobalt blue body dancing in a halo of flames, baring fangs in a furious demeanour, his big, hanging belly bursting with power, Vajrapani embodies the raw, untameable force of spiritual energy – an energy that burns through delusion and ignorance. With his raised vajra – the thunderbolt of clarity – poised to strike at any obstacle, he represents the exuberance of the awakened mind, obliterating inertia and confusion.

Far from representing mundane power or aggression, figures like Vajrapani are symbols of our capacity to transform passion into compassion, anger into wisdom, and chaos into clarity. Spiritual growth is not always a gentle process, but sometimes requires fierce resolve, honest confrontation, and the daring to harness our most visceral energies in service of Awakening.

Bachelard highlights the deep symbolic and metaphysical resonances of fire across human culture.[168] In earlier cosmologies, fire was not just an earthly power, but integral to the celestial order. In this symbolic universe, fire was associated with purity, spirit, and the upward movement of energy. It was not the destructive fire of a forest conflagration, but the primordial flame of the heavens, a medium through which the divine communicated and inspired. Bachelard sees in this vision a reflection of a deeper longing that he calls the 'Novalis complex', after the Romantic poet who dreamed of a primordial unity. Fire, in this context, evokes a memory of that unfallen world, a trace of pre-Creation, before spirit and matter were torn apart.

Fire invites reverie. As we yield our gaze to its flames, we begin to imagine unforeseen possibilities. Fire fascinates and hypnotizes. As it paints colours that rise into the air, it draws us into an oneiric reality, a spiritual realm beyond our ordinary consciousness, a purified world in which images of renewal are sketched out in flames. It speaks to something in us that yearns – not for the world as it is, but for an immemorial, radiant order. This is no mere nostalgia – it's a spiritual impulse, a reaching towards the primordial flame. This archetypal fire underlies inspiration, creativity, and transformation.

Contemplating fire

In the stupa, the fire element appears as a red cone balanced on the white sphere, pointing upwards. The fire element invites us to ask: what are our sources of inspiration? What does initiation mean for us? And how might we liberate the radiance within?

Air: The Dream of Flight

While unseen, air – or wind – is a pervasive force, breathing life into both the outer and the inner world. A breeze lifts a curtain, stirs a leaf, or sends a scrap of paper into motion – modest gestures that reveal an invisible presence at work. It evokes images of clipper ships on the high seas, their sails billowing, rushing towards land with precious cargos to unload; kites soaring and diving in the sky; 'the hurl and gliding'[169] of birds' wings beating against the wind. In this way, air becomes a symbol of the unseen forces that transport us beyond our mundane selves – a metaphor for a transcendent mode of conditionality that carries us beyond the reach of the ego.

This sense of air or wind as an invisible yet powerful force is captured in a short poem by Christina Rossetti:

> Who has seen the wind?
> Neither I nor you.
> But when the leaves hang trembling,
> The wind is passing through.
>
> Who has seen the wind?
> Neither you nor I.
> But when the trees bow down their heads,
> The wind is passing by.[170]

While fire moves upwards in a single direction, air represents energy released outwards, expanding simultaneously and continuously in all directions. In *Air and Dreams*[171], Bachelard interprets air as the element of elevation, imagination, and inner flight. He speaks of 'aerial reverie' as the dream of rising above the world, of shedding weight and constraints. For Bachelard, air is not only breath or atmosphere, but the very medium of poetic dreaming – the invisible current that carries us inwards and upwards. In this light, the air element invites us to attune to the whisper of something beyond form: the soaring freedom of the awakened mind.

In Mesoamerican myth, the god Ehécatl – the divine wind – is a manifestation of Quetzalcóatl, the feathered serpent. He is the breath in living beings, the wind that brings the rain, the invisible messenger that connects heaven and earth. As a creator god and a mover of worlds, Ehécatl symbolizes a power that does not cooperate with the mundane will but lifts us beyond it.

In Buddhist thought, the element of air finds its echo in the bodhicitta – the awakened heart-mind, a suprapersonal force that elevates and dignifies us beyond ourselves. Like the wind, the bodhicitta cannot be grasped, but its momentum can be felt. It is the current of compassion rising through us, a soaring force that carries us towards Awakening. It uplifts, refines, and unfurls us – just as sails are filled and guided by an unseen breath, just as birds are carried upon the winds.

But air has its shadow side too. It can be highly destructive, as in hurricanes and violent storms. When unbalanced or disconnected from the grounding element of earth, it can become superficial, erratic, even alienated – movement without meaning or purpose. To be 'airy' can mean to lack seriousness, to have one's head in the clouds.

The element of air evokes freedom, lightness, and unbounded movement. This quality finds its most vivid expression in tantric symbolism through the figure of the *dakini* – a wild, untamed presence embodying the liberation of our suppressed energies. She is naked, dancing, her limbs whirling in ecstatic abandon, unbound by inhibition. She manifests when the mind begins to open to its own boundless nature.

The word *dakini* stems from a Sanskrit root suggesting flight or soaring. In Tibetan, it becomes *khandroma* – a word compellingly rendered as 'sky-walker' or 'space-dancer'. The *dakini* symbolizes this complete, unqualified freedom of movement – an unimpeded flow of energy within the vast expanse of awareness. She is not merely a being, but a principle: a way of understanding how mind itself moves when it sheds clinging and resistance, becoming awake, alive, and profoundly receptive.

The *dakini*s are those surges and tremors that pulse through the depths of the psyche – visceral stirrings, flashes of intuition, piercing moments of clarity or delight. At times, they may rise from the unconscious as expressions of the deeper intuitions of the mind, disrupting our complacency to call us towards liberation.

Contemplating air

The element air is symbolized by a dish of shimmering, emerald light – a kind of sacred vessel – balanced on the tip of the red cone. To connect with the air element, step outside and feel the breeze on your skin, notice each breath you take, or just listen to the rustling of leaves in the trees. Watch how it carries birds aloft.

Space and the Elemental Mystery

The four material elements – earth, water, fire, and air – are usually considered primary. Yet the fifth element – space or *akasha* – is both the most subtle and the most foundational. It contains the other four, not just as a passive container, but as their enabling condition: it allows them to move, to combine, to manifest. Without space, there is no possibility of fire to radiate, air to expand, water to flow, or earth to settle. Space is the luminous, open dimension from which all forms and experiences arise – and into which they eventually dissolve.

Lama Govinda describes *akasha* as 'all-pervading ether and all-containing space, the synthesis of all that exists, and therefore the symbol of the essential unity of cosmic, psychic, and physical energies'.[172] Space is not simply a backdrop – it is the very domain of ultimate reality, the *Dharmadhatu*: the sphere of phenomena as they truly are. In Mahayana philosophy, this is none other than *shunyata*, or emptiness – not a barren void, but a pregnant fullness beyond all fixed identity, a dynamic field of potential, the womb of all arising.

The energy of space transcends conceptual thought, evoking a dimension beyond duality. The *Vimalakirti Nirdesha Sutra* hints at this mystery when it compares the entrance to non-duality to space itself: 'it has no entrance and no exit'. There is no threshold to cross, no point of arrival. Just like space, it is already at hand – vast, open, and indivisible.[173] It opens out in every direction without ceasing – limitless, omnipresent, and unobstructed. Space thus becomes a profound metaphor for the enlightened mind: open, indivisible, and radically creative. It has no edges, no seams, no obstructions – nothing to push against, and nothing to grasp.

Rilke's poem 'Entrance' evokes something of this infinite openness:

Whoever you are: step out of doors tonight,
Out of the room that lets you feel secure.
Infinity is open to your sight.
Whoever you are.
With eyes that have forgotten how to see
From viewing things already too well-known,
Lift up into the dark a huge, black tree
And put it in the heavens: tall, alone.
And you have made the world and all you see.
It ripens like the words still in your mouth.
And when at last you comprehend its truth,
Then close your eyes and gently set it free.[174]

Rilke's invitation to 'step out of doors' and 'make the world' affirms the boundless potential inherent in space, mirroring the mind's creative power to give birth to reality. In this light, space is not merely what surrounds us – it is what we are: limitless, free, and ceaselessly creative.

Contemplating space

In the architecture of the stupa, space is symbolized by the flaming drop, the *bindu*. It is the seed of all manifestation, the source of infinite possibilities. The element of space invites us to ask: what does it mean to embrace boundless potential? How do we cultivate a mind as open, as unobstructed, as luminous as space itself? What does it mean to 'course' in the realm of reality – the *Dharmadhatu* – with nothing to grasp and nothing to resist?

Introduction to the Stupa Contemplation Practice

Why contemplate the stupa? In this practice, we explore progressively more refined forms of energy, which establish a hierarchy of subtlety. In the first instance, the stupa contemplation practice serves as a *shamatha* practice. It enables us to begin to gather our scattered energies into an integrated whole. We can understand it as a form of *kasina* contemplation, which uses a specific object of attention to create a state of concentration.

As we work with colour, form, and symbolism, the stupa becomes a mirror, helping us to understand ourselves more fully. As we contemplate the stupa, we deepen our awareness of the elements and their role in our inner and outer lives. We begin to align our energies, refine our inner experience, and clarify our orientation towards the ideal of Enlightenment.

The Contemplation of the Stupa

1. First, expand into the pristine vastness of the infinite, blue sky – the open dimension.
2. From within the clear blue sky, a cube of yellow light emerges – the symbol of the earth element (solidity, resistance, and potential).
3. Above the yellow cube, there is a white sphere – the symbol of the water element (fluidity and transparency).
4. Above the white sphere, imagine a red cone – the symbol of the fire element (heat and inspiration).
5. On top of the red cone is an emerald-coloured dish – the symbol of the air element (lightness and mobility).
6. On top of the emerald dish, there appears a flame-shaped drop, iridescent with shimmering rainbow colours – the symbol of space (expansion, infinite extension, and freedom).
7. The flame-shaped drop slowly dissolves into the emerald dish.
8. The emerald dish slowly dissolves into the red cone.
9. The red cone slowly dissolves into the white sphere.
10. The white sphere slowly dissolves into the yellow cube.
11. The yellow cube slowly dissolves into the blue sky.
12. Finally, allow the blue sky itself to gradually fade, thus concluding the practice. Sit for a while absorbing the fruits of the practice.

8

Roaming Outside the Frame: Meditation

> The object of meditation is to transform oneself, not to have good meditations.[175]

Calm and Insight

Samadhi encompasses what we typically refer to as meditation. Literally, it refers to the gathering or settling of the mind upon a single object – one-pointedness. But this isn't a forced or rigid focus; rather, it's a natural coalescing of the psyche's energies. Habitually, our energies are dispersed, even diluted. It's rare for us to be fully concentrated mentally, emotionally, and physically at the same time. *Samadhi* involves bringing the whole of ourselves into a unified, coherent field of awareness.

When I first learned to meditate, I had no idea what to expect. I'd been experiencing a lot of anxiety and even a disconnection from reality. A friend suggested I try meditation because it might bring me peace of mind. The main effect I noticed was that one of my legs went to sleep, so when I got up from the cushion I had intense pins and needles. As I began to meditate more regularly, the pins and needles thankfully subsided, and I slowly began to feel more 'together', more present, more aware of myself – especially of self-destructive thoughts – and of what was around me.

While meditation is widely regarded as the signature Buddhist practice, the vast majority of Buddhists don't spend all day on the cushion, and many don't meditate at all. Yet, in the Western reception of Buddhism, meditation seems to have been elevated above all other forms of commitment and practice. In some cases, it has been removed altogether from its traditional context of beliefs and put in service of secular goals. At a basic level, meditation could be described as the cultivation of creative or 'skilful' mental states. That is to say, mental states that are characterized by generosity, benevolence, and clear understanding. This highlights that it isn't necessarily confined to sitting on a cushion with our eyes closed. At the advanced level, meditation involves transforming our underlying views and desires so that they harmonize with reality. In this way, we cease to resist the way things are, which is the primary cause of our suffering. In traditional terms, these two levels or dimensions correspond to calm (*shamatha*) and insight (*vipashyana*).

The cultivation of calm is sometimes regarded as a preparatory stage, but it can also be seen as *complementary*. We cultivate calm in order to create the necessary stability and focus to contemplate the nature of reality in a sustained way. Exalted intuitions no longer pass like mist across the mind, but settle and become absorbed into the fabric of our consciousness. Calm is associated with practices like the mindfulness of breathing and the cultivation of loving-kindness, whereas insight is linked with the six-element practice, reflection on death, reflection on the three marks of existence, and the contemplation of *shunyata*, amongst others.

While the distinction between calm and insight can be useful, it can give the impression that they are separate and hierarchical. This is not necessarily so. Practices traditionally regarded as favouring insight can help to stabilize the mind, thereby developing stillness, clarity, and emotional resilience. Equally, practices generally categorized as calming – and sometimes dismissed as preliminary or basic – can function as contexts for insight. After all, it is said that the Buddha himself gained Awakening while grounded in the simple exercise of contemplating the breath. If it was good enough for him, it should be good enough for us. Yet the lure of apparently more 'advanced' practices lingers, causing us to fall victim to spiritual materialism. Merely collecting supposedly advanced practices does not automatically elevate us to the status of advanced practitioners. As the saying goes, there are no higher teachings, only deeper understandings. Even the simplest of teachings can result in profound transformation if we are sufficiently receptive; we really don't need anything too complicated. As one spiritual teacher puts it: 'Whether or not meditation and spiritual practices are powerful depends on the practitioner more than the form of the practice.'[176] We may do well to remember the Buddha's warning that his teachings are like a snake: if grasped wrongly, they may turn around and bite us.[177]

The Five Dimensions of Practice

Within the Triratna Buddhist Community, we follow a fivefold model of spiritual practice that may be applied more specifically to meditation.[178] The five elements of this system are:

- Integration
- Positive emotion
- Spiritual death
- Spiritual rebirth
- Receptivity.

Each element can be seen as progressive, but, equally, the five aspects can be understood as a mandala, each of which we practise simultaneously at ever-increasing levels of depth and intensity. Before exploring this framework in more detail, it is worth pausing to note that meditation cannot function in a vacuum. Whatever meditation technique we adopt forms part of an overall programme of spiritual training. To extract a practice from the framework within which it functions, and assume that it will be just as effective as a stand-alone technique, is to misunderstand how meditation works. In the same way that an athlete will follow an integrated training regime to be ready for race day, the spiritual practitioner embraces a complete programme that not only includes meditation but also addresses every aspect of his or her life in order to get to grips with the habitual mind. In this way, he or she trains in more creative patterns of thinking, feeling, and acting.

If we extract a practice from its framework, it's not that it will have no effect – an athlete doing only push-ups will still build strong triceps – but we're likely to develop in a one-sided way. Our spiritual practice becomes unbalanced and partial, making us more susceptible to spiritual materialism, spiritual bypassing, and whimsy. It's all too easy to use meditation to deepen our delusion rather than resolve it, leading us to believe we're making huge advances – even nearing Awakening – when in reality we're stuck in a fantasy, intoxicated with narcissism. Such dangers highlight not only the importance of embracing a comprehensive system of practice but also the crucial role of the human context. Ideally, this means practising within a spiritual community where we have a range of spiritual friendships, including healthy relationships with mentors.

This theme is comically illustrated by the story of Meghiya.[179] While living as the Buddha's companion, Meghiya hankered for a life of intensive meditation, convinced that this was where 'real practice' lay. One day he spotted a mango grove that he thought ideal for his purposes, and asked permission to go and meditate there. The Buddha discouraged him, indicating that Meghiya's needs would be best served by remaining at his side. Being a wilful, perhaps even arrogant, young man, Meghiya insisted. Ignoring the Buddha's gentle warning, he plunged into the forest, eager to immerse himself in sublime states of meditation. Or so he thought. Predictably, Meghiya could not concentrate. His mind was assailed by numerous distractions, and he sank into self-destructive mental states. When he returned to the Buddha, chastened and humbled, his teacher set out five progressive steps that would enable Meghiya to reach liberation. This training begins not with meditation, but with spiritual friendship, followed by a more intensive practice of ethics, Dharma study, then meditation, and finally wisdom.

Integration

Integration is the process of becoming more aware of ourselves, of revealing our hidden corners, of developing greater congruence and depth. The everyday mind is splintered, dispersed; its capacity to pay attention is weak. Through the process of integration, we become more complete, more conscious, even more real. This can be accomplished through practices such as the mindfulness of breathing, which help us to gather together the scattered parts of the mind in a harmonious whole.

When this harmony matures, it results in meditative absorption, an elevated state of consciousness known as *dhyana*, in which all our energies are unified. Early Buddhism speaks of a series of progressively more subtle levels of *dhyana* as the mind becomes more refined, more integrated, more whole. Although these are sometimes described in analytical terms – which can seem rather dry and technical – we should remember that they are elevated, dynamic, unfolding states of consciousness. *Dhyana* bestows a radiant and nurturing calm that, in turn, enables us to enter into sustained contemplation. The Buddha evoked the experience of these increasingly subtle states through similes, each one highlighting a specific quality: integration, inspiration, permeation, and radiation.[180]

For the first *dhyana*, the Buddha offered this analogy:

> Suppose you take a plateful of soap powder, then gradually mix your soap with water and knead it all together until you have a ball of soap absolutely saturated with water, so that there is not a single speck of soap powder that is still dry, and not a single drop of water trickling free of the ball.[181]

This simile illustrates how, when we sustain this level of meditative concentration, we become completely saturated with higher consciousness. A blissful peace permeates every part of our being, just as the powder is permeated by the water. No energy is lost or left unintegrated. It's a state of harmony and peace, where the energies of the conscious and unconscious mind are unified, just like the soap powder and water. It is a state of *integration*.

For the second *dhyana*, the Buddha proposes the image of a pool of perfectly clear, pure water constantly refreshed by a subaqueous spring. Similarly, the second *dhyana* is a clear, pure state of consciousness into which rapture and joy are perpetually bubbling up from deep within. It is a state of *inspiration*.

The third *dhyana* is likened to lotus flowers immersed in a pond of fresh water. Their stalks, leaves, blossoms, and seed pods are all permeated by the water, yet remain distinct. In the same way, in this superconscious state, we are completely pervaded and nourished by an all-encompassing bliss, while still retaining clarity. It is a state of *permeation*.

Finally, the Buddha illustrates the fourth *dhyana* with another classic Indian image. Imagine a hot, dusty day: you bathe in cool water and then wrap yourself in a clean, white sheet. You sit, calm and refreshed, enveloped from head to toe. In this *dhyana*, we similarly wrap ourselves in a purified consciousness that insulates us from all harm, and the dust of worldly distraction. It is a state of *radiation*. Together, these similes point to a progressive unification and refinement of consciousness – a blossoming of awareness that is inwardly enriching and transformative, as well as outwardly radiant.

Integration has both a horizontal and a vertical dimension. That is to say, we may integrate the mind at its present level, which can lead to fairly immediate experiences of concentration, but we also want to work towards integrating the mind on a vertical level, which may involve discovering, or rediscovering, hidden prejudices, fears, aspirations, and obstacles. For this reason, meditation is likely to become more nuanced – even more challenging – as we gain access to a greater range of possible experience. At times this can become uncomfortable. But, as we tap into untold wellsprings of inspiration, we integrate the heights as well as the depths. This gives us greater access to skilful emotions like joy, loving-kindness, and equanimity.

While the cultivation of *dhyana* may express a healthy process of refining consciousness, it is not immune to misuse. Many people who are approaching meditation for the first time are not seeking to know themselves better, but rather looking for a shortcut to some blissful state in which they won't have to confront the messy reality of being an imperfect human being. They may seek to leapfrog themselves into some apparently higher state of consciousness – and it can even work, up to a point. But it comes at a cost: uncomfortable, unresolved feelings and emotions are likely to be ignored, even repressed, and so the underlying experience of disintegration is aggravated rather than healed. Everything may appear tranquil on the surface, but this tranquillity is purchased at the price of alienation from oneself. Experience is held at arm's length, a stance that can harden into self-delusion and distort our sensitivity to others. For this reason, the cultivation of *dhyana* should form part of a balanced pattern of spiritual practice.

Positive Emotion

Meditation is 'weighty' karma – it is the cultivation and reinforcement of skilful mental states. The cultivation of skilful attitudes is exemplified by a family of practices known collectively as the *brahma vihara*s, or divine abodes. These attitudes may be cultivated not only through specific meditation practices but also in daily life. The root emotion is *metta* or *maitri*, which is an impartial feeling of benevolence and goodwill towards all beings. Regardless of whether others are 'good' or 'bad', or whether they like or dislike us, serve our aims, agree with us, or help us, we affirm their intrinsic worth. Aquinas expressed this rather beautifully when he wrote, 'love has the quality of a first gift, through which all other free gifts are given'.[182] *Metta* is a gift that has no expectation of reciprocity. When it is put this way, we may begin to see how much of our goodwill towards others depends on some kind of contract. So long as someone acts in a way that we approve of, we affirm them; yet, as soon as they diverge from our expectations, that approval is promptly withdrawn.

With a firm foundation of *metta*, we can then cultivate the other *brahma vihara*s: *mudita* or sympathetic joy, *karuna* or compassion, and *upekkha* or equanimity. *Mudita* arises when our *metta* comes into contact with someone who is happy because they are leading an ethical, creative life. A common response to such people is envy or even a desire to see them fail. We may sometimes feel that, if someone else is happy or successful, it somehow diminishes us, as though there were only so much happiness to go round. In contrast, *mudita* rejoices in the good done by others, in their accomplishments, and in whatever benefits come to them as a result.

Karuna arises when our *metta* meets suffering. We don't cultivate compassion in isolation; rather, when our *metta* encounters suffering, it naturally gives rise to a desire to alleviate it. *Upekkha* is the most refined and complete of the *brahma vihara*s because it expresses awareness of both the happiness and suffering of others and how this happiness and suffering are produced through causes and conditions. While equanimity might sound like a detached or 'cool' state of mind, it, too, expresses love – a love deeply informed by a profound understanding of life's complex realities. It is a love not blown about by circumstance, able to embrace life's 'ups and downs' by recognizing that individuals are always more than their merits or faults.

Integration and positive emotion can be equated with *shamatha*; however, as already noted, so-called *shamatha* practices can also serve a *vipashyana* function. This is particularly true of the *brahma vihara*s, which invite us to transcend self-identification, move beyond our own needs, and drop the illusion that we are the centre of the universe. Moreover, they involve outgrowing personal likes and dislikes, and relating instead to others on the basis of our shared humanity and potential for Awakening.

The cultivation of positive emotion also refines our moral sensibility, extending our scope as 'ethical agents'. This means recognizing how our actions – of body, speech, and mind – transform us and our world, and also impact others. Rather than blaming others for our experience, we begin to see how, moment by moment, we are constructing a reality that leads us towards either suffering or joy. Moreover, through meditation, we can tenderize our conscience as we discover with greater clarity the ethical tone of our actions. This can be chastening, especially where we begin to see the negative impacts we have on others.

Spiritual Death

Spiritual death is associated with insight practices. What this really means is the death of the egocentric attitude, our neurotic self-obsession, which is a primary cause of our suffering. While 'dying' spiritually may initially sound somewhat bleak and drastic, it points to letting go of the fixed views that we have about ourselves, shedding our limiting patterns of thinking, feeling, and behaving. Spiritual death is, therefore, about moving towards greater freedom.

Spiritual death occurs when we renounce our false sovereignty over experience. Yet this is not something we exactly *decide*; rather, it comes upon us through exposure to *shunyata* – the elusive, mysterious, ungraspable nature of all experience. This nature bears comparison with what Jean-Luc Marion calls the 'irregardable', that which is so immersive, so overwhelming that we cannot hold it in view.[183] It is limitless. We have no prepared categories that might enable us to pin it down or domesticate it. As it exceeds our interpretive capacities, we no longer have authority over what appears. Our habitual initiative is revoked. We surrender our illusory identity as a prior self – an ego that seeks to marshal experience – and become instead a 'luminous witness'.[184] As witness, we are amazed by the glory of the saturated instant. It bestows upon us a superabundance and, ultimately, a new life – a new self – that we are always in the process of taking in. Experience is liberated from the confining verdicts of our habitual ways of seeing.

The six-element practice is one way to engage with spiritual death.[185] We have already looked at the five elements as forms of the progressive liberation of energy. Here, we successively contemplate each of the six elements as objects of attachment that we need to let free. We contemplate earth, water, fire, air, space, and consciousness, recognizing that they do not belong to us, they are not ours, but borrowed. Sooner or later, we must give them back. As we cannot identify ourselves with any of the six elements, we can relinquish our attachment to them; in doing so, we let go of our ego-clinging and permit a new way of being to emerge, one that honours our interconnection with the world, that recognizes with gratitude how life is constantly remaking us.

Spiritual death may also be cultivated by contemplating the three marks of existence: suffering, impermanence, and lack of fixed self-nature. While we have already looked in detail at the topic of suffering, reflecting on impermanence is a means through which we can begin to loosen our attachment. Contemplating our lack of fixed self-nature tackles the habitual self directly – the self that we constantly cherish and defend – and allows us to recognize that it is, in a sense, a fiction. This enables us to attune to the evanescent, ungraspable nature of experience.

Spiritual Rebirth

Spiritual death is intimately connected with spiritual rebirth; they are really two sides of the same coin. Without due emphasis on spiritual rebirth, however, spiritual death is likely to seem an unwelcome and even depressing prospect. Spiritual rebirth is symbolized by the Buddha himself and also by the archetypal buddhas and bodhisattvas, who encapsulate our most exalted possibilities. Through visualizing and contemplating them, we open ourselves to wisdom and compassion and, through our individual actions, may begin to function as channels for their influence. Ultimately, we are not separate from the buddhas and bodhisattvas since they epitomize the spiritual potential latent within all of us.

There are many contemplative practices that incorporate the intricate visualization of archetypal figures and the recitation of mantras, but all can be traced back to the practice of recollecting the Buddha (*Buddhanusmrti*), which we explore in more detail in Chapter 9. In essence, this practice evokes the spiritual qualities that the Buddha exemplifies so that we may begin to incorporate them into our own conduct. By identifying ourselves with our spiritual potential more deliberately, we deepen our confidence in the possibility of Awakening.

Spiritual rebirth may be understood as the dawning of a sacred horizon – the arising of a new mode of consciousness. Perhaps its most exalted expression is evoked by the notion of the bodhicitta: the 'urge towards Awakening'. The bodhicitta is a compassionate impulse that arises as though from elsewhere. Sangharakshita extols it as 'a sort of higher power [...] which works through you when you are open and receptive'. At the same time, he cautions, 'It's not "yours" in the ordinary sense [...] it's something that takes you over.'[186] He goes on to equate this selfless volition as the impulse that underpins *all* Buddhist practice:

> the whole spiritual life manifests from the *bodhicitta*, is the *bodhicitta* at work. It's us in a sense, but it isn't us. It isn't literally an outside force which takes possession of us [...] but it's so different from the ordinary 'me' that it seems almost like something apart from that 'me', or even opposed to that 'me'.[187]

The bodhicitta never becomes a possession of the self because it arises when the ordinary self ruptures. In the arising of the bodhicitta, we enter into a new mode of life, we become sons and daughters of the Buddha entrusted with the cosmic mission of helping lead all beings towards Awakening.

Anuttara puja, or supreme worship, is a traditional method for cultivating the bodhicitta. One form of this is the sevenfold puja, a sublime ritual that guides us through a sequence of devotional moods. In essence, *puja* is the turning of the mind towards the Buddha – saturating our awareness with the living presence of Awakening. The Buddha appears vividly before us, perhaps embodied in a sacred image (*rupa*) or evoked through the imagination. Every act within the *puja* – each gesture, each offering, each verse – draws us towards a greater intimacy with the Buddha. Through devotional practice of this kind, we become increasingly receptive to the qualities of Enlightenment, opening the heart and mind to the compassionate impulse of the bodhicitta.

Receptivity

It is usual to emphasize that meditation requires effort. An entire stage of the eightfold path is devoted to the elaboration of the four aspects of 'right effort'. Moreover, we talk about the 'cultivation' or 'development' (*bhavana*) of skilful mental states; they don't just happen by themselves – we have to put the work in. Even so, this approach has its shortcomings. All too readily, effort in meditation can become somewhat forced, even rather dry and joyless. After some time, this can provoke resistance, a loss of inspiration, and even physical symptoms such as headaches. Besides this, meditation can degenerate into a kind of papering over the cracks where, instead of genuinely deepening into our experience, we merely smear a layer of positivity over it. Our meditation remains superficial and, still worse, we may fall victim to alienated awareness (see Chapter 10). Our desire to find happiness may cause us to flee the instant, which is unsatisfactory, in search of some future in which we believe we will be happier. This can result in a fantasy spiritual life. In the context of our meditation practice, we seem to escape for a while, but nothing really changes because we avoid engaging with the root of the problem.

For this reason, it is important to balance cultivation with receptivity. This is exemplified in the practice of just sitting, where we dwell in awareness of the present moment without trying to accomplish anything in particular. We might characterize this as a posture of listening, of waiting, of allowing experience to ripen organically rather than restlessly chasing after it. This can be a very fulfilling state of mind, in which our imagination begins to unfold spontaneously and deeper intuitions rise to the surface of consciousness. It is helpful to follow a practice of active cultivation with at least a short session of just sitting. Receptivity can also be encouraged in other ways, notably through devotional practices.

According to Dōgen, meditation practice is not a means to an end but itself *manifests* that end. Awakening is neither a fruit of the past nor a hope for the future, but perpetually reveals itself in the present. Awakening is not something gained by means of meditation, because it does not arise at an instant in time; rather it points to a reality that stands outside time as we normally conceive of it. Dōgen expresses this beautifully in his usual, mystical idiom:

> When we solely sit in zazen [...] relying now on exactly the same posture as the Buddha, and letting go of the myriad things, then we go beyond the areas of delusion, realization, emotion, and consideration, and we are not concerned with the ways of the common and the sacred. At once we are roaming outside the [intellectual] frame, receiving and using the great state of *bodhi*.[188]

Enemies of Meditation

Like the other spiritual faculties, *samadhi* has both near and far enemies. Some of its far enemies are obvious: agitation, distraction or mental dispersion, and unwise attention. But one of its near enemies is what Sangharakshita has called 'pseudo-spiritual technicism' – a weighty phrase that merits unpacking.[189]

Pseudo-spiritual technicism is a kind of fundamentalism in relation to select methods of liberation – most often, meditation techniques. Buddhist culture has at times been disfigured by this reductive attitude, from Nichiren's frantic insistence on exclusive recitation of the *daimoku* and belligerent dismissal of all other practices, to modern *vipassana* approaches that effectively narrow the entire path to a single attentional protocol. Contemporary 'focus-hack' mindfulness likewise treats awareness as a neutral psychotech that will deliver guaranteed benefits regardless of context. In this mindset, the technique itself is granted a kind of quasi-magical status. Transformation is attributed to the inherent power of the method rather than individual effort, the surrounding conditions, or the interpretive framework through which the technique is understood and applied. But the impact of any practice is shaped as much, if not more, by its context as by its technical features. Practice is less about virtuosity than about immersing ourselves in a transformative milieu.

Sangharakshita describes pseudo-spiritual technicism in the following terms:

> We think that if we can only find the one right, infallible method or technique, it will automatically give us the experience. Or else we believe that we have actually found such a method or technique, and then of course we become very dogmatic and intolerant about it. All other methods are dismissed as worthless. Only our own technique, only the method to which we ourselves have recourse, is the right and efficacious one.[190]

Such an attitude is likely to breed a sense of superiority about one's own allegiance and focus, as well as a sense of pity, or even contempt, for those who do not follow the same approach. One is likely to see oneself as one of the elect and others as stumbling around, deprived of the one true way. If we dismiss other methods as worthless, then we will not accord them value and much less practise them. Even where we do continue to practise them, somewhat half-heartedly and perhaps out of a sense of resentful obligation or loyalty, we will fail to recognize how they contribute towards our process of spiritual maturity. So focused are we on the one, special technique that we are convinced will lead us to the crucial experience, we may fail to notice the subtle process of reorientation that results from a commitment to a holistic regime of spiritual life.

Obstacles in Meditation

Given their repetitive, routine nature, we may easily become bored or dissatisfied with particular meditation practices. Who wants to spend year after year counting to ten as the mindfulness of breathing directs us to do? Yet boredom is more likely a symptom of superficiality than a genuine need for novel practices. If we are bored, it often means we are not truly engaged with ourselves. Interest and curiosity are lacking – we're skating across the surface rather than plumbing our depths.

Besides, boredom may be enriching. Walter Benjamin praised it as 'the dream bird that hatches the egg of experience'.[191] Boredom is a mode of incubation. It interrupts compulsive routine and allows space for the new to arise. Instead of reaching for what seems more exciting or 'advanced', we may need to return to our basic purpose and remember why we are meditating in the first place. This can help rekindle our enthusiasm.

While, earlier in this chapter, I outlined the superconscious states that we may access through meditation, this is by no means the experience of most people. In fact, many meditators, myself included, often struggle to develop settled concentration. This can readily engender a sense of failure and dejection. However, meditation is not only about what we notice at the surface of the mind; it is also a process that reorganizes our psyche at a deeper level. I am often struck by how my meditation can seem completely distracted, even aimless; yet, at the end of it, I feel calmer and more collected. This suggests that, even when the surface of our mind feels turbulent, the intentionality and process of integration that we are cultivating in meditation is still having an effect at a deeper level. It also points to the importance of favourable conditions. Many of us are more likely to experience concentrated states of mind on a retreat than amidst the busyness of our everyday routine.

9

Imagining a Cosmos

> The imagination is not [...] the faculty for forming images of reality; it is the faculty for forming images which go beyond reality, which *sing* reality. It is a superhuman faculty.[192]

It's striking that there is no single word in Buddhism that directly corresponds to the English word 'imagination'. There are, however, terms that relate to what we might call the negative aspects of imaginative capacity – such as the tendency to distract ourselves with fantasy or to become entangled in self-destructive thinking (*prapanca*). While *sati*, in its aspect of 'recollection' or 'remembrance', clearly draws on some of the creative functions of the imagination, perhaps the closest term is *samadhi*, which we habitually translate as 'meditation'. *Samadhi*, then, isn't a passive state, but an active, imaginative process in which we *intentionally* harness the mind's creative capacities to transform our emotions, our attitudes, and even our actions. While this process is less prominent in early Buddhism, given its more analytical orientation, it comes into full bloom in Mahayana and Tantric traditions – especially through the Mahayana sutras and the practice of *sadhana*, which centres on the contemplation of archetypal figures that symbolize the qualities of the enlightened mind. Rather than through words and ideas, the imagination perceives through images and symbols.

My teacher Sangharakshita distinguished between what he called the 'horizontal imagination', corrupted by self-interested emotion – plotting, scheming, and catastrophizing – and the 'vertical imagination', which ascends in search of higher realities.[193] He associated the latter with the understanding found among the Romantic poets.[194] While acknowledging that Buddhism lacks a direct equivalent to the term 'imagination', Sangharakshita proposed that the divine eye (*divya-chakshu*) corresponds to it. Through this 'Eye of Imagination', the Buddha beheld humanity as a lake of lotus flowers, each person at a different stage of unfolding.[195] He saw in every individual the potential for growth, which inspired him to proclaim the Dharma. In this sense, imagination is integral to the bodhisattva ideal, which seeks to recognize, nurture, and serve this potential so that all beings may fulfil it.

Refining the Imagination

Meditation can be understood as an imaginative journey into our deepest interiority. Indeed, Sangharakshita proposes that we can articulate the entire process of self-understanding as just such a journey. He describes the imagination as 'a faculty for the perception of images',[196] and invites us to notice how certain images capture our attention because they evoke a symbol, which in turn reveals an archetype, which in turn points to a subtle, spiritual reality.[197] This process may begin through the contemplation of art.

As an example, Sangharakshita explores the archetypal significance of the figure of St Jerome. Throughout his life,

Sangharakshita was repeatedly drawn to paintings of this Christian saint, discerning in this image an embodiment of the archetype of the wise old man as 'translator' and 'alchemist'. More deeply, something within him 'corresponded' to the image; in St Jerome, Sangharakshita saw a reflection of himself. He affirms that the symbolic impact of images isn't limited by belief systems, because they connect with something primordial and universal within us. In summing up the archetypal meaning of St Jerome, Sangharakshita remarks that he symbolizes 'man as interpreter and creator, bringing into consciousness what he has experienced in the depths of his own being and giving it appropriate expression for the benefit of all'.[198]

Sangharakshita goes on to propose 'a hierarchy of levels of the imagination, or imaginal faculty, corresponding to a hierarchy of levels of images and archetypes, or imaginal world'.[199] Moreover, he argues that to speak of the imagination as a faculty among faculties isn't quite correct, since 'when one truly perceives an image one perceives it with the whole of oneself, or with one's whole being.'[200] In contemplating an image deeply, we're transported to the world where that image belongs; we even become an inhabitant of that world. Ultimately, he argues, 'in perceiving an image what one really perceives is, in a sense, oneself'.[201] Thus, the imaginative engagement with archetypal images becomes a process of self-exegesis and ultimately of self-transcendence.

Through his meticulous contemplation of the figure of St Jerome and its associated motifs, Sangharakshita invites us to embark on a similar journey of image interpretation, which amounts to an education and refinement of our imaginative powers. Stimulated by his creative imagination, our own capacity to find meaning in images may be awakened and, in turn, serve to reveal more of ourselves to ourselves. In this way, it contributes to a process both of deepening self-integration and of profound, intuitive connection with reality.

An image that has long called my attention comes from a nested story in John Fowles' novel *The Magus*. Conchis (the magus), then a young doctor, travels to a remote Norwegian-fir forest, drawn by reports of Gustav Nygaard, a bird expert. There he learns of Gustav's estranged brother, Henrik, who lives in a spartan cabin on a remote promontory, seemingly mentally ill. Now almost blind, he is 'waiting to be visited by God'. Conchis catches a glimpse of Henrik's gaunt figure, with fierce, protruding blue eyes – eyes of madness. When he offers assistance, the hermit attacks him with an axe.

Some nights later, Conchis hears a cry from across the water. It is Henrik calling out to God: 'Do you hear me? I am here.' The narrator approaches to find the hermit standing, legs astride, with his feet in the water. He hears Henrik cry '*Takk*' – thanks. Henrik then falls to his knees in the shingle, adopting a watchful posture. Witnessing this mystical scene, Conchis comments ruefully:

> I would have given ten years of my life to have been able to look out there to the north, from inside his mind. I did not know what he was seeing, but I knew it was something of such power, such mystery, that it explained all.[202]

It then dawns on the narrator that Henrik isn't merely *waiting* to meet God, but is actually 'meeting God'. He discerns that Henrik is undergoing an experience utterly beyond the scope of his own scientific knowledge. This provokes an epiphany:

> But in a flash, as of lightning, all our explanations, all our classifications and derivations, our aetiologies, suddenly appeared to me like a thin net. That great passive monster, reality, was no longer dead, easy to handle. It was full of a mysterious vigour, new forms, new possibilities. The net was nothing, reality burst through it.[203]

The Unifying Function of the Imagination

Subhuti emphasizes imagination's *unifying* function: it integrates both the objects of perception and the subject of those perceptions.[204] First, from the torrent of perceptual input, imagination creates a coherent, intelligible whole. This unification has two aspects: quantitative and qualitative. Quantitatively, perception coordinates the objects of experience into a single, experienced world. Qualitatively, imagination transforms all perceptions into symbols, giving rise to a new mode of perceiving – a distinct language that mediates experience symbolically.

Second, imagination unifies the subject – that is, us. It draws together and elevates the mind's ordinary faculties, resolving their habitual conflicts and dissonances. It integrates our cognitive, emotional, and volitional dimensions with a refined sensation, enabling a single, harmonious act of awareness. This stands in stark contrast to our usual fragmented state, in which we might know what is good but lack the will to act, feel deeply yet become overwhelmed by emotion, or act impulsively without mental clarity. In its integrative mode, imagination aligns these functions: thought becomes felt, feeling becomes intelligent, and action flows naturally from both. This gives rise to a profound sense of well-being, harmony, and even love. This is precisely the unification implied by the term *samadhi*.

Imagination not only discloses deeper dimensions of reality – it actively draws us towards them, guiding us into increasingly refined and luminous modes of perception. It doesn't merely embellish reality; it lifts us beyond mundane preoccupations, connecting us with the transcendent. It fulfils a kind of sacred exegesis, revealing the hidden meaning of symbolic forms.

In the Buddhist tradition, we might trace this imaginative ascent through the three realms (*loka*s), understood not only cosmologically but also experientially. The *kamaloka* refines sensual experience to the point of an exquisite aesthetic responsiveness – a heightened sensitivity to beauty and vitality. In the *rupaloka*, the imagination opens to visionary form and symbolic resonance, radiant with meaning. At the level of the *arupaloka*, even form dissolves; the imagination now rests in pure qualities of awareness – felt rather than seen, known directly rather than conceptualized.

At each level, there's a deeper harmony, a more unified consciousness. Aesthetic delight and cognitive clarity begin to converge. Yet even this level of awareness isn't transcendental; it depends on favourable conditions, on karmic momentum, and is thus liable to fade. Only when imagination aligns with wisdom (*prajna*) – with the nature of things as they truly are –

does it become a reliable compass. Then, imagination becomes not just a guide, but pure revelation – Awakening itself.

Imagination as Cosmic Reverie

Gaston Bachelard approaches the imagination from a phenomenological and poetic standpoint. He characterizes it as 'essentially *open* and elusive. It is the human psyche's experience of *openness* and *novelty*.'[205] He also points to the quality of wonder that is inherent in imaginative experience, describing the imagination itself as 'a wild hope of unbounded seeing'.[206]

For Bachelard, imagination isn't a faculty that merely reproduces past perceptions (as memory does); rather, it creates new possibilities of being, governed by what he calls the 'unreality principle' – a generative, future-oriented capacity that allows new worlds to emerge. As he writes: 'A world takes form in our reverie, and this world is ours. This dreamed world teaches us the possibilities for expanding our being within our universe.'[207]

More specifically, Bachelard connects the imagination with what he calls 'cosmic reverie', which bears some relationship with the notion of *samadhi*. This is not idle daydreaming but 'an ever-emanating universe, a fragrant breath that issues from things through the dreamer'.[208] He proposes that 'imagining a cosmos is the most natural destiny of reverie'.[209] Reverie is a sacred mode of awareness that 'puts us in the state of a soul being born'.[210] Finally, he declares that 'Reverie sacralizes its object.'[211]

In reverie, time is suspended. The world becomes so majestic that 'nothing any longer happens there; the world reposes in its tranquility'.[212] This timeless stillness induces what Bachelard calls an 'ante-perceptive' state – a condition prior to subject–object duality, where image precedes perception and initiates a new mode of seeing.

According to Bachelard, 'The human psyche creates itself by means of images.'[213] Imagined images aren't mere reproductions of external forms; they are sublimated archetypes. Such images are *immediate*, and thus a single image can give birth to an entire imaginative universe. They become the very units of reverie, capable of sustaining entire worlds of symbolic meaning. Bachelard characterizes reverie as a state of lightness, repose, and well-being.

The Active Imagination and the Earth of Visions

Persian mysticism accords a central role to the imagination and celebrates its transformative power. The French scholar Henry Corbin sharply distinguishes between mere fantasy – which he views as a distortion of reality or escapism – and what he terms the 'active imagination' (*imaginatio vera*).[214] This active imagination is a subtle faculty, capable of perceiving a dimension of reality that transcends both sensory experience and abstract conceptual thought. Far from fabricating illusion, the active imagination uncovers profound layers of truth.

Through this faculty, we gain access to a visionary realm known as Hurqalya – the 'earth of visions'. Hurqalya mediates between the sensible and the invisible, functioning as what Corbin calls an *interworld*. Within this subtle domain, archetypal realities are disclosed – not as subjective projections but as real events, as *hierophanies*: revelations of sacred meaning. Hurqalya is the realm in which genuine spiritual events unfold – a luminous ground where reality reveals itself in symbolic form. Here, images serve not as decorative fictions but as radiant lattices through which the light of ultimate truth shines.

Corbin associates this mode of perception with the practice of *ta'wil*, a type of spiritual hermeneutics central to certain strands of Islamic thought. *Ta'wil* is the process of uncovering the inner, symbolic, or hidden meanings of perceived forms. It bears comparison with *prajna*, understood as luminous, creative discernment that brings ultimate truths into the light of awareness. It is not a flight from the world but a penetration into its symbolic depth. In this sense, imagination functions as an organ of knowledge – one that harmonizes the emotional, volitional, and cognitive faculties in a single act of visionary discernment.

In many respects, the realm of Hurqalya resonates with the *sambhogakaya* ('enjoyment body') of Buddhist tradition – the dimension of visionary forms, accessible not through the senses but through purified imagination.[215] Here, in this world-between-worlds, far from being a distorting veil, the imagination serves as the lens through which reality's radiant glory pours forth, sacralizing all perception.

We are accustomed to dignify the world of outer perception as 'objective reality', often relegating the inner world of imagination to mere subjective creation. However, if we are to deepen our meditation practice and harness the creative powers of the imagination, we must take these capacities more seriously – even recognizing them as integral to the process of spiritual Awakening.

The Vertical Imagination and Compassion

The vertical imagination 'lifts us out of ourselves', enabling us to identify with others and even step into their shoes.[216] This capacity is essential for developing ethical sensitivity and many Buddhist attitudes, most notably compassion. While the word 'imagination' does not appear in Mahayana texts, this faculty clearly serves as a powerful instrument for creative transformation. The *Bodhicharyavatara*, a classic presentation of the bodhisattva ideal and the arising of bodhicitta, explicitly uses the creative powers of imagination as its primary contemplative tool for eliciting transformation.

While Shantideva draws upon both the 'horizontal' and the 'vertical' tendencies of imagination to inspire deeper commitment and far-reaching transformation, in the chapter on the perfection of meditation (*samadhi*), he primarily employs the vertical imagination to stimulate awareness, empathy, and compassion for other beings. This is especially evident in the sections where he introduces contemplations on 'equalizing self and other' and 'exchanging self and other'.

Shantideva introduces 'equalizing self and other' as a meditative contemplation to encourage us to step beyond our self-preoccupation and recognize that others are just like us.[217] First, we reflect that they experience happiness and suffering just as we do. Thus, he affirms:

> I should dispel the suffering of others because it is suffering like my own suffering. I should help others too because of their nature as beings, which is like my own being.[218]

If others seek happiness and fear suffering just as I do, Shantideva reasons, why should I prioritize my own happiness before theirs, or protect only myself from suffering and not others?[219] The broader intention is to recognize that the needs of others are just as important as our own. In this way, we begin to understand our unique individuality within a universal context: we are just one among countless beings who all seek happiness and want to avoid suffering.

Confronted with the objection that compassion may bring personal discomfort and thus should be avoided, Shantideva counters that, in the larger scheme of things, if a minor inconvenience on our part can alleviate the suffering of many, we should be more than willing to endure it. To illustrate this, he evokes the image of a bodhisattva plunging into the darkest hells 'as geese into a cluster of lotus blossoms'.[220] This vivid image serves as a reminder of vigour, one we might recall the next time we find ourselves grumbling about performing a small kindness to ease another's burden.

The practice of 'exchanging self and other' takes our imaginative capacity even further.[221] In part, the aim is to help us see how our self-preoccupation is, in fact, the root cause of our own suffering. Paradoxically, by giving up the self-centred pursuit of our own happiness and instead devoting ourselves to easing the suffering of others, we may discover a deeper and more lasting happiness. In this meditative contemplation, we imagine that, as another, we are faced with ourselves.[222] It is quite an unnerving reflection. We adopt three perspectives: imagining what someone who regards themselves inferior, equal, or superior to us might think and feel as they encounter us. Through these imaginative exercises we break free of our self-referential concern, intensify our awareness of the inner life of others, and become more sensitive to their struggles. This serves a dual purpose: first, reducing our own suffering by shedding excessive self-concern; and second, opening our hearts with compassion to the suffering of others. As Shantideva puts it:

> If one does not let go of self one cannot let go of suffering, as one who does not let go of fire cannot let go of burning.
>
> Therefore, in order to allay my own suffering and to allay the suffering of others, I devote myself to others and accept them as myself.[223]

The *Samadhi* of Seeing the Buddhas

Mahayana Buddhism developed contemplative practices that harness the transformative power of imagination. Among these is the *samadhi of seeing all the buddhas*, a visionary form of *Buddhanusmrti*, or recollection of the Buddha. Rather than relying on conceptual analysis, this practice activates the imagination to evoke a vivid, symbolic presence – one that subtly redraws the contours of our perceived world in the light of our ultimate concern.

The instructions are fairly simple. The *Pratyutpanna Samadhi Sutra* describes it in these terms:

> One should find a quiet, solitary place and bring to mind the presence of Amitabha Buddha in the western direction. One should imagine that, countless buddha-fields away, in the Pure Land of Sukhavati, Amitabha is surrounded by bodhisattvas and expounding the Dharma. In this way, one should maintain an ongoing recollection of the Buddha.[224]

This mode of perception is likened to dreaming: a man sees his loved ones and treasured possessions in a dream and delights in them. Upon waking, the memory moves him so deeply that he sheds tears. The emotional impact of imagined presence is real.

The practice teaches that, by invoking Amitabha in this way, we cultivate the conditions to be reborn in the Pure Land. Simply hearing the Buddha's name, and turning our attention towards any direction, enables us to behold *all* the buddhas – each like a radiant gem, set upon polished beryl.

Numerous similes are offered to clarify the nature of this vision. For instance, a monk contemplates bones – now green, now white, now red, now black – not brought from anywhere, not materially existent, but arising entirely in the mind. Likewise, the appearance of the Buddha does not come from outside but arises due to three factors: the Buddha's spiritual power, the meditative concentration he bestows, and the practitioner's own merit.

Another image compares the meditator to a handsome young man gazing at his reflection in a clear mirror, polished crystal, or calm water. The reflection does not enter from without; it arises because the right conditions are present. In the same way, the vision of the Buddha arises within the purified mind – not as illusion, but as symbolic manifestation.

In reflecting on a visionary encounter like this, we may ask ourselves: 'Where did the Buddha come from? Where did I go to?' Then one sees clearly: 'The Buddha came from nowhere, and I too went nowhere.'[225]

This insight culminates in a radical statement of mind-only doctrine:

> Whatever I think, that I see. The mind creates the Buddha. The mind itself sees him. The mind is the Buddha. The mind is the Tathagata. The mind is my body, the mind sees the Buddha.[226]

Empowered by the Buddha's numinous presence, and firmly grounded in meditation, the bodhisattva gazes eastwards and beholds hundreds, thousands, even innumerable buddhas. Just as the bodhisattva sees the buddhas of the east, so too do the buddhas of all ten directions come into view, for such perception is no longer confined by time or space.

A final simile compares this to looking up at the night sky: a person sees countless stars and later recalls them clearly. In the same way, the meditator, even after rising from meditation, can *vividly remember* and speak of the buddhas they have seen.

While the text encourages us to take the forms that appear within meditation seriously, it also reminds us that their true nature is emptiness – *shunyata*. This means not that they are mere fictions but that they share the nature of all phenomena: everything is conditioned; nothing has inherent existence. The text cautions us not to cling to the visions of buddhas that arise in meditation since this leads to suffering. To illustrate this, the text compares the situation to a woman contemplating her own image in a newly polished mirror or in a bowl filled with oil.[227] Seeing her reflection, she becomes utterly infatuated with herself – much like Narcissus in Greek mythology:

> She pursues what is not real, rejecting the Dharma for nothing.
>
> On account of form she runs about, setting her body on fire.[228]

The teaching is thus a subtle one: while the imagination has the power to evoke the Buddha and effect deep transformation, we must not reify its creations. The forms it brings forth are not distractions, but neither are they ends in themselves. They are symbolic forms – gateways that guide the mind towards more expansive and elevated states of consciousness.

Imagination in the *Surangama Samadhi Sutra*

The *Surangama Samadhi Sutra*, the scripture concerning the *samadhi* that bestows 'heroic progress' (*surangama*) on the path to Enlightenment, is an early Mahayana work dating from around the second century CE.[229] In both themes and style, it bears comparison with the better-known *Vimalakirti Nirdesha*.[230] Although the Sanskrit source has been lost, the text survives in Chinese and Tibetan translations. Using light, space, multiplicity, imagery, and boundless time, the sutra expands and purifies our consciousness by drawing us into a series of contemplations that overwhelm our habitual perceptual categories. As we surrender to its bedazzling scope, the text opens up a visionary horizon that transforms us. It evokes a realm of incalculable vastness, miraculous possibilities, inconceivable depths, and inexhaustible brilliance.

The *Surangama Samadhi Sutra* is sometimes classified as a 'meditation sutra', yet the '*samadhi* of heroic progress' is not merely an exalted state of concentration but virtually a synonym for Enlightenment itself; it constitutes the spiritual condition of the most advanced bodhisattvas. Throughout the sutra, the *samadhi* seems to hover above and beyond the scene as a transcendent possibility or dimension – constantly gestured towards yet never fully visible or assimilated, always beyond the self's capture. By rehearsing the sutra's visionary scenes, we begin to anticipate a glorious consciousness whose scope we can never circumscribe.

As we immerse ourselves in the scripture, we are confronted with the ineffable glory of this *samadhi*. While stealing all our admiration, it defies every attempt to encapsulate it. Its splendour continually exceeds our interpretive reach – and this is precisely the point. The *samadhi* symbolizes a constant overwhelming of our panoptic urge; it never permits us to rise above it – like some surveillance drone mapping the territory below – and so impose our ready-made understanding upon it. Instead, it remains just out of reach, granting only fleeting glimpses of its brilliance. Resistant to our interpretive calculation, its ultimate majesty remains forever deferred. Such elusiveness characterizes our encounter with the transcendent, which, by its very nature, surpasses the confines of dualistic perception.

How might we best prepare ourselves to approach such a sutra? And what can we hope to gain? Mahayana sutras can seem excessive, confusing, and ultimately frustrating. They resist our subsuming tendency – our impulse to domesticate the unfamiliar. They cannot be consumed, assimilated, and then filed away; rather, they call us into question. The philosopher Jean-Luc Marion defines a work of art not as something one simply sees, but as something that one sees *again* – that is, to which one *returns*. A painting, for instance, reveals 'an exceptional realm of visibility'. Moreover, 'The more I see it, the more it will give me to see, and the more my concepts will lag behind.'[231] In a similar way, we can never 'master' or control a Mahayana sutra; instead, we must yield to its wondrous power and allow it to disclose its marvels. If we accept its call to follow the imaginative itinerary it opens for us, we will enrich our consciousness. A Mahayana sutra resists objectification; it is not a spectacle but rather a milieu within which we become immersed and through which we become enlarged. Again, following Marion, we might say that a sutra functions by way of a 'counter-intentionality' that summons our gaze and floods us with vision. It opens onto a magnitude beyond anything we can anticipate.

Early in the sutra, a vision of limitless multiplicity serves to expand consciousness. The participants of the cosmic assembly gathered around the Buddha – which includes brahmas and shakras (different types of celestial being), as well as world-protecting kings – react with surprise and delight, since they have never heard of the *surangama samadhi* but are inspired to learn about it. Each then conceives the idea of offering a splendid lion throne for the Buddha to sit upon and expound the *samadhi*. The perspective of each is self-referential, since each believes that it is they alone who will offer the throne to the Buddha and no one else. Each throne is strewn with precious fabrics, covered with spectacular canopies, banners, and exquisite parasols, surrounded by a balustrade of precious jewels; its top is scattered with all kinds of wonderful flowers, perfumed with celestial incense, and embellished with precious metals and stones.

All of a sudden, an innumerable host of lion thrones appears before the Buddha. Each participant sees only the lion throne that they offered, unaware of the countless others, and so believes that they alone have made an offering. Then, 'desiring to demonstrate a little of the potency' of the *samadhi*, and so inspire the assembly to adopt the Mahayana path, the Buddha opens out a cosmic vision for all to see of innumerable lion thrones, on each of which he is seated simultaneously.[232] The entire assembly is filled with wonder and experiences great joy. They rise from their seats and pay homage to the Buddha. Having witnessed this spectacular vision of multiplicity, they conceive the bodhicitta – the impulse towards Awakening for the benefit of all beings. A stunned brahma god asks which of the innumerable buddhas is real. The Buddha answers that *all* of them are real.

The initial position depicts our habitual state: self-oriented, confined by our own desires, goals, and parameters. The vision revealed by the Buddha is a transformation of consciousness, one that can never settle into habit. Bachelard writes that 'there is a growth of being in every instance of consciousness'.[233] This cosmic scene broadens our perceptual horizon, rehearsing the boundless openness that is Enlightenment. By evoking limitless multiplicity, the sutra anticipates the infinite riches of the enlightened mind.

Later in the sutra, the main protagonist, the bodhisattva Drdhamati, asks a shakra god called Bearer of Meru's Summit

(Merusikharadhara): 'What universe do you come from?' The shakra replies:

> A bodhisattva who possesses the *Surangama Samadhi* dwells in all the buddha fields, but is not attached to a dwelling-place, does not perceive a dwelling place, and does not see a dwelling place.[234]

Another god named Kaushika then questions Meru's Summit about his attainment of the *samadhi* and his reputed capacity to appear in all the palaces of the shakra gods. How is it, he asks, that he has never seen him? Meru's Summit replies that, if he were to show his true body, Kaushika would no longer feel any joy in his own palace. Nonetheless, Kaushika insists on seeing the body of this perfected being. When Meru's Summit displays his true and marvellous body, all those present in the assembly who have not yet realized the *surangama samadhi* become invisible. His body – lofty as Mount Meru itself – shines, gleams, and is resplendent. Moreover, the Buddha's body becomes doubly luminous. The astonished Kaushika comments that the colours of Meru's Summit's body are pure, marvellous, and unequalled, its brilliance eclipsing the splendour of all the gods. The overwhelming visibility and extreme light of Meru's Summit's body (which is, of course, his mind) render ordinary reality so dim as to be invisible. The sutra thus invites us towards a greater intensity of perception, a kind of saturated awareness. In Rilke's words, 'whatever is present is utterly and urgently present'[235] – not only in detail, but in scope and in glory.

Kaushika then introduces a superlative image to further evoke this sense of inconceivable brilliance. He mentions a necklace of jewels that he wears in his god realm, which eclipses the light of all the devas there. The Buddha then amplifies this analogy. Suppose the entire universe were filled with jewels of the brilliance of Kaushika's necklace; there is still another jewel that would eclipse them all, known as 'Brilliance of All the Gods'. Supposing the entire universe were filled with jewels of that kind, there is still another, 'Diamond Brilliance', which would eclipse them all. If the entire universe were filled with those jewels, there is another still, 'Assemblage of All the Brilliances', which outshines them entirely. The Buddha points out that Meru's Summit wears this jewel and asks Kaushika if he can see it. He replies, 'Yes, but the brilliance of that jewel is so violent that my eyes cannot bear it.' The Buddha then affirms that bodhisattvas who have realized the *surangama samadhi* all wear a necklace of jewels of such inconceivable splendour.

This series of superlative comparisons offers us an imaginative itinerary that orients us towards the transcendent. It invites us to open ourselves to an ever-widening vista of insight – one that we cannot encompass because it surpasses our capacity to envision it. It saturates our awareness with an overwhelming intensity and so evades all rehearsed objectification. The *Surangama Samadhi* dazzles us and reconstitutes us in the light of its overpowering glory.

The sutra also employs the motif of unbounded duration to disrupt our parochial measures of time. Despite Meru's Summit's being an advanced bodhisattva, it turns out that he is still not yet a perfect buddha. The Buddha of the sutra predicts that in sixty-two *kalpa*s (about a billion years) this great bodhisattva will become a cosmic buddha named 'King

Glory of Unstained Brilliance', and will create a Pure Land called 'Pure Vision'. He will live for ten small *kalpa*s (168 billion years). After his passing, his Dharma will endure for a hundred thousand *koti*s of years (a *koti* being 10 million). Awakening thus defies our lilliputian time horizon; it is inconceivable.

Properly speaking, all experience is inconceivable: it is like being drenched by a wave we cannot stand back from and admire. It envelops us, saturates us, even perfumes us. This precise moment of consciousness is inexhaustible in its depths and riches. What opens before us always supersedes our capacity to formulate it. The glory that the transcendent deigns to let us glimpse can never be made ours, but rather provokes amazement, wonder, and reverence. In giving its inexhaustible brilliance, it seizes our prescriptive agency and bestows a new subjectivity, purified of ego-grasping. The *surangama samadhi* is not a distant world, but rather hints at a sacralizing mode of perception. The imagination has a transformative capacity that invites connection with what can never fully be held in focus or calculated.

A further theme evoked in the sutra is nonduality: more particularly, the non-difference between ignorance and wisdom, or between samsara and nirvana. The trickster Mara – who basically symbolizes everything that stands in the way of awakened awareness – reappears in several chapters. It is affirmed that Mara himself will eventually reach perfect Awakening: an immensely optimistic vision given his status as the enemy of the spiritual path. Moreover, the distance between his domain and the *surangama samadhi* is collapsed. In one comical scene, Mara complains that he has lost command of his entourage since it has been exposed to the *surangama samadhi*. His followers assure him that they have not abandoned him because 'Between the *maradhatu* and the *buddhadhatu* there is neither duality nor difference.'[236] Crestfallen, Mara returns to his palace, only for a bodhisattva to follow him and suggest that he offer everything he possesses to the Buddha. Mara agrees, and in that very moment 'the whole assembly was in his residence and the Buddha was expounding the *Suramgamasamadhi*'.[237]

10

Myriad Things Come Forth: Mindfulness

> If we weren't so single-minded
> about keeping our lives moving
> and could maybe do nothing for once
> a huge silence might interrupt this sadness
> of never understanding ourselves,
> of threatening ourselves with death;
> perhaps the earth could teach us;
> everything would seem dead
> and then be alive.[238]

Awareness is our most fundamental reality. Yet much of the time we are only dimly present to our experience. We often lack continuity of intention and purpose. Our attention is habitually reductive – so much so that we often inhabit only a narrow band of our potential awareness. Like the smug frog in his well who believes he spans the full range of the universe, we believe we reach across the entirety of ourselves – when in fact we live in just a tiny corner. Our awareness is also fragmented and brittle: easily scattered, lacking depth, and prone to distraction. Like a restless butterfly flitting from flower to flower, always looking for the next fix, the mind constantly flies off – into fantasies of the future, into regrets about the past. Rarely is our attention simply here. We imagine that satisfaction lies elsewhere, and so flee the present moment in search of it. In mindfulness (*sati*), instead of evading the present we turn towards it – even begin to savour it.

The tendency to flee the present is not merely a private failing – it is culturally reinforced. In many ways, the modern world seems designed to keep the mind dispersed and restless. Social media and digital technologies constantly pull at our already fragile attention, even when we begin with more constructive intentions. A familiar scene might unfold like this: we sit down to read a book. After half a page, we need the toilet. As we return, the phone rings. A friend wants to know if we've seen their latest Facebook post. We haven't – so we check. Then we check other posts. Then email. We remember a friend we meant to write to. We feel thirsty, so we make tea. And only then do we recall... we were supposed to be reading that book.

A traditional Buddhist image likens the mind to an elephant in rut, maddened by its urgent desires.[239] Sometimes it feels that way – our mind out of control, dragging us along behind it. Mindfulness helps us to recapture our agency, to tether the elephant. Little by little, we expand our capacity for self-direction. Rather than being helpless victims of our mental states, we can cultivate clarity about what is happening and how our decisions construct our experience. This enables us to intervene skilfully, shifting our mental state – and then our actions – in a more creative direction. Without awareness, we cannot even see what is happening – let alone recognize the patterns of reactivity that keep us stuck.

Given how saturated contemporary well-being and self-help discourse is with the language of 'mindfulness', it's easy to forget that mindfulness is, above all, a core element of Buddhist practice. Sangharakshita extols it as 'the defining quality of all Buddhist practice'.[240] He goes on to say that 'Mindfulness harmonizes and unifies every aspect of Buddhist practice into a concentrated, responsive awareness.'[241] In light of this integrative role, within the context of the five spiritual faculties, mindfulness (*sati*) functions as the *regulating* faculty – helping to balance the others and bring them into harmony. While often associated with meditation, mindfulness is a quality of awareness that we can cultivate in every moment. At a basic level, it enables us to be fully present, right now. As Bachelard observed, 'Any awareness is an increment to consciousness, an added light, a reinforcement of psychic coherence [...] there is a growth of being in every instance of awareness.'[242] That, in essence, is mindfulness.

Traditionally, mindfulness is articulated in terms of four foundations (*satipatthana*): mindfulness of the body and its movements, of sensations, of thoughts, and of Dharma principles (such as the four noble truths).[243] In this chapter, however, we will explore a broader model that characterizes mindfulness in terms of four *dimensions*: mindfulness of self, of others, of the environment, and of reality.[244] These dimensions offer a more complete vision of what mindfulness can become – reaching beyond personal calm and self-awareness towards an ethically engaged attention, responsive to others, and sensitive to the environment. Ultimately, mindfulness is a vivid engagement with the nature of reality. As Simone Weil wrote, 'Absolutely unmixed attention is prayer.'[245] She also remarked that 'Attention only reaches its true dimensions when it is religious.'[246] Taken together, her reflections reveal why, in its full scope, mindfulness cannot be reduced to a merely secular mode of awareness.

1. Mindfulness of Self

Mindfulness of self means bringing more of ourselves into view – coming to know ourselves in our breadth and depth, our light and shade. It includes awareness of the body, of sensations and emotions, and of thoughts. The development of mindfulness highlights a crucial contrast between two modes of awareness: *alienated awareness*, which calls for healing, and *integrated awareness*, which is wholesome and to be cultivated.

In alienated awareness, we may be aware of our thoughts or emotions without experiencing them. In its extreme form, it becomes an awareness of *non-experience* – a disturbing sense of being present yet hollow, monitoring our lives as if from the outside. For some, especially those who mistake mindfulness for a kind of stoic detachment, this alienated state is even conflated with spiritual progress. In reality, it produces a deep disconnection from oneself and others – leaving us isolated and emotionally absent, floating above rather than grounded within ourselves.

By contrast, integrated awareness is an embodied, affective connection to experience. It allows us to fully inhabit our emotional and bodily states – even difficult ones – while remaining attentive and receptive. Because we are truly present, experience is able to unfold and resolve in its own time. Mindfulness implies intimacy, not surveillance.

Three modes of experience

To clarify this crucial distinction, let's explore how awareness plays out in daily life through three modes of experience:

experience without awareness, awareness without experience, and experience with awareness.

Experience without awareness

Experience without awareness is perhaps our most habitual state. We feel pleasure, anger, longing, fear – but without fully understanding what is happening. We are swept along, lost in the intensity of experience. Think of moments of rage: later we may say, 'I lost myself.' Or moments of anxiety, where we feel paralyzed without knowing why. In such states, we are not present to ourselves. We are submerged in emotion but without conscious recognition and so unable to alter course. Experience has us; we don't have it.

Awareness without experience (alienated awareness)

Here, we perceive our experience as though it were happening at arm's length – as if it belonged to someone else. We may speak of anger, sadness, or even love, but these emotions feel distant, as if being played on a screen. This kind of awareness feels cold, sterile. It may arise from a habit of self-censoring, reinforced by social expectations or even trauma. In Buddhist practice, it can be mistaken for genuine non-attachment and equanimity.

People often approach meditation and Buddhist teachings looking for a fix to their problems. They want to find inner peace or to experience love. But their excessive focus on the goal can lead to a kind of spiritual bypassing, whereby they ignore, and even repress, feelings that don't correspond to their spiritualized image of themselves. Wanting to feel that they are advancing – evolving – they push away anything that complicates the picture. Unwelcome emotions like jealousy, loneliness, and dejection are blocked from awareness in order to sustain the illusion of ascent. Instead of acknowledging and integrating complex emotions, they attempt to leapfrog them – perhaps even unconsciously.

Becoming more aware means awakening to the full range of ourselves. This includes joy, peace, and other positive emotions, but, crucially, it also means recognizing inconvenient, even ugly, emotions like anger, craving, and even hatred. As Rilke puts it: 'Let everything happen to you: beauty and terror. Just keep going. No feeling is final.'[247]

Developing mindfulness of our sensations and thoughts – our interior landscape – can feel like turning over a large stone and uncovering a nest of ants. Everything seemed fine while we remained oblivious to what lay beneath. With mindfulness, we begin to recognize what is happening in the mind moment by moment: the constant chatter, self-criticism, negativity towards others, circling thoughts, and obsessing about nothing in particular. At times it can feel like a horror show. Yet this interior melee goes on regardless of whether we notice it, shaping our emotions, decisions, and actions. Remaining unaware may feel neater, more convenient, but, without awareness, we cannot change. Without awareness, we have no real agency and so remain at the mercy of the habitual mind, trapped in the patterns of the past.

Experience with awareness (integrated awareness)

In this state, we not only have the emotion, but we know we are having it. Awareness isn't alienated from experience (on the outside looking in) – it saturates the experience, like dye permeating a fabric. We may be angry, but we know we are angry and allow ourselves to feel it fully, without denial or suppression.

This is well illustrated in the *Satipatthana Sutta*:

> [W]hen feeling a pleasant feeling, a bhikkhu understands: 'I feel a pleasant feeling'; when feeling a painful feeling, he understands: 'I feel a painful feeling.' [...] When feeling a worldly pleasant feeling, he understands: 'I feel a worldly pleasant feeling'; when feeling an unworldly pleasant feeling, he understands: 'I feel an unworldly pleasant feeling.'[248]

The Buddha's teaching here affirms a vivid, embodied recognition of our emotional states – not watching them from afar, but knowing them directly. This fusion of awareness and feeling permits transformation.

Similarly, the *Satipatthana Sutta* describes mindfulness as awareness deeply immersed within activity:

> Just as a skilled turner or a turner's apprentice knows, when making a long turn, 'I am making a long turn', or knows, when making a short turn, 'I am making a short turn', so too a bhikkhu [...] abides independent, not clinging to anything in the world.[249]

Both passages affirm that genuine awareness is not distant, clinical, or detached, but intimate, embodied, and integrated – a knowing that arises from being fully immersed within our lives.

Purpose, means, and vigilance

Mindfulness is not just about being in the moment to the exclusion of the past and anticipation of the future; it also includes a sense of purpose – both immediate and existential. We might be acutely aware of the texture of the tiles beneath our feet, yet have forgotten why we were walking in the first place. We've lost touch with our intention.

Mindfulness also includes an awareness of means – using appropriate methods to accomplish a task. Trying to knock a nail into a wall with a slipper won't work. The same principle applies spiritually: if we wish to deepen our meditation, we must also consider the wider conditions of our life. A dispersed, over-busy lifestyle may undermine our efforts, regardless of what happens on the cushion.

Finally, mindfulness of self includes ethical vigilance: the capacity to discriminate between skilful and unskilful mental states. This sensitivity enables us to act appropriately to transform the mind. In this way, mindfulness becomes not just a mirror but a means of transformation. As the *Dhammapada* puts it: 'Mindful among the unmindful, wide awake among the sleeping, the man of good understanding forges ahead like a swift horse outdistancing a feeble hack.'[250]

2. Mindfulness of Others

True awareness of others requires humility, imagination, and the willingness to let go of assumptions. This is not easy, especially when we're caught up in our own concerns or lack self-awareness. Our capacity to empathize and identify with others is in large part an extension of our ability to understand ourselves as sensitive, meaning-discovering beings. If we're alienated from ourselves – unaware of our deeper feelings, lacks, and aspirations – we're unlikely to truly perceive others, certainly not in their depths or possibilities. We inevitably see others through the lens of our own experience – what else could we do?

Empathy is a function of the imagination. By activating our imagination, we may notice that, although others are similar to us in many ways, they often experience things differently. This may help us to recognize that we don't always know what others are thinking and feeling. A certain level of humility is in order, lest we impose upon others the feelings we merely project onto them.

Some years ago, I was on retreat at Chintamani, giving a talk about the nature of reality – the three *lakshana*s. A woman at the back of the shrine room raised her hand. A clarifying question, I imagined. 'So, the reality is that you are angry?' she asked. I was completely thrown. At first, I assumed I had misunderstood her Spanish, so I repeated back what I had heard. 'Yes', she affirmed. 'The reality is that you are angry.' I reviewed my conduct to see what she might have interpreted as anger. I concluded that it was nothing more than my focused manner when speaking about a matter of importance. Perhaps it was also a question of cultural perception. When I later shared this incident with a Spanish friend, she reported the same experience; once, a student interrupted her lecture to suggest she smile more. Hearing this, a Mexican friend added that, since childhood, people have repeatedly asked her why she is so sad. Projections are universal – I wasn't being singled out.

These everyday examples show the pitfalls of assuming we know what others are thinking and feeling, and of imposing that view on them. In a sense, this is a subtle act of violence. But, while I am quick to judge when someone presses their projection upon me, I sometimes fall into the same trap. Not long ago, a man who participates in an online study group I teach became erratic in his attendance. What's more, he didn't communicate why. I began to speculate: *he doesn't care, this is disrespectful, he lacks commitment*. Such was the verdict of my judgemental mind. Eventually, we spoke. He shared that he was struggling with a stressful job, a crisis in his marriage, and depression; his health was also suffering. I immediately saw how insensitive and lacking in empathy my speculative thoughts had been. But I'm not alone. We all create stories about others that bear little relation to the facts. Recognizing such moments enables us to open out into a broader, more compassionate awareness.

This pervasive tendency to project our own narratives onto others is often entangled with how we present ourselves to the world. If we're not careful, we default to a mode of social interaction where we offer only a facade, greeting people with ready-made answers rather than truly engaging with them. We adopt a social mask and merely go through the motions. While this may shield us from hurt, it inevitably blocks deeper connection. And when others approach us, comfortably obscured behind their own masks, how do we respond? Do we collude in the pretence or do we stand in our authenticity – a position that may, at times, be uncomfortable – and respond with sincerity? This choice can transform the very nature of our communication and relationships.

My friends will tell you that I often carry an intense look about me – perhaps this is what the lady mentioned above misread. There was a phase when people would regularly approach me with concern: 'Nagapriya, what's wrong? Why are you so serious?' It happened so often that it became irritating; at times I voiced my exasperation. Here in Mexico, it's customary to smile and then ease into conversation with a little chit-chat. Since that isn't my natural mode, I began to feel somewhat misunderstood.

But other kinds of interactions convinced me that my apparent seriousness was actually an advantage: people in difficult situations approached me in order to share their burdens. The following is just one example: a young woman approached me and asked if we could talk. 'Of course', I replied. We went into the garden. 'I've been in hospital this last week because I slit my wrists in an attempt to kill myself.' Her admission left me in shock. This beautiful, intelligent young woman, who outwardly seemed to have everything going for her, was so unhappy she had taken recourse to such drastic action. We talked for a while, and I believe she felt relieved to have shared her secret pain. She began to do better.

This experience underscored a sobering truth: we never truly know what burdens people are carrying, or when they might desperately need us to witness them. To do that, we must be congruent, receptive, and capable of setting aside our social mask. We need to be able to truly listen – not just wait for the other person to finish speaking so that we can talk about ourselves.

Emmanuel Levinas gave voice to moments like this, when someone pierces our habitual armour. He characterized our encounters with others in terms of a profound *appeal* – a summons that confers upon us a responsibility to respond.[251] From this perspective, others do not appear as mere objects to be categorized or ignored. Instead, they break into our visibility as a radiance so vivid and unforeseen that it interrupts our comfortable self-absorption. We are unsettled, dazzled by a presence that we cannot fully grasp, control, or reject. Such encounters draw us into a new awareness, in which our sense of self arises in response to the other's call. We find ourselves already 'convoked' – singled out and addressed – before any resort to our own initiative.

Being fully attentive means not just listening to others, but recognizing their potential, rather than only their failings. At times we may collude, minimizing the context of our shared ultimate concern. This may stem from awkwardness, embarrassment, or simply having low expectations of others. But it is part of our responsibility to other human beings to relate to them on the basis of their ultimate potential. This is what *metta bhavana* calls on us to do. This is precisely what the Buddha exemplified when he looked upon humanity as a pond of lotuses in various stages of unfolding.[252] He affirmed the enlightened potential of all.

3. Mindfulness of the Environment

Mindfulness of the environment extends beyond our immediate surroundings, encompassing the natural world and our cultural milieu. Integral to mindfulness is an increasing sensitivity not only to the beauty of things but also to ugliness, fostering a refinement of aesthetic awareness.

To be mindful of the environment means to attune to what is around us. It also means understanding how surrounding conditions impact our mental states and even our actions. For instance, a chaotic urban environment might foster anxiety, while a peaceful natural setting can calm the mind. This means being aware of interconnection, recognizing that we don't live in a bubble but are profoundly affected by our circumstances, for better or worse.

This highlights the importance of being selective about the kinds of stimuli we expose ourselves to, as they can disperse our attention, agitate emotions, and even provoke unskilful reactions. This is not to defend being overly delicate or avoidant; we must, of course, be robust in dealing with what life throws our way. But we live in a world saturated with input: news, social media, even the technical complexity of daily transactions. All this stimulus can weigh on us, leading to a sense of mental overload and disconnection. Many of us no longer know what true silence feels like – or what it's like to spend time offline. Making conscious choices about what we let into the mind is central to mindfulness and relates to what is traditionally called *apramada* or 'vigilance'. Shantideva compares the mind to a wound – tender, easily aggravated, and in need of protection. If we protect a physical wound from further harm, why not do the same with the vulnerabilities of the mind?[253] As the *Dhammapada* reminds us: 'A guarded mind brings happiness.'[254] To protect the mind is not to shield it from life, but to give it space to deepen. Like a nest, the mind requires a certain insulation, a certain quietness, to become a cradle of living reverie. The guarded mind is not closed or fearful, but *reverent* – a space of stillness that favours depth. Mindfulness needs a certain shelter and spaciousness – qualities steadily eroded by the overstimulating conditions of modern life.

Extending the same awareness to the natural world means deeply acknowledging the elements – their unique properties and limits. It also entails recognizing our profound impact on the planet, challenging us to become responsible stewards rather than agents of destruction. As someone recently commented, in nature there's no rubbish. I found this humbling – especially when I consider how many materials we produce do not return to the elements but instead pollute the environment.

This aspect of mindfulness means being sensitive to the fact that we live not in a world of inert matter but in one where everything pulses with life. The early scriptures depict the Buddha as deeply attuned to natural forces. At the moment of his Enlightenment, for example, he touches the earth and calls upon the Earth Goddess to bear witness to his Awakening. Later, as he absorbs the significance of his realization, a great rainstorm breaks and a naga king (serpent deity) appears to shelter him from the downpour. These mythic scenes reflect a vision of the Buddha as in profound communion with the living world around him.

When we are in a state of mindfulness, everything seems to slow down and, simultaneously, becomes richer, more vivid. Colours seem brighter, forms more intense, sounds more precise and evocative. When we're more gathered, this permits a more intimate engagement with the environment. We sense our interconnection with the natural world. Awareness itself becomes aesthetically pleasing – feeling the sun on our face, the cool surface of the tiles beneath our feet, the aroma of incense... Instead of being exploitative, awareness becomes contemplative and appreciative. Awareness opens itself entirely to amazement.

Compared with the beauty of the states of superconcentration, and intimations of the transcendental, the world around us can sometimes seem quite ugly. As our consciousness becomes more refined, it's natural to withdraw from crude stimuli and to cultivate a beautiful and ordered world around us. While Buddhism emphasizes renunciation, this doesn't mean that beauty has no place. Contact with beauty can uplift and refine our awareness. Visiting an art gallery, for instance, is one way in which we can stimulate our imagination and so open up a new way of seeing the world. The painter Mark Rothko is renowned for creating highly abstract compositions that consist of bands or stripes of colour, often laid over a monochrome background. There is no narrative, no recognizable form, which initially may hinder a deeper appreciation of the qualities of the works. What are they 'about'? But, with time and repeated viewing, Rothko's paintings exude a contemplative quality, enabling contact with deeper feelings within ourselves. In Buddhist terms, the paintings seem like visual parallels of states of meditation, and invite us into just such a mood. Rothko's works have a liminal, sacred resonance that inspires a sense of awe, of heightened awareness, clarity of purpose, and enriched emotion. His paintings transport us into a new imaginative universe – an infinite dimension of contemplative stillness.

An elevated aesthetic awareness infuses some aspects of Zen, where nature is treasured as a manifestation of reality, revealing the beauty of impermanence (*wabi-sabi*). This appreciation, while tinged with melancholy, nevertheless offers the promise of spiritual insight. Zen art converts everyday items and experiences into icons – windows through which the truths of the Dharma are revealed. Something as seemingly innocuous as a gravel garden reveals a deeper message. It works directly on consciousness, bringing us into greater intimacy with experience. Zen poetry captures this vivid, reflective encounter with reality through nature, as evoked in this subtle haiku by Bashō:

White chrysanthemums
looked at closely
no dust at all.[255]

Through opening ourselves to the sensory world, we begin to appreciate the wonderful, ungraspable, evanescent nature of experience. The cracking cement, the shrub growing out of the drain, even the crumbling wooden bench – all reveal impermanence. Through contact with the natural world, we enter into deeper communion with our interior world.

4. Mindfulness of Reality

What does it mean to be awake to reality? The phrase can sound abstract, as though 'reality' were some hidden layer behind appearances – an esoteric truth waiting to be uncovered. But it's not about revealing a secret. To be mindful of reality is not to access a definitive, metaphysical truth, but to open ourselves to the full implications of our existence – to its constraints and its possibilities. It means to be alive to our ultimate concern, to attend to what calls us towards the beyond rather than to ignore or suppress it. While life often bears the marks of tragedy, it also offers a rare and precious opportunity for Awakening. To be mindful of reality is to recognize that every moment is a threshold into a richer dimension of perception. Rather than running away from ourselves or the world, we open ourselves to the truth of things – even when that truth is uncertain or painful.

In traditional terms, mindfulness of reality includes reflecting on the three *lakshana*s: all conditioned things are impermanent (*anicca*), unsatisfactory (*dukkha*), and lacking a fixed essence (*anatta*). These are not dogmas to be dutifully affirmed, but rather lenses through which we may begin to clarify our perception. They help us see that much of our suffering stems from clinging to what is unstable, vainly hoping it will bring lasting satisfaction.

Through contemplating *shunyata* – often translated as 'emptiness' – we may extend this insight still further. But emptiness doesn't mean that reality is a void or a lack. On the contrary, it suggests that reality is teeming, open, glimmering, and fundamentally relational. To see things as empty is to see them as alive in their contingency and interdependence. Reality teems not with fixed substances, but with ever-shifting patterns of co-arising. As the *Heart Sutra* puts it: 'Form is emptiness; emptiness is form.' Emptiness indicates not absence or nothingness, but rather a mysterious excess that resists any final definition.

Beyond rational analysis, this dimension of mindfulness also blossoms through imagination and reverence. Contemplating emptiness need not lead to detachment – it can awaken a poetic, even devotional sensibility. This is where the symbolic dimension comes in. Through images, sounds, and gestures, we begin to resonate with this deeper register of knowing.

One way this depth of mindfulness is cultivated is through mantra. A mantra is a sonic symbol that doesn't so much name reality as evoke it – inviting us to resonate with a participatory, non-conceptual mode of awareness. Similarly, the vajra – ritual thunderbolt – reminds us that Awakening is not something soft or vague, but brilliant, piercing, unshakeable. Symbolic perception is a kind of contemplative dwelling, a way of *being with* mystery, not trying to fix or solve it.

Mindfulness of reality also means recognizing that our ordinary perception is often distorted. The *viparyasa*s – perceptual distortions – describe how we habitually mistake the impermanent for the permanent, the painful for the pleasurable, the non-self for the self, and the impure or ugly for the pure or beautiful. These errors are not simply cognitive mistakes, but deeply ingrained patterns of perception. Mindfulness of reality, then, involves untangling the knots we have tied ourselves in. It is a kind of deconstruction – a clearing away that allows reality to shine forth in its splendour.

To be mindful of reality is to live in ever-unfolding wonder – an astonished receptivity to what can never be fully captured. In Dōgen's richly evocative words: 'To carry the self forward and illuminate myriad things is delusion. That myriad things come forth and illuminate the self is awakening.'[256] We are striving not to master reality, but to meet it more fully. In the words of Mary Oliver: 'I was a bride married to amazement [...] the bridegroom, taking the world into my arms.'[257] Mindfulness of reality implies a kind of reverent attention: a willingness to be reshaped by what calls to us from beyond our present horizon.

The Halo of the Present

The present moment, as popularly conceived, is sometimes unduly reduced and so risks being isolated, stripped of its context, and thereby deprived of its possible meanings. If we are reading *Les Misérables* and find ourselves transported to the Battle of Waterloo, are we absent from the present moment? Should we suppress our reverie – our creative imagining of this historical episode that we never lived through? Clearly not; to do so would make reading the book pointless. Accepting Hugo's invitation to enter the world of his imagination – Napoleonic France – does not pull us away from the present moment; rather, it reveals that what counts as the present moment should not be restricted to immediate sense perceptions, thoughts, and feelings.

If we're strongly inclined to distraction and alienation, then attending to the body, sensations, and the flow of thoughts can indeed enhance our self-awareness, opening us to spaciousness, and even to wonder. It's certainly beneficial to be attentive: if we're washing dishes, we can be fully aware of that act. But this isn't the only admissible mode of perception. Why prize the present moment more than an ever-renewing past or an anticipated future? While turning towards the past or future sometimes leads us astray from the present, resulting in dispersion – and even alienation – it can just as readily open up new sources of orientation, empathy, and meaning.

Likewise, we can attend to the intimations of one of Pindar's odes, allowing it to carry us into a glorious, imagined world of Greek gods and heroes.

An overly prescriptive notion of being in the present moment risks overvaluing immediate sensory experience while diminishing the creative powers of the spiritual faculties, which open an expanded field of perception and meaning. It may also encourage an idea of the present as a discrete, self-contained point. Yet the present is itself a dynamic construction – something we imagine into being rather than an isolated atomic instant. The present is a breaking open.

The notion of a 'thick present' is central to Edmund Husserl's account of time. He argued that our perceptions don't arise as isolated, snapshot moments, but rather belong to a continuous, lived flow. Husserl proposed that our experience of the 'now' isn't just about what's immediately present (what he called 'primal impression'). Instead, the present moment is always interwoven with two other immediate forms of awareness: primary remembrance (also called 'retention') – an ever-renewing grasp of what has just passed – and 'protention' – a subtle, anticipatory awareness of what is about to come. This means the present is always infused with both an immediate past and an immediate future. Primary remembrance 'bears in itself the heritage of the past',[258] giving temporal depth to the present, while protention shapes our continuous movement towards the future. Thus, even as one immediate impression fades, and is replaced by another, these processes of remembrance and anticipation continuously carry moments forward, constituting the dynamic flow of the present.

To illustrate these subtle, temporal distinctions, Husserl uses the analogy of the sounding of a bell, whose intensity gradually diminishes until it becomes only reverberation. Our immediate awareness of the fading sound of the bell is retention (primary remembrance), while our subtle anticipation of the coming silence is protention. Both of these – this immediate lingering and this immediate leaning forward – are integral dimensions of our direct, flowing experience of the 'now'. Crucially, these immediate forms of awareness are different from our more deliberate acts of recollection or conscious expectation. To consciously *recollect* the bell's sound later is not simply to access its fading reverberation. Instead, a recollected sound is a mental recreation, a distinct experience from the original sensation or its automatic echoes in primary remembrance and protention. Similarly, a conscious expectation (like explicitly waiting for the next song to begin) is different from the pre-reflective pull of protention. Retention is the ongoing awareness of the present as it passes; recollection – memory proper – is the awareness of the past as past, revived and recreated in the present. Thus, the 'now' is never a bare, isolated point, but is always surrounded by a 'temporal halo' – a dynamic continuum of the just-past and the imminent future. The now is embedded in time.

This vision of time, in which the present radiates a 'temporal halo', expands the reach of mindfulness beyond isolated, present-moment awareness. While grounding our attention in bodily sensation and immediate experience is important as a foundation for self-awareness and integration, the deeper purpose of these practices is not simply to contract attention to a static instant. Husserl's model suggests that our experience of the 'now' is always textured by the lingering echo of what has just passed and the subtle anticipation of what is yet to come. In this light, mindfulness becomes not a restriction of perception, but an expansion – a receptive attunement to the unfolding dynamics of experience as a whole.

This recovered understanding of mindfulness allows us to honour the imaginative, ethical, and relational dimensions of awareness – dimensions carried by memory, aspiration, and purpose, through which deeper meanings reveal themselves as life unfolds. Rather than a static point, Husserl characterizes the present as the *new*: 'The now moment is characterized above all as the new. The now that is just sinking into the past is no longer the new but that which the new has pushed aside.'[259] Irrepressible, the now wells up, pushing aside what *had been* now and granting it a new mode of appearance – that of the past. Sangharakshita highlights a striking distinction between the 'horizontally new' and the 'vertically new'. While the horizontally new is simply the novel or unprecedented in time, the vertically new is that which 'has no connection with time but which irrupts into, or manifests within, the temporal process, from another dimension'.[260] Recognizing the vertically new allows us to become aware of moments that interrupt the mundane flow of time and disclose possibilities beyond habitual perception, opening the way for a mindfulness of the transcendent.

Anticipation: The Unending Gift

While future orientation can sometimes pull us away from what is unfolding in the present, anticipation remains a valid mode of consciousness – one that can give rise to inspiration, orientation, and even transformation. This is suggested in Borges' remarkable poem 'The Unending Gift':

> A painter promised us a picture.
>
> Here, in New England, having learned of his death, I felt once again the sadness of recognizing that we are but shapes of a dream. I thought about the man and the picture, both lost.
>
> (Only the gods can make promises, for they are deathless).
>
> I thought about the place, chose in advance, where the canvas will not hang.
>
> Later, I thought: if it were there, wouldn't it in time become one thing more – an object, another of the vanities or habits of the house? Now the picture is limitless, unending, capable of taking any form or color and bound to none.
>
> In some way, it exists. It will live and grow, like music, and will remain with me to the end. Thank you, Jorge Larco.
>
> (Men can make promises, too, for in a promise there is something that does not die.)[261]

In this sublime meditation, Borges shows how the open future becomes a source of richness, meaning, and satisfaction, even – or perhaps especially – when it will never be fulfilled. In fact, it is precisely the fact that the future will not be realized that constitutes its inexhaustible riches. If the narrator had received the picture, their horizon of expectation would have closed down – shrinking to a particular image and the restricted palette of interpretations it would permit. Eventually, it would assimilate into the bland gaze of daily routine. But while the picture remains an imagined future, it offers infinite potential: an open field for reverie that continuously reshapes inner experience. Such possibilities invite a transformative comportment towards the future. The future, then, is not just fantasy but may confer order and direction upon the present.

A similar dynamic appears in the thought of the Protestant theologian Rudolf Bultmann, who defines the future Kingdom of God as:

> a power *which, although it is entirely future, wholly determines the present.* It determines the present because it now compels man to decision; he is determined thereby either in this direction or in that, as chosen or as rejected, in his entire present existence.[262]

Just as Borges' anticipated picture continuously reshapes the narrator's inner world, Bultmann's future Kingdom, though never materialized as a historical event, exerts a powerful, immediate gravity on our existence and decision in the present. As Bachelard puts it, the future is 'a perspective of expectation'.[263] We might say that the Kingdom of God functions as a kind of horizon that orients but is never reached in time precisely because it belongs not to time, but to what lies beyond it. Its existential meaning denotes the ever-present prospect of an end to secular, inauthentic existence and the entrance into an authentic, sacred life.

Since the Kingdom is always in the process of arising, it becomes an *ever-present call*, even a challenge, rather than merely a distant consolation.

For both Borges and Bultmann, the ungraspable future, precisely because it resists consolidation, retains its openness as a perpetually unfolding gift – one that infuses the present with intensity, meaning, and purpose. When we cultivate an open, patient attentiveness, the bedazzling glory of the new can lift us out of routine, offering the possibility of contact with the transcendent.

11

The Past Falls Open Anywhere

> Remembrance advances from small to smallest details, from the smallest to the infinitesimal, while that which it encounters in these microcosms grows ever mightier.[264]

> Only forgetting makes possible the exaltation of memory.[265]

While mindfulness is often characterized as simply 'being in the present moment', it is also bound up with recollection or memory.[266] The meaning of any particular instant isn't merely *given*; it's actively shaped by what we remember and what we anticipate. Far from being a distraction from the present, memory is essential – not only for making sense of our individual lives but also for sustaining human culture. It's also vital to the process of spiritual awakening. Still, it's important to distinguish between skilful and unskilful ways of engaging with the past. Unskilful memory often takes the form of rumination – endlessly replaying past hurts, dwelling on regrets, or projecting unresolved anxieties into the future. In contrast, skilful memory involves deliberate reflection: recalling experiences to draw lessons, cultivate gratitude, celebrate transformation, and inspire compassion.

What would life be like stripped of memory? It's an unsettling thought, yet it shows just how deeply memory underpins our sense of self and our capacity to make sense of the world. Without memory, the coherent threads of our identity would unravel, leaving us marooned in an ever-resetting present, unable to find our bearings under a barrage of unfamiliar impressions. While Buddhism emphasizes that we have no fixed self, it also stresses that there is a degree of stability within experience. Without memory, however, we would have no sense of continuity across time. Each moment would arise in isolation, severed from what came before, then dissolving away with no trace left behind. Life would be merely a succession of isolated moments – fleeting micro-stories that never coalesce into a larger narrative.

Sustained learning would be impossible. Without the capacity to recall and integrate past experiences, we could not adapt, develop new skills, or build upon previous knowledge. We would not be able to build enduring relationships. Human connection accumulates over time – through difficulties overcome, remembered glances, shared joys, and the slow, deliberate building of trust. Without memory, each person would remain unfamiliar to us, no matter how often we met them. We might exchange pleasantries, but the sense of intimacy and loyalty that deepens with time would be impossible. Social life would be fragmentary; each encounter would be new, but not in the enlivening sense of novelty – rather, a disquieting parade of strangers.

Even the choices we make depend on memory. We decide what to do by reviewing past outcomes, recalling what worked, and what didn't. We scrutinize our past mistakes and, having acknowledged their negative impact, use them as motivation to do better in future. Without access to that archive of experience, we would be condemned to repeat our errors, not through perversity or stubbornness but through amnesia.[267]

Emotion, too, draws its depth from memory. Our present joys and sorrows are shaped by recollection – by our capacity to return to what moved us, hurt us, or gave us hope. Without memory, emotion would lose all context. We might still feel, but it would be a surface ripple rather than a deep current.

Even the most mundane tasks rely on memory. Cooking, taking medication, bathing – these actions depend upon continuity, routines, and recall. Without memory, even basic functioning would become difficult. Life would be bewildering, overwhelming in its immediacy and novelty.

It is true that, stripped of memory, we would be free of the burden of past regrets and future anxieties. But equally we would lose the possibility of learning from those regrets and the sense of purpose afforded by anticipation. Memory is not a fixed record of the past; it is the lens through which the present becomes meaningful.

Memory isn't merely a distraction from the present moment but a key source of continuity, meaning, and identity. It enables us to weave together the disparate moments of our existence into a story we can recognize as our own. Without it, we would lose our capacity for enduring relationships, our ability to learn, and our possibility of growth. We might still possess consciousness, but we would hardly be persons in any meaningful sense. Consequently, authentic mindfulness seeks in no way to sever us from memory, nor from our sense of the future, but to engage wisely with both. Through conscious recollection and thoughtful foresight, the present moment gathers depth and colour. New possibilities open before us, allowing us to inhabit a life that is intelligible, purposeful, and guided by ethical sensitivity.

Consider the simple act of mindfully drinking a cup of coffee. While I might focus on the warmth of the mug, the aroma, the bitter taste, and other present-moment sensations, the experience is profoundly enriched by memory. The moment takes on the weight of all the previous mornings I have prepared and drunk coffee: the friend who gifted me the mug, conversations had over similar beverages, even the origins of the beans. These layers of remembrance don't pull me *away* from the moment; rather, they enrich the present with a filigree of detail, of consequence, and of gratitude. In these ways, the 'here and now' ceases to be a mere temporal slice and takes on ever greater majesty.

Black Ice and Rain

In 'Black Ice and Rain', Michael Donaghy offers a poignant and compelling contemplation on memory. The poem depicts how one reminiscence may trigger another in a torrent of associations, even when, on the surface, those memories share no obvious connection. It also illustrates how memories can rekindle complex emotions, like grief and longing, and even cause us to relive trauma. I would love to quote the entire poem but for now will cite just the first few lines.

> Can I come in? I saw you slip away.
> Hors d'oeuvres depress you, don't they? They do me.
> And cocktails, jokes... such dutiful abandon.

Where the faithful observe immovable feasts
– boat races, birthdays, marriages, martyrdoms –
we're summoned to our lonely ceremonies any time:
B minor, the mouldiness of an old encyclopedia,
the tinny sun snapping off the playground swings,
these are, though we can't know this, scheduled
to arrive that minute of the hour, hour of the day,
day of every year. Again, regular as brickwork
comes the time the nurse jots on your chart
before she pulls the sheet across your face. Just so
the past falls open anywhere – even sitting here with
you.[268]

The poem opens, it would seem, at a party of some sort, in a room apart from the main event where a woman – and now the narrator – has sought refuge from the melee. The narrator contrasts 'immovable feasts', such as marriages and funerals, with 'our lonely ceremonies', to which we are summoned not at ordered times but at any moment. If the 'immovable feasts' are to mark important social occasions, then the 'lonely ceremonies' are epiphanic instants. They are often arranged in 'B minor', which the composer and pianist Ernst Pauer describes as 'that very melancholy key [which] tells of a quiet expectation and patient hope'.[269] Such moments are 'lonely' not only because they may be tinged with melancholy and nostalgia, but because they recall our unique, untransferable memories. There follows a series of disconnected flashes, as emotionally charged recollections pop up, unannounced, like surprise guests.

The poem suddenly leaps into an unexpected scene – 'the nurse jots on your chart'. We are transported from the party into a hospital where the narrator accompanies someone gravely ill, until the nurse 'pulls the sheet across your face'. We must assume that the person died. But who is this figure? The poem later reveals that this person is the narrator's abusive mother. In the melange of memories that swirl to the surface throughout the poem are the dark reminiscences of a childhood lived with a violent parent. The narrator concludes, 'the past falls open anywhere' – a structural motif that holds the poem together. Donaghy shows how remembering erupts through the cracks of intention, returning us to painful moments that can feel as vivid now as they were terrifying then. There is also a quality of witnessing in the poem; in particular, the narrator witnesses some of the experiences of his younger self with a certain compassion and evident sadness.

Towards the end of the poem, Donaghy reflects:

each night contains all others,
nested mirror-within-mirror, stretching back from then
to here and now.[270]

Donaghy's startling metaphor of 'mirror-within-mirror' challenges the notion of memory as a process of mechanical retrieval. In an image that evokes the famous tower of Vairochana from the *Gandavyuha Sutra*, each night – each 'mirror' – *contains* all others, suggesting that the present moment is not isolated, but intimately interwoven with the entire tapestry of our past. Memory is not a static playback but a dynamic, associative capacity that weaves scattered moments into coherent meaning. *Now* is saturated with the resonance of all that has come before – not as an encumbrance, but as an essential part of its significance. This creates a seemingly infinite layering, where experience discloses its inexhaustible richness and profound depth. To be truly present is to recognize how the now is shaped by all that has gone before – an interconnected awareness that invites a more imaginative, nuanced, and compassionate response to this moment. While Donaghy's cascade of memories is anything but mindful – almost suffocating – his poem still points to the creative power of memory.

Bearing Witness

One way we can understand mindfulness in its function of remembrance is through 'bearing witness'. This goes far beyond mere recollection; it is a moral imperative – a profound attentiveness to the past that shapes the present in order to safeguard the future. Few have articulated this with greater authority than the Holocaust survivor Elie Wiesel. For Wiesel, remembrance is not a personal indulgence but a sacred responsibility.

In his Nobel Prize acceptance speech, he famously asserted,

> Remembering is a noble and necessary act [...] It is incumbent upon us to remember the good we have received, and the evil we have suffered [...] [T]he rejection of memory becomes a divine curse, one that would doom us to repeat past disasters, past wars.[271]

This underscores memory's dual function: it is essential both for gratitude and for learning from positive experiences but, perhaps even more urgently, it serves as a reminder of the dark excesses of the past, forewarning against their repetition.

Wiesel insisted, 'Without memory, there is no culture. Without memory, there would be no civilization, no society, no future.'[272] He passionately stressed the importance of actively remembering the despicable acts of the Nazis – not to wallow in despair, but to honour those who suffered and to ensure such evil is never normalized or repeated. This active role of remembrance aligns with our earlier exploration of memory as a dynamic capacity – rather than a process of mechanical retrieval – that directly informs our present and future ethical sensitivity.

Wiesel further acknowledged the personal cost of this commitment, suggesting that some Holocaust survivors believed they were spared only to bear witness to the gruesome realities of the camps. Moreover, he expressed a profound anxiety:

> I am afraid that memories suppressed could come back with a fury, which is dangerous to all human beings, not only to those who directly were participants but to people everywhere, to the world, for everyone.[273]

This 'fury' of suppressed or discarded memories manifests not only individually but collectively. When a society fails to confront and commemorate its past traumas and injustices, those unaddressed memories do not vanish. Instead, they may seek other, disguised outlets for expression – perhaps as cycles of prejudice, persistent grievances, or even the normalization of hatred. Bearing witness, in this light, becomes an act of moral vigilance, indispensable for living a truly dignified, meaningful, and ethically informed human existence.

'We Could See Again More Than We Have Seen'

Memory may even become a primary mode of perception – one that reveals aspects of experience not evident at the time. The poet Paul Valéry remarked that 'Memory has frequently been utilized to perceive *for the first time* events so brief that direct perception has been almost nil and useless.'[274] And, as Friedrich Hölderlin wrote:

> What happened before, scarcely sensed,
> Becomes apparent now for the first time.[275]

Memory doesn't simply recall; it also sees and creates. Some experiences are so rich and subtle that their complexity slips through the net of the moment. As Chrétien puts it, memory makes it possible that 'We could see again *more* than we have seen.'[276] Memory thus becomes a second lens through which certain experiences make their first – or fuller – *appearance.*

Thus memory is far more than a mere echo of a lived instant; the remembered moment can supplement – and even surpass – the original perceptual act, both in intensity and in significance. This resonates with Bachelard's insight that reverie, often taking memory as its point of departure, reveals dimensions of reality inaccessible to sensory attention alone. As he puts it, 'The imagination ceaselessly revives and illustrates the memory.'[277] This possibility is central to Proust's spectacular meditation on memory, *In Search of Lost Time*, where a taste – of the famous madeleine – unlocks an entire world of significance and reverie that is deeper than anything accessible directly through sense perception. Proust suggests that true remembering is not merely a superficial return to a past moment, but a profound exploration of its depths, triggered by sensory experiences and leading to a more complete understanding of oneself and one's history. Bachelard underlines the dynamic quality of memory when he affirms that, 'like a forgotten fire, a childhood can always flare up again within us'.[278] Memories are not just passively stored but actively break through towards the present moment of consciousness. He also writes, 'the past is not stable; it does not return to memory either with the same traits or in the same light'.[279] This is because the remembered past is not simply a past of perception, but rather a function of the imagination.[280]

In challenging the conventional view of memory, Louis Lavelle argues that the past is never a 'lost present'.[281] The only present we truly 'lose' is the fleeting, instantaneous moment, which vanishes as quickly as it arrives. In contrast, the past is an enduring 'present experience', one that we are guaranteed to retain. We cannot sever it from our ongoing life as it is perpetually available to us, an inseparable and active dimension of our being in the 'now'.

The past is not a series of closed jars arranged neatly on a shelf, each containing a discrete event salted away for later. A past event can gather momentum over time. It can even function as a kind of *terma* – a hidden treasure text – whose deeper significance is revealed much later. While in the moment we may lack the horizon of understanding to receive its full intensity, with time and distance it may begin to disclose its deeper meaning. This is especially true of repeated rituals. When I participate in the sevenfold puja, or some other ceremony, I am not always emotionally engaged. My mind sometimes drifts into petty worries, reminiscences, or planning. The ritual can feel forced, even mechanical. Yet afterwards its impact begins to reveal itself to me, as if something dormant awakens. Even a ritual performed years before can burst into awareness, suffused with unforeseen colours and shades. Rituals are not experiences that simply recede into oblivion; they rush, unsolicited, towards the present, like forgotten ships storming into port, laden with untold spicy riches.

In writing of revelation, Jean-Luc Marion describes it as 'like a tremendous explosion', affecting all who witness it – from those at its origin to those at its remotest fringes.[282] He stresses how each person, regardless of how much they initially grasp, is tasked with actively making sense of their experience – an unfolding process that is never truly complete. Some experiences are so unexpected, so far beyond our habitual frames of reference, that their meaning can only be discerned retrospectively – and even then, always just in part. They call us back, again and again, soliciting new understanding. Like ritual, memory doesn't so much preserve as reveal. Again and again, it brings into view what we are only just becoming able to understand.

The Ten Recollections

Buddhist tradition harnesses the transformative power of memory in a series of contemplative practices known as the *anusati*s (recollections or remembrances). Sometimes presented as a list of ten, the recollections are more commonly grouped into two complementary sets.[283] The first includes the three jewels – Buddha, Dharma, and Sangha – along with ethics, generosity, and the gods. The second comprises recollection of death, the body, breathing, and peace.

Recollection, or *sati*, in this context means paying close, deliberate, and sustained attention to an object of spiritual significance. This lends the object of interest greater weight, drawing it closer to us – or, indeed, drawing us closer to it. In this way, that object becomes more intimate, familiar, and treasured. As the mystic Novalis wrote, 'Every beloved object is the centre of a Paradise.'[284] In recollecting the three jewels, we deliberately engage both memory and imagination to deepen our orientation towards them – or, in traditional terms, to express and intensify our going for refuge to what we regard as having ultimate value.

Recollection of the Buddha

Recollection of the Buddha takes many forms, from daily moments of reflection to richly imaginative and devotional practices. One of the most common approaches involves recalling the Buddha's enlightened qualities by reciting and reflecting on epithets described in traditional texts. This method is particularly associated with the *Tiratana Vandana*, an early Buddhist chant that evokes the first three *anusati*s: the Buddha, the Dharma, and the Sangha.

In addition to such epithets, another way to recollect the Buddha is through the rich narratives of his life. This might involve studying the early scriptures, which offer glimpses of his spiritual biography, or engaging with later devotional and poetic retellings, such as Ashvaghosa's *Buddhacarita*.[285] These stories enable us not only to imagine the Buddha's life but also to empathize with his struggles and rejoice in his liberation. We can recall, for instance, the four sights that inspired him to go forth in search of the transcendent, his victorious battle with Mara (which is evoked in Chapter 6), and his calling the Earth Goddess to witness his Enlightenment. This helps us to see how our own path recapitulates archetypal themes exemplified in the Buddha's own life, and so take heart that we too can overcome the obstacles that he overcame.

A widely practised form of recollection involves contemplating an image of the Buddha. Whether through statues, paintings, or visualization in meditation, such images serve as focal points for receptivity, devotion, and faith. In gazing upon or inwardly contemplating the Buddha, we open ourselves to the sublime qualities that he embodies – serenity, wisdom, and boundless compassion.

Other practices move into the realm of ritual and devotion, such as *puja* – acts of symbolic offering and veneration – and chanting. Mantra recitation, including the repetition of the Buddha's name or a sacred phrase, helps to concentrate the mind and to resonate with the qualities of the enlightened state. These practices deepen our connection to the Buddha through body, voice, and heart.

Within Pure Land Buddhism, the recollection of the Buddha centres on the cosmic figure of Amitabha. This practice often takes the form of invoking or contemplating Amitabha Buddha with the aspiration to be reborn in his Pure Land. Calling on Amitabha is regarded as especially important at the time of death. If a strong connection is established through lifelong practice, it's believed that Amitabha – accompanied by his retinue of bodhisattvas – will appear to us at the moment of death in order to guide us to the Pure Land, where we will gain complete Enlightenment without fail. This exalted scene is known as *raigo*: 'welcoming descent'.

Some traditions follow more advanced contemplative practices, such as meditating on the Buddha's thirty-two marks of a great man (*mahapurisa-lakkhana*), or the sixteen exquisite visualizations of Amitabha and his Pure Land found in the *Contemplation Sutra*.[286] These intricate exercises involve structured visualization, designed to elevate our perception. Through them, we encounter the Buddha not as a historical person but as a cosmic principle – a symbol of the awakened mind, of the highest potential of our being. Such practices activate what we might call the 'vertical imagination', enabling us to orient ourselves towards what is of transcendent value.

Recollection of the Buddha builds trust in the Blessed One as the supreme exemplar of Enlightenment and as the guide towards that goal. It becomes a profound source of confidence and inspiration, quickening our aspiration to fulfil our own potential for liberation. By focusing on such elevated qualities, our mind is uplifted and purified, which counteracts debilitating mental states like doubt, confusion, and dejection. It also fortifies our commitment to ethical practice, as we aspire to emulate the conduct of the Awakened One. In this way, recollecting the Buddha becomes a means of reorienting our entire being towards the path of Awakening, inspiring us to follow in his footsteps.

The Gift of Forgetting

At first glance, forgetting seems one of the most intimate – and most pernicious – forms of loss. Memories are not stored in any external archive; they live within us, woven into the fabric of our subjectivity. To lose a memory, then, feels like a permanent loss – like the only print of a photograph consumed by fire. In forgetting part of our past, we seem to lose part of ourselves.

Yet what if forgetting were not a loss of self, but a loosening of its grip? We tend to associate memory with our identity, meaning, and continuity – what holds us together over time. But memory can also bind us too tightly to the past; it can hold us captive. Without the possibility of forgetting, Nietzsche warned, the past becomes 'the grave digger of the present'.[287]

Would we truly want to recall *everything*? This haunting possibility is the subject of Borges' short story 'Funes the Memorious'.[288] After falling from a horse, Funes acquires the unlikely capacity to remember every moment in exhaustive detail. His memory becomes infallible. About this Borges comments: 'To think is to forget a difference, to generalize, to abstract. In the overly replete world of Funes there were nothing but details, almost contiguous details.'[289] Funes is overwhelmed by the infinite precision of his memory. Unable to forget anything, he becomes incapable of discerning which details actually matter. Though prodigious, his memory is useless. It cannot serve his deepest concerns, but simply engulfs him. As Chrétien puts it, 'To be unable to forget is to be unable to digest, to be unable to assimilate.'[290]

This invites us to consider: might forgetting *not* be the enemy of memory? Could it be instead that memory must negotiate with forgetting – groping towards the right measure, the proper balance between holding on and letting go? What if forgetting were not a failure, but a gift? As Pindar wrote, 'But with good luck oblivion may come, for a malignant pain perishes in noble joy.'[291]

Beyond the realm of sheer information, forgetting plays a vital role in our moral and relational lives. To forget a moral debt, or a moral hurt, for instance, is not a failure of care but a renunciation of continued resentment. This perspective leads us to the topic of forgiveness, understood as a form of *moral forgetting*. Amnesty (from the Greek *amnestia*, 'forgetfulness' or 'passing over') is an act of grace – a gift, a generous forgetting of offence and of the demand for justice.

According to Hannah Arendt, resentment and revenge bind us to the past, whereas forgiveness cuts us loose.[292] Resentment seeks to get even; forgiveness lets go. Both the offended and the offender participate in a form of absolute forgetting: the infringement is waived, the debt is pardoned. Forgiveness means we are not eternally held captive by the past; its weight is lifted, allowing for a new past and a new future. It breaks the cycle of retaliation and karma – the logic of *samsara*. Forgiveness is not deserved, nor does it impose a new debt. Instead, by forsaking the comforting righteousness of victimhood, it ushers in an economy of grace. It abandons all calculations and expectations of reciprocity, embodying boundless compassion.

When seen not as a failure of attention but as an active, ethical surrender, intentional forgetting reveals a profound creative and spiritual potential. The poet Fernando Pessoa gestures towards this when he writes: 'No one tires of dreaming, because to dream is to forget, and forgetting does not weigh on us; it is a dreamless sleep throughout which we remain awake.'[293] Here forgetting does not oppose remembrance, but enables a vital quality of presence – one that is simultaneously active and receptive. It is a relinquishing – a renunciation – that allows what is unbidden to come forward.

Such forgetting is not a rejection of memory, but a selective loosening of its grip. Intentional forgetting, in this sense, clears a space within experience. It is a giving-way that precedes the new, not by erasing the past, but by releasing us from its settled judgements. The genuinely new does not inevitably surge forth; it arrives only after we have been bedazzled by the unsolicited. What we later name as *unforgettable* often concerns precisely such moments – encounters with what was never hoped for and can never be fully assimilated into memory. Letting go makes new responses possible. This orientation is echoed by Paul in his letter to the Philippians: 'But one thing I do, forgetting those things which are behind and reaching forward to those things which are ahead.'[294] In this light, selective forgetting is not a loss of meaning, but a condition for its renewal.

Alongside conscious acts of renunciation and forgiveness, healthy forgetting plays a crucial role in letting go of the baggage of the past and opening up possibilities for rejuvenation. Imagine remembering every mistake you ever made, every wrong done to you, with unrelenting intensity. Such a state would be not only intolerable but a recipe for persistent guilt and obstinate resentment. We would be stuck in our sense of hurt, not able to get past it. Healthy forgetting allows for genuine resilience, enabling us to move forward without being weighed down by the past. It's a vital – often unconscious – process that supports healing and frees us to engage more fully with the present and future.

We may also forget ourselves in the presence of a work of art, such as a painting or a musical performance. In such moments, we loosen the tight grip of self, surrender control, and give way to what overflows us. We forget our self-referential cares and commend ourselves to the summons of the artwork. This letting go, this momentary renunciation of ego-clinging, enables a deeper receptivity and a more intimate encounter with the world.

Ultimately, these various forms of beneficial forgetting – whether the selective operation of healthy forgetting or the profound forgetting of the self through renunciation – are not erasures but acts of liberation. They clear space to pay full attention to what truly matters. By relinquishing what binds us – be it the tyranny of overwhelming detail, the weight of grievance, or the insistent grip of ego – we open up the possibility of a more profound transformation. We forget and leave behind the habitual self, and embrace instead what is unforgettable. This transformative forgetting is not an enforced loss, but an active and courageous engagement with our possibilities of greater freedom.

The Immemorial and the Unforgettable

While Elie Wiesel emphasized the sacred responsibility to remember and commemorate historical events – not only those we've lived through ourselves, but also the triumphs and, especially, the tragedies of previous generations – many cultures affirm a myth that we have somehow primordially forgotten something vital that needs to be recovered. This recalls e.e. cummings' ironic affirmation that he loves humanity because 'you are perpetually putting the secret of life in your pants and forgetting it's there'.[295]

Yet, in a deeper sense, this 'primary forgetting' is not an event in time that might be recalled. Rather, it's an integral aspect of our existential condition. The 'immemorial', therefore, belongs not to the order of time, but to its rupture, to its transcendence. It isn't recovered from a distant past but bursts in on us; it overwhelms us, continually evading the grasp of ordinary thought and recollection. It pierces the flow of time, interrupts it, and unconditionally offers itself from a realm beyond our habitual self. As Emmanuel Levinas wrote, the immemorial cannot be assimilated to conventional memory and history: it's 'a responsibility that comes from before'.[296] Primarily, Levinas understood this as an ethical responsibility to others, arising prior to any conscious commitment. Our duty to them is not chosen but *antecedent*, he writes, like an order slipped into our consciousness by a thief, smuggled in, 'as though it were formulated before every possible present'.[297]

According to Marion, the immemorial is, strictly speaking, 'unthinkable' because it escapes all finite thought. It cannot be inspected or aimed at. He proposes instead the possibility of 'great thought', which would not grasp for an object but 'know how to let what it thinks come to it, weigh on it, and be exercised over it'.[298]

This understanding of the immemorial invites a radical receptivity, a being-given-to-oneself that supersedes – even precedes – the self-directed will. As Marion suggestively puts it:

> I am each time that, as lover and as gifted, I let the immemorial come over me, as a life *that does not belong to me* and that, for that very reason, inhabits me more intimately than myself.[299]

This highlights how the deepest aspect of our being isn't contrived or remembered in the conventional sense, but instead *received* through a reverent attentiveness to something beyond our habitual awareness.

Conceived as a radical givenness that disrupts and reconstitutes the self – an 'overcoming' of the ego by something transcendent – the immemorial resonates deeply with the notion of Other Power (*tariki*) in Pure Land Buddhism. The liberating grace of Amitabha Buddha is understood not as something that we attain through our own merit or effort, but as something *gifted*, a blessing that overflows the limits of our self-generated striving and conventional identity. It's a compassionate force that interrupts and surpasses our deliberate measures, instigating liberation through profound receptivity rather than self-driven exertion. Other Power represents the ultimate expression of the immemorial, as it's a boundless compassion that is primordially active, prior to our subjectivity, patiently awaiting us to turn towards it. It's an unconditional gift that depends not on recollecting our ethical trajectory, but on our continuous openness to its infinite grace.

This experience of something both utterly familiar and entirely beyond the scope of historical memory is vividly captured in Sangharakshita's account of his initial, transformative encounter with Buddhist teachings:

> To me the *Diamond Sutra* was not new. I had known it and believed it and realized it ages before and the reading of the *Sutra* as it were awoke me to the existence of something I had forgotten. Once I realized that I was a Buddhist it seemed that I had always been one, that it was the most natural thing in the world to be, and that I had never been anything else.[300]

Reflecting on memory also invites the question: are there things that cannot be forgotten? Not in the sense that they are perfectly preserved in memory, and so always available to awareness, but in the sense of something that 'does not lend itself to forgetting'.[301]

The 'unforgettable' is not a matter of any nostalgic relationship with the past; instead, it concerns our present, our future, and our ultimate ends. It impinges upon us not as something we dredge up from the deep wells of memory, but as something that is persistently and urgently present for us, that overruns us, that claims us. What else would we try to forget, if not the unforgettable itself? Yet the unforgettable can be neither truly lost nor entirely abandoned. Even when we flee from its call or resist its claim upon us, it persists as a promise that 'shines from the brilliance of the future'.[302] Because the unforgettable incessantly exceeds the capacity of our memory, it calls for a fidelity that is always new. Paradoxically, it is only through forgetting, in Dōgen's sense of 'forgetting the self' – that is, through letting go of ego-clinging – that the unforgettable can make an appearance. As Chrétien emphasizes:

> The unforgettable is a light [...] whose excessive radiance makes the light of our candles disappear and be lost, but without this being a matter of wiping out traces, imprints, or residue.[303]

This radiance does not merely shine; it envelops our attention. For Chrétien, the unforgettable is 'not what we perpetually grasp and what cannot withdraw from memory, but *what does not cease to grasp us* and from which we cannot withdraw'.[304] This recalls Shinran's affirmation that we are 'grasped never to be abandoned' by Other Power, by the Buddha's compassionate gift. To lose touch with the unforgettable is not merely to forget, but to be cut off from what ultimately matters. Fidelity to this gift consists not in possession but in receptivity – a readiness to receive ever more and to move towards what it promises. This requires a forgetfulness that frees us from stubborn habit, clearing the way to respond to the unforgettable by renouncing all that stands in its path.

And all that matters
Is of the moment of late, fine morning
When the world's yellow is of burning sands
Leading down to the penultimate blue
Of, say, the Ionian Sea whose waves
Gave light that had to have been of their own
And which, when darkened momently by the
Cool shadows of our gaze, plucked up the deep
Hues of our gleaming feet at the bottom
Of our golden bodies in their purest
And most revealing element at last.[305]

12

What Shimmers Ungraspably Through Everything

> If you turn downwards, worms and maggots and everything that crawls, all sentient beings, each and every one emits great shining light, each and every one towers like a wall miles high.[306]

The Spiritual Senses

The metaphor of 'spiritual senses' or faculties is not found only in the Pali canon, nor is it confined to Buddhism. It is a widely used figure to evoke an extended range of perception, especially a sensitivity to the sacred dimension of human experience. In Christianity, for instance, the patristic scholar Origen speaks of a 'divine sense', which 'only the man who is blessed finds on this earth'.[307] The function of the spiritual sense, or senses, is to discern and savour the presence of this sacred dimension. Writing of his own relation with the transcendent, St Augustine also draws on the metaphor of interior, subtle senses:

> There my soul receives a radiance that no space can grasp; there something resounds which no time can take away; there something gives a fragrance which no wind can dissipate; there something is savoured which no satiety can make bitter; there something is embraced which can occasion no *ennui*.[308]

This passage underlines how, in speaking of what is transcendent, and how we might intuit it, we are compelled to fall back on language drawn from familiar, sensory experience. In Augustine, and other Christian writers, the spiritual senses are modelled directly on the analogy of the physical senses, and may even overlap with them. Such merging of the ordinary and spiritual senses is especially vivid in the Eastern Orthodox notion of the Taboric Light: an 'uncreated light' through which the Divine becomes manifest, and which spiritualizes or transfigures whoever is blessed to perceive it. This capacity is not the achievement of the calculating self but a gift of grace, allowing access, in the words of St Gregory Palamas, to the 'superluminous splendour of the beauty of the Archetype'.[309] He elaborates on this mystical condition:

> He who participates in the divine energy, himself becomes, to some extent, light; he is united to the light, and by that light he sees in full awareness all that remains hidden to those who have not this grace; thus, he transcends not only the bodily senses, but also all that can be known by the intellect.[310]

Palamas speaks of a 'light beyond light'. He argues that true apprehension of the sacred dimension involves a direct, intuitive perception that transcends not just the physical eyes but even the powers of the intellect. He likens those who rely upon reasoning alone to blind people who can feel the warmth of the sun, but refuse to believe that the sun is also radiant.[311] This powerful analogy underscores how a genuine encounter with the transcendent calls upon spiritual senses that reach beyond the scope of the ordinary mind.

The five spiritual faculties draw upon the metaphor of the physical senses only in a broad or suggestive sense; they do not map directly onto them but constitute distinct organs of contemplative perception that enable a more profound and subtle apprehension of what bears ultimate value. They do not negate or erase the physical sense faculties; instead, they both suffuse and expand upon them, allowing for the perception of truths and realities that the raw, physical senses alone cannot intuit. The spiritual faculties enable not merely a greater quantity or range of perception but, rather, a greater *quality* and *depth*; most especially, they enable us to receive and absorb intuitions of transcendent value.

But what, then, does it truly mean to perceive something, particularly when we speak of truths that transcend the ordinary? With Gustav Siewerth, we might affirm that 'Openness is the essence of the senses.'[312] But to take something into ourselves is not to consume it, nor to reduce it to our ready-made categories. Instead, it means 'to empty oneself out more deeply to the stream of light of the real'.[313] Perception is neither acquisitive nor accumulative, like squirrels burying nuts away for later: it is inherently *transformative*. To perceive means to surrender to the new, to be changed, remade under the force of its revelation.

Are the Five Spiritual Faculties Comprehensive?

The five spiritual faculties amount to a kind of *phenomenology of awakened perception*. Far from being an anodyne list of virtues, they evoke the structure and texture of how awakened perception manifests. They aren't really separate faculties at all, but rather combine to form a complete, integrated mode of spiritual apprehension.

But why these five qualities and not others? After all, the Buddhist tradition contains a wealth of lists elaborating a profuse array of spiritual virtues – the eleven positive mental events, the seven factors of Awakening (*bodhyangas*), or the six perfections (*paramitas*). Several important qualities found in these other lists are not explicitly included among the five faculties: patience and fearlessness, for instance. Likewise, highly skilful attitudes like *metta*, joy, and equanimity don't figure here. Still, many of these can be meaningfully related to one or more of the spiritual faculties. Fearlessness, for instance, was touched upon in considering *virya*.

Perhaps the most striking omission is an explicit treatment of ethics. The development of a tender conscience – one that draws back from unskilfulness as if recoiling from a red-hot coal – is central to the emergence of more subtle, awakened consciousness. However, while not directly named, ethics is clearly implied. *Virya*, for example, is defined as energy directed towards the good, and is traditionally articulated in terms of the four right efforts: to prevent the arising of unskilful states, to abandon those already arisen, to cultivate skilful states, and to maintain them once developed. In this light, *virya* becomes almost synonymous with ethical cultivation.

There is also a strong link between *samadhi* and ethics: one definition of meditation is the uninterrupted development of skilful mental states – and skilful mental states naturally incline towards skilful action. Finally, *sati*, especially in the mode of *apramada* (vigilance), also bears an ethical dimension. This ethical dimension of mindfulness is affirmed in the *Bodhicharyavatara*, which vividly portrays the dangers of neglecting vigilance, as well as the benefits of cultivating it:

> Rutting elephants roaming wild do not cause as much devastation in this world as the roaming elephant, the mind, let free [...] But if the roaming elephant, the mind, is tethered on every side by the cord of mindfulness, every danger subsides, complete prosperity ensues.[314]

Golden Splendour Hovering All About

The sacred is not above or apart from this world but reveals itself whenever our senses are awake to it, since, as Wallace Stevens writes,

> What is divinity if it can come
> Only in silent shadows and in dreams?[315]

The shining of the sacred through all things can be approached through the symbolism of gold.

Before his final Awakening, the Buddha Amitabha made a series of forty-eight cosmic vows, which would be fulfilled only if he reached the ultimate goal. His third vow reads as follows:

> May I not attain unsurpassed, perfect Awakening if, when I have attained Awakening, any of the living beings who are born in my buddha-field are not of a single colour, the colour of gold.[316]

At first glance, the idea of all beings having golden bodies may seem a rather strange prospect – perhaps even a little kitsch. I'm instantly transported to Las Ramblas in Barcelona, where street performers daub themselves gold and pose, frozen like statues, until someone offers up a coin and they spring to life. Here too, in Mexico, a fire juggler, gilded from tip to toe, plies his improbable trade at an anonymous intersection. But gold is not just decorative or lucrative – it carries deep, symbolic resonance. It adorns icons, Buddha images, and all manner of ritual objects. Gold is the colour of reverence. In their gold-drenched bodies, even street performers echo something primordial and sacred: the longing to embody radiance.

In eastern temples, it is customary for devotees to apply sheets of gold leaf to Buddha statues as an act of devotion, and to accumulate spiritual merit. Over time, these images become sheathed in golden skin. Gold leaf is gossamer thin, about thirty times thinner than human hair. It is like sunlight that has taken material form. Within Buddhism, gold signifies purity and ultimately Awakening itself. Gold is brilliant, incorruptible, and precious. Gold is immune to rust, and so symbolizes what is indestructible, eternal, and sacred. In ancient Egypt, gold signified the flesh of the gods. The pharaohs adorned both themselves and their palaces with gold. They were even buried with gold. Throughout history, gold has evoked abundance, health, beauty, royalty, and ultimately the holy.

According to Indian mythology, gold ennobles all it touches. To have a golden body therefore signifies spiritual elevation and purity, a purity that is both radiant and incorruptible. In this, we can discern a symbolic and sacred anatomy at work, whereby physical characteristics attest to a sacred identity. Gold has a shining, shimmering quality that evokes what is holy, what is numinous. By means of colour, gold calls forth the sacred dimension.

This symbolic power of gold has also captivated philosophers. Heidegger, for example, was particularly drawn to the mythic and poetic resonance of gold in Pindar's *Isthmian Ode* 5:

> Mother of the Sun, Theia of many names
>
> Because of you men value gold [*chryson*] as mighty above all other things.[317]

Heidegger proposes that gold is not simply 'mighty' in comparison with all other things but reveals something *more present*, even more real. For him, gold highlights the unique radiance or *gleam* (*Glanz*, *glänzen*) that allows each particular being, as well as the entirety of all being, to shine forth, to reveal what it is. For Heidegger, Pindar's ode 'thinks Being in the name of gold'.[318]

Heidegger writes:

> Gold is thus in no way named only as one gleaming thing among others [...] Rather, gold is named because, thought in Greek terms, the essence of Being consists in *shining*, so that this being that we call 'gold' is in a certain way the Being of beings.[319]

In this sense, we can say that gold symbolizes, and even reveals, the nature of reality. Gold, says Heidegger, 'is the gleam of the true'.[320] Gold is the colour of the holy; it symbolizes the capacity of human awareness to relate to everything in the light of its deepest dimensions and significance, a capacity that opens to the shining forth of truth itself.

This radiance is not abstract – it shimmers in the world around us. Heidegger turns to Hölderlin's late poem *Autumn* (*Der Herbst II*), which evokes a golden presence suffusing the world as summer yields to autumn:

> Nature's gleaming [*Glänzen*] is higher revealing,
> Where with many joys the day draws to an end,
> It is the year that completes itself in resplendence
> [*Pracht*],
> Where fruit come together with beaming radiance
> [*Glanz*].
>
> Earth's orb is thus adorned, and rarely clamours
> Sound through the open field, the sun warms
> The day of autumn mildly, the fields lie
> As a great wide view, the breezes blow
>
> Through boughs and branches, rustling gladly,
> When then already to emptiness the fields give way.
> The whole meaning of this bright image lives
> As an image, golden splendour hovering all about
> [*das goldne Pracht umschwebet*].[321]

The noun *Glänzen* (normally a verb) may be translated as 'shining', 'gleaming', 'glistening', 'sparkling', and even 'brilliance'. It suggests that nature reveals something beyond itself: the transcendent, the holy that shimmers all around. Hölderlin also uses the noun *Pracht*, which means 'splendour' or 'glory'. He gestures towards a hierophanic sensibility that discerns the holy as revealed in the midst of nature. Heidegger highlights how this splendour is *golden* and comments:

> 'Golden' names the *highest and richest gleaming*, the most luminous and most pure shining. The golden gleaming hovers about the whole, forms its wholeness, and is the completing [...] it brings forth in the first place the orb of the wholeness of the whole that hovers about everything, just as a shining wreath 'wreathes' everything that appears.[322]

Gold evokes the overflow, the excess of presence. According to Heidegger, 'The gleaming of nature is not a state but a *happening*.'[323]

The theme of sacred, symbolic anatomy also runs through Dōgen's poetic intimations of the transcendent. He regularly speaks of Enlightenment as attaining 'the sixteen-foot golden body'.[324] This powerful image evokes not only the imposing stature of a giant buddha, but also a symbolic expansion beyond our current dimensions – an alchemical transmutation of the whole body into gold, the most radiant and precious of substances. In realizing this spectacular form, we become luminous agents in the Enlightenment of the entire cosmos.

In the imagery of Shin Buddhism, the arising of *shinjin* – deep entrusting – is likened to base materials being transmuted into gold. Shinran writes that 'we, who are like bits of tile and pebbles, are turned into gold'.[325] To be turned into gold is to be spiritualized, raised up, to be united with the mind of the Buddha, to become intimate with Amida's heart-mind, and a channel for the revelation of Awakening. Amida is usually depicted as having a golden body, as are the bodhisattvas of his Pure Land. This underlines both their exalted nature and their intimacy with the deepest aspect of reality. Gold is not only the colour of their skin – it is the glow of Awakening made visible. Gold is used liberally in the imagery relating to the geography of the Pure Land itself.

A little further ahead in the sutra, the beings of the Pure Land are described in the following way:

> They are all of one form, without any differences, but are called 'heavenly beings' and 'humans' simply by analogy with states of existence in other worlds. They are of noble and majestic countenance, unequaled in all the worlds, and their appearance is superb, unmatched by any being, heavenly or human. They are all endowed with bodies of naturalness, emptiness, and infinity.[326]

To be 'golden' is not only to be radiant, but to participate in a different order of reality altogether: beyond decay, beyond separation, beyond duality. Gold, then, is not ornamentation but transcendent radiance, the sheen of reality, which gleams with a beauty of elsewhere. It is the glitter of the sacred, the overflow of Awakening. The golden splendour that hovers all about is nothing less than the shining forth of the true, which gives itself in effortless blessing – perhaps even at an anonymous intersection. It shimmers ungraspably through all things.[327]

In awakening the five spiritual faculties, we incline ourselves to continual amazement before the unfolding mystery of our existence. Reality assumes the character of revelation – always already present, yet always new. Revelation disconcerts our expectations and surpasses our ready schemes of interpretation. What is revealed is disproportionate and incommensurable, expanding the horizon beyond any settled measure. Thus it never ceases to bedazzle us, confound us, and so enlarge us.

Notes and References

Preface

1 *The Complete Works of Sangharakshita*, 27 vols, Windhorse Publications, 2016–24, vol.17, p.60.
2 Friedrich Schleiermacher, *On Religion: Speeches to Its Cultured Despisers*, K. Paul, Trench, Trübner & Co., Ltd, 1893, p.33.
3 Mary Oliver, in *Devotions: The Selected Poems of Mary Oliver*, Little, Brown, 2017, p.85.

Epigraph

4 From Mary Oliver, 'Sometimes', in *Devotions*, p.105.

Chapter 1

5 *Samyutta Nikaya* 48:18, in *The Connected Discourses of the Buddha: A New Translation of the Samyutta Nikaya*, trans. Bhikkhu Bodhi, Wisdom Publications, 2000, pp.1675–6.
6 For a study of Shinran (1173–1263) see Nagapriya, *The Promise of a Sacred World: Shinran's Teaching of Other Power*, Windhorse Publications, 2022.
7 *The Collected Works of Shinran*, trans. Hongwanji International Center Translation Committee, vol.1, Jodo Shinshu Hongwanji-ha, 1997, p.429.
8 The *Larger Pure Land Sutra* (T360). See Ratnaguna and Shraddhapa, *Great Faith Great Wisdom: Practice and Awakening in the Pure Land Sutras of Mahayana Buddhism*, Windhorse Publications, 2016, p.294. Amitabha (Infinite Light) is also known as Amitayus (Infinite Life) and in Japanese Pure Land Buddhism as Amida (Infinite).

9 Throughout this book, I give the relevant Sanskrit, Pali, or Japanese term in italics.
10 *Samyutta Nikaya* 12:65.
11 *Complete Works of Sangharakshita*, vol.11, pp.53–71.
12 See Julian Pas, *Visions of Sukhavati: Shan-tao's Commentary on the Kuan Wu-Liang-Shou-Fo-Ling*, SUNY Press, 1995, pp.147–9. See also *Collected Works of Shinran*, pp.89–91.
13 John D. Caputo, *The Weakness of God: A Theology of the Event*, Indiana University Press, 2006, pp.109–10.
14 The science here is disputed. While some propose that a dog's sense of smell is even more powerful than suggested here, others have counterargued that we underestimate human olfactory capacities. See John P. McGann, 'Poor human olfaction is a 19th-century myth', *Science* 356:6338 (12 May 2017), doi: 10.1126/science.aam7263. The differences may also vary according to specific odours.
15 See, for instance, Jackie Higgins, *Sentient: What Animals Reveal about Our Senses*, Picador, 2021.
16 *The Blue Cliff Record*, trans. Thomas Cleary and J.C. Cleary, Shambhala, 2005, p.73.
17 R.M.L. Gethin, *The Buddhist Path to Awakening*, Oneworld Publications, 2001, pp.105–6.
18 The equivalent terms in Pali are: *saddha*, *panna*, *viriya*, *samadhi*, and *sati*. In what follows, I will use English terms to refer to the five spiritual faculties. Various English translations are used interchangeably to designate the faculty in question.
19 *Samyutta Nikaya* 48:10, in Bhikkhu Bodhi, *The Connected Discourses of the Buddha*, pp.1671–3.
20 *Complete Works of Sangharakshita*, vol.1, p.279.
21 *Complete Works of Sangharakshita*, vol.1, p.393.
22 *Complete Works of Sangharakshita*, vol.13, p.329.
23 *Complete Works of Sangharakshita*, vol.11, p.478.
24 The full list comprises seven categories: the four foundations of mindfulness (*satipatthana*), the four right efforts, the four bases of spiritual power, the five spiritual faculties, the five powers, the seven factors of Awakening (*bodhyanga*s), and the noble eightfold path. See Gethin, *The Buddhist Path to Awakening*.

25 *Samyutta Nikaya* 48:51.
26 *Samyutta Nikaya* 48:52.
27 Bhadantacariya Buddhaghosa, *The Path of Purification* (*Visuddhimagga*), trans. Bhikkhu Ñāṇamoli, 3rd ed., Buddhist Publication Society, 1991, p.125.
28 Buddhaghosa, *The Path of Purification*, p.125.
29 Buddhaghosa, *The Path of Purification*, p.125.
30 *Complete Works of Sangharakshita*, vol.12, p.284.
31 See Thomas Aquinas, *Summa Theologica*, first part of the second part, question 62.
32 See also Subhuti and Sangharakshita, *Seven Papers*, 2nd ed., Triratna InHouse Publications, undated, pp.52–3.

Chapter 2

33 From the poem 'A path in the woods' by Anna Kamieńska (1920–86), in *Astonishments: Selected Poems of Anna Kamieńska*, trans. Graźyna Drabik and David Curzon, Paraclete Press, 2008, p.xix.
34 Jean-Louis Chrétien, *The Call and the Response*, Fordham University Press, New York, 2004, p.10 (emphasis added).
35 Chrétien, *The Call and the Response*, p.15.
36 Subhuti, *Mind in Harmony: The Psychology of Buddhist Ethics*, Windhorse Publications, 2015, p.111.
37 Elsewhere, Sangharakshita writes: 'Faith is the emotional counterpart of reason. What you understand with your intelligence you must feel also with your emotions. The two go together, and cannot be separated.' *Complete Works of Sangharakshita*, vol.6, p.424.
38 Subhuti, *Mind in Harmony*, p.112.
39 *Complete Works of Sangharakshita*, vol.3, p.263.
40 Paul Tillich, *Dynamics of Faith*, Harper Torchbook, 1958, p.4.
41 *Complete Works of Sangharakshita*, vol.6, p.506.
42 See Jean-Luc Marion, *The Rigor of Things*, Fordham University Press, 2017, p.111.
43 From the poem 'Ariadne's thread' by Maria Pawlikowska-Jasnorzewska (1891–1945), available at https://polskapoeta.

wordpress.com/2023/07/30/brief-encounters-14/, accessed on 24 January 2026.

44 *Puja: The Triratna Book of Buddhist Devotional Texts*, Windhorse Publications, 2008, p.27.

45 Byung-Chul Han, *The Disappearance of Rituals*, Polity Press, 2020, p.8.

46 *Complete Works of Sangharakshita*, vol.11, p.49.

47 Buddhaghosa, *Visuddhimagga*, p.479.

48 *Samyutta Nikaya* 22:84, in Bhikkhu Bodhi, *The Connected Discourses of the Buddha*, p.929.

49 Tillich, *Dynamics of Faith*, p.22.

50 *Majjhima Nikaya* 47.

51 *The Middle Length Discourses of the Buddha: A Translation of the Majjhima Nikaya*, trans. Bhikkhu Ñāṇamoli and Bhikkhu Bodhi, Wisdom Publications, 1995, p.418.

52 *Mumonkan* 1.

53 Bertrand Russell, *The Problems of Philosophy*, Oxford University Press, 1912, chapter XV, pp.242–4.

54 *Notes on Once Calling and Many Calling*, in *Collected Works of Shinran*, p.480 (emphasis added).

55 *Collected Works of Shinran*, p.93.

56 Tillich, *Dynamics of Faith*, p.105.

57 *Collected Works of Shinran*, p.79.

58 John Caputo, 'Spectral hermeneutics: on the weakness of God and the theology of the event', in John Caputo and Gianni Vattimo, *After the Death of God*, ed. Jeffrey W. Robbins, Columbia University Press, 2007, pp.47–85 and 180–90 (p.183, n.4).

59 Jean-Luc Marion, 'The event, the phenomenon, and the revealed', *Danish Yearbook of Philosophy* 40 (2005), pp.57–78 (60).

60 Jean-Luc Marion, 'They recognized him; and he became invisible to them', *Modern Theology* 18:2 (April 2002), pp.145–52 (150).

61 This is a phrase borrowed from Hélène Cixous in her *Reading with Clarice Lispector, Theory and History of Literature*, vol.73, University of Minnesota Press, 1990, p.126.

62 *Collected Works of Shinran*, p.72.

Chapter 3

63 From Mary Oliver, 'The fourth sign of the zodiac,' in *Blue Horses*, Penguin, 2014, p.63.
64 *Self-Portrait Dedicated to Paul Gauguin*, 1888.
65 See *Complete Works of Sangharakshita*, vol.13, pp.71–87.
66 *Notes on Once Calling and Many Calling*, in *Collected Works of Shinran*, p.481 (emphasis added).
67 *Passages on the Pure Land Way*, in *Collected Works of Shinran*, p.304.
68 *Passages on the Pure Land Way*, in *Collected Works of Shinran*, p.305.
69 Wendell Berry, 'A native hill', *The Hudson Review* 21:4 (winter 1968–9), pp.601–34.
70 Ted Hughes, *Collected Poems*, ed. Paul Keegan, Faber and Faber, 2005, p.182.
71 Mary Oliver, 'The summer day', in *Devotions*, p.316.
72 Rainer Maria Rilke, *Letters on Cézanne*, Fromm International Publishing Corporation, 1985, p.50.
73 *Bashō: The Complete Haiku*, trans. Jane Reichhold, Kodansha USA Publishing, 2008, p.132.
74 Rilke, *Letters on Cézanne*, p.43.
75 Jean-Luc Marion, *The Crossing of the Visible*, Stanford University Press, 2004, p.57.
76 Marion, *The Crossing of the Visible*, p.62 (emphasis added).
77 Marion, *The Crossing of the Visible*, p.75.
78 Vow 21. See Ratnaguna and Shraddhapa, *Great Faith Great Wisdom*, p.260.
79 *Garava Sutta*, in *Samyutta Nikaya* 6:2.
80 From 'Some reflections on the *Garava Sutta*', in *Complete Works of Sangharakshita*, vol.26, p.628.
81 'Some reflections on the *Garava Sutta*', in *Complete Works of Sangharakshita*, vol.26, p.630.
82 Sangharakshita, *Through Which Reality Shines: A Commentary on D.T. Suzuki's Outlines of Mahayana Buddhism*, Windhorse Publications, 2025, pp.81–2.
83 *The Lotus Sutra*, chapter 23. The bodhisattva supposedly went on to become the Medicine Buddha.

84 Henry Corbin, 'Theophanies and mirrors: idols or icons?', trans. Jane Pratt and A.K. Donohue, *Spring: An Annual of Archetypal Psychology and Jungian Thought* (1983), pp.1–2 (2).

Chapter 4

85 *Anguttara Nikaya* 10:121.
86 Buddhaghosa, *Visuddhimagga*, p.125.
87 Anaïs Nin, *Seduction of the Minotaur*, Swallow Press, 1961, p.124.
88 *Majjhima Nikaya* 117.
89 See Sangharakshita, *The Ten Pillars of Buddhism*, in *Complete Works of Sangharakshita*, vol.2. See also Subhadramati, *Not About Being Good: A Practical Guide to Buddhist Ethics*, Windhorse Publications, 2013.
90 *Anguttara Nikaya* 3:61.
91 *Majjhima Nikaya* 9.
92 *The Debate of King Milinda: An Abridgement of the Milinda Panha*, ed. Bhikkhu Pesala, Motilal Banarsidass, 1991, p.3.
93 *Samyutta Nikaya* 41:3.
94 *Majjhima Nikaya* 2.
95 *Majjhima Nikaya* 72, in Bhikkhu Ñāṇamoli and Bhikkhu Bodhi, *The Middle Length Discourses of the Buddha*, p.591.
96 *Majjhima Nikaya* 72, in Bhikkhu Ñāṇamoli and Bhikkhu Bodhi, *The Middle Length Discourses of the Buddha*, p.591.
97 *Majjhima Nikaya* 63, in Bhikkhu Ñāṇamoli and Bhikkhu Bodhi, *The Middle Length Discourses of the Buddha*, p.536.
98 *Majjihima Nikaya*, in Bhikkhu Ñāṇamoli and Bhikkhu Bodhi, *The Middle Length Discourses of the Buddha*, p.592.
99 *Majjhima Nikaya* 22.
100 *Digha Nikaya* 23.
101 *Samyutta Nikaya* 56:11.
102 During writing, Frutos Prohibidos closed down. Happily, it turned out that this was only for refurbishment and so chilaquiles are back on my Roma breakfast menu.
103 *Samyutta Nikaya* 36:6.
104 See Nagapriya, *Seeing Like a Buddha: The Four Noble Truths*, Triratna Inhouse Publications, 2020, pp.98–168.

105 See, for instance, *Majjhima Nikaya* 117.
106 *Majjhima Nikaya* 56.
107 Bhikkhu Ñāṇamoli and Bhikkhu Bodhi, *The Middle Length Discourses of the Buddha*, p.485.

Chapter 5

108 *The Perfection of Wisdom in Eight Thousand Lines and Its Verse Summary*, trans. Edward Conze, Sri Satguru Publications, 1994, p.135.
109 *Complete Works of Sangharakshita*, vol.1, p.183.
110 Cited in Baldwin Wong, 'Careful, patient, and modest citizens: facilitating civic education through Zhu Xi's method of deep reading', *Educational Philosophy and Theory* 57:4 (2025), pp.374–84 (376).
111 Wong, 'Careful, patient, and modest citizens', p.377.
112 Wong, 'Careful, patient, and modest citizens', p.377 (emphasis added).
113 Wong, 'Careful, patient, and modest citizens', p.377.
114 Han, *The Disappearance of Rituals*, p.7.
115 Han, *The Disappearance of Rituals*, p.8.
116 Hans-Georg Gadamer, *Truth and Method*, trans. Joel Weinsheimer, Crossroad, 1975, p.269.
117 Killer Mike, *R.A.P. Music* [studio album], Williams Street, 2012.
118 Gadamer, *Truth and Method*, p.310.
119 Robert H. Sharf, 'The rhetoric of experience and the study of religion', *Journal of Consciousness Studies* 7:11–12 (1998), pp.267–87 (271).
120 *Complete Works of Sangharakshita*, vol.11, p.79.
121 *Complete Works of Sangharakshita*, vol.3, p.227.
122 *Shobogenzo: The True Dharma-Eye Treasury*, trans. Gudu Wafu, 4 vols, BDK America, 2007–2008, vol.1, pp.5–6.
123 Chrétien, *The Call and the Response*, p.10.
124 *Pythian* 8. The odes were originally sung, accompanied by dance. This particular ode was commissioned to celebrate the victory of a wrestler at the Pythian Games of 446 BCE.

Christopher Childers, *The Penguin Book of Greek and Latin Lyric Verse*, Penguin Classics, 2024, unpaginated e-book.

125 *Udana* 1:10.

126 Maurice Merleau-Ponty, *Phenomenology of Perception*, Routledge, 2012, p.95.

127 Jean-Luc Marion, *In Excess: Studies in Saturated Phenomena*, Fordham University Press, 2002, p.113; as cited (and modified) in Christina M. Gschwandtner, *Degrees of Givenness: On Saturation in Jean-Luc Marion*, Indiana University Press, 2014, p.7 (original emphasis).

128 Marion, *In Excess*, p.72.

129 Marion, *In Excess*, p.72.

130 A portion of the text in this chapter, 'Seeing things as they really are', appeared in *Tricycle* magazine in May 2024.

Chapter 6

131 *Dhammapada*, verse 327, in *Complete Works of Sangharakshita*, vol.15, p.45.

132 *Complete Works of Sangharakshita*, vol.22, pp.363–4.

133 For an account of the noble eightfold path see Nagapriya, *Seeing Like a Buddha*.

134 *Anguttara Nikaya* 6:55.

135 Gampopa, *Jewel Ornament of Liberation*, trans. Herbert V. Guenther, Shambhala Publications, 1971, p.182.

136 *Majjhima Nikaya* 4.

137 This narrative is actually found in the *Nidana-Katha*, which introduces the commentary on the *Jataka*s, and probably influenced the narrative structure of the *Mahavastu*. See *Buddhist Birth-Stories, the Commentarial Introduction Entitled Nidana-Katha: The Story of the Lineage*, trans. T.W. Rhys-Davids, George Routledge and Sons, 1925, p.194.

138 *Sutta Nipata* 3:2, available at https://suttacentral.net/snp3.2/en/sujato, accessed on 27 January 2026.

139 *Dhammapada*, verse 40, in *Complete Works of Sangharakshita*, vol.15, p.13.

140 *Anguttara Nikaya* 5:57.

141 *Complete Works of Sangharakshita*, vol.1, p.332.
142 *Complete Works of Sangharakshita*, vol.1, p.347.
143 *Complete Works of Sangharakshita*, vol.15, p.552.
144 Simone Weil, *Waiting for God*, Harper and Row, 1973, pp.194–5.
145 Michael Taussig, 'What colour is the sacred?', *Critical Inquiry* 33:1 (autumn 2006), pp.28–51 (31).
146 Denise Levertov, 'The avowal', in *Selected Poems*, New Directions, 2003, unpaginated e-book.
147 *The Bodhicaryavatara*, trans. Kate Crosby and Andrew Skilton, Oxford University Press, 1995, chapter 7, verse 3, p.67.
148 Shantideva, *Bodhicaryavatara*, chapter 7, verse 71, p.73.
149 Gampopa, *Jewel Ornament*, p.183.
150 Sangharakshita, *Complete Works of Sangharakshita*, vol.17, p.675.
151 Gampopa, *Jewel Ornament*, p.183.
152 From *Discourses of Rumi*, Discourse 4, available at https://www.rumi.org.uk/discourses/, accessed on 27 January 2026.
153 Byung-Chul Han, *Vita Contemplativa*, Polity Press, 2024, pp.1–2.
154 Han, *Vita Contemplativa*, p.11.
155 *Complete Works of Sangharakshita*, vol.17, p.676.
156 Shantideva, *Bodhicaryavatara*, chapter 7, verse 65, p.73.

Chapter 7

157 *Complete Works of Sangharakshita*, vol.2, p.93.
158 Gaston Bachelard, *Earth and Reveries of Will: An Essay on the Imagination of Matter*, Dallas Institute of Humanities and Culture, 2002, p.2.
159 Simone Weil, *Gravity and Grace*, Routledge Classics, 2002, p.33.
160 Gaston Bachelard, *Water and Dreams: An Essay on the Imagination of Matter*, Dallas Institute Publications, 2021, p.47.
161 Bachelard, *Water and Dreams*, p.31 (original emphasis).
162 Museo Sorolla, Madrid.
163 Museo Sorolla, Madrid.
164 From Rosario Castellanos, 'Lamentación de Dido'. See *El amor, el sueño y la muerte en la poesía mexicana*, ed. Jaime Labastida, Siglo XXI Editores, 2015, pp.203–7. This poem is a dramatic monologue inspired by Canto IV of Virgil's *Aeneid*.
165 Cited in Bachelard, *Water and Dreams*, p.31.

166 See https://books.openedition.org/pus/33203?lang=en, accessed on 28 January 2026.
167 Gaston Bachelard, *The Flame of a Candle*, Dallas Institute Publications, 1988, p.41.
168 Gaston Bachelard, *The Psychoanalysis of Fire*, Routledge & Kegan Paul, 1964.
169 See Gerard Manley Hopkins, 'The windhover', available at https://www.poetryfoundation.org/poems/44402/the-windhover, accessed on 27 January 2026.
170 Christina Rossetti, 'Who has seen the wind?', available at https://www.poetryfoundation.org/poems/43197/who-has-seen-the-wind, accessed on 27 January 2026.
171 Gaston Bachelard, *Air and Dreams: An Essay on the Imagination of Movement*, Dallas Institute Publications, 2011.
172 Lama Anagarika Govinda, *Psycho-Cosmic Symbolism of the Buddhist Stupa*, Dharma Press, 1976, p.97.
173 Robert Thurman, *The Holy Teaching of Vimalakirti: A Mahayana Scripture*, Pennsylvania State University Press, 1987.
174 Translated from the poem 'Eingang' by Dana Gioia in *99 Poems: New and Selected*, Graywolf Press, 2001. See also Rainer Maria Rilke, *The Book of Images*, trans. Edward Snow, North Point Press, 1994.

Chapter 8

175 *Complete Works of Sangharakshita*, vol.26, p.47.
176 Tenzin Wangyal, *Healing with Form, Energy and Light: The Five Elements in Tibetan Shamanism, Tantra and Dzogchen*, Snow Lion Publications, 2002.
177 See *Majjhima Nikaya* 22.
178 This model is based loosely on the five chief paths.
179 *Udana* 4:1.
180 *Complete Works of Sangharakshita*, vol.11, p.150.
181 These similes are found in many places in the Pali canon, for instance in *Majjhima Nikaya* 39. See Bhikkhu Ñāṇamoli and Bhikkhu Bodhi, *The Middle Length Discourses of the Buddha*, pp.367–9.

182 Aquinas, *Summa Theologica*, first part, question 38, article 2, conclusion.
183 Jean-Luc Marion, *Being Given: Towards a Phenomenology of Givenness*, Stanford University Press, 2002, p.212. See also the discussion of the 'event' in Chapter 2, above.
184 Marion, *Being Given*, p.217.
185 *Complete Works of Sangharakshita*, vol.3, pp.134–6 and 348–50.
186 *Complete Works of Sangharakshita*, vol.4, p.241.
187 *Complete Works of Sangharakshita*, vol.4, p.265.
188 Dōgen, *Shobogenzo*, vol.1, pp.10–11.
189 'Enlightenment as experience and non-experience', in *Complete Works of Sangharakshita*, vol.11, p.85.
190 *Complete Works of Sangharakshita*, vol.11, p.85.
191 Walter Benjamin, *Illuminations*, Schocken Books, 2007, p.91.

Chapter 9

192 Bachelard, *Water and Dreams*, p.16 (original emphasis).
193 *Complete Works of Sangharakshita*, vol.11, pp.724–5.
194 Coleridge, for instance, writes of the 'esemplastic power of the imagination', 'esemplastic' meaning 'shaping into One'. Samuel Coleridge, *Biographia Literaria*, ed. Adam Roberts, Edinburgh University Press, 2014, p.205.
195 *Vinaya Pitaka* 1:6. See *The Book of the Discipline, part 4*, trans. I.B. Horner, Pali Text Society, 1996, p.9.
196 *Complete Works of Sangharakshita*, vol.26, p.266.
197 *Complete Works of Sangharakshita*, vol.26, p.302.
198 *Complete Works of Sangharakshita*, vol.26, p.306.
199 *Complete Works+ of Sangharakshita*, vol.26, p.271.
200 *Complete Works of Sangharakshita*, vol.26, p.271.
201 *Complete Works of Sangharakshita*, vol.26, p.271.
202 John Fowles, *The Magus*, rev. ed., Jonathan Cape, 1977, chapter 44, unpaginated e-book.
203 Fowles, *The Magus*, chapter 44, unpaginated e-book.
204 Sangharakshita and Subhuti, 'Reimagining the Buddha', in *Seven Papers*, pp.88–9.
205 Bachelard, *Air and Dreams*, p.1 (original emphasis).

206 Gaston Bachelard, *Earth and Reveries of Repose: An Essay on Images of Interiority*, Dallas Institute Publications, 2011, p.12.
207 Gaston Bachelard, *The Poetics of Reverie: Childhood, Language, and the Cosmos*, Beacon Press, 1971, p.8.
208 Bachelard, *Water and Dreams*, p.7.
209 Bachelard, *Poetics of Reverie*, p.23.
210 Bachelard, *Poetics of Reverie*, p.15.
211 Bachelard, *Poetics of Reverie*, p.36.
212 Bachelard, *Poetics of Reverie*, p.173.
213 Bachelard, *Earth and Reveries of Will*, p.3.
214 This summary is mainly based on Henry Corbin, *Spiritual Body and Celestial Earth: From Mazdean Iran to Shi'ite Iran*, Princeton University Press, 1977.
215 See *Complete Works of Sangharakshita*, vol.2, pp.41–3.
216 *Complete Works of Sangharakshita*, vol.11, p.725.
217 Shantideva, *Bodhicharyavatara*, chapter 8, verses 90–6, p.96.
218 Shantideva, *Bodhicharyavatara*, chapter 8, verse 94, p.96.
219 Shantideva, *Bodhicharyavatara*, chapter 8, verses 94–6, p.96.
220 Shantideva, *Bodhicharyavatara*, chapter 8, verse 107, p.97.
221 Shantideva, *Bodhicharyavatara*, chapter 8, verses 120–65, pp.99–103.
222 Shantideva, *Bodhicharyavatara*, chapter 8, verses 140–54, pp.100–2.
223 Shantideva, *Bodhicharyavatara*, chapter 8, verses 135–6, p.100.
224 *The Pratyutpanna Samadhi Sutra and the Surangama Samadhi Sutra*, trans. Paul Harrison and John McRae, Numata Center for Buddhist Translation and Research, 1998, p.21.
225 Harrison and McRae, *The Pratyutpanna Samadhi Sutra and the Surangama Samadhi Sutra*, p.25.
226 Harrison and McRae, *The Pratyutpanna Samadhi Sutra and the Surangama Samadhi Sutra*, p.26.
227 Harrison and McRae, *The Pratyutpanna Samadhi Sutra and the Surangama Samadhi Sutra*, p.40.
228 Harrison and McRae, *The Pratyutpanna Samadhi Sutra and the Surangama Samadhi Sutra*, p.41.

229 See Etienne Lamotte, *Suramgamasamadhisutra, The Concentration of Heroic Progress: An Early Mahayana Buddhist Scripture*, trans. Sara Boin-Webb, Curzon Press, 1998.
230 See, for instance, *The Vimalakirti Sutra*, trans. Burton Watson, Columbia University Press, 1997.
231 Jean-Luc Marion, 'What we see and what appears', in *Idol Anxiety*, ed. Josh Ellenbogen and Aaron Tugendhaft, Stanford University Press, 2011, pp.152–68 (163).
232 Lamotte, *Suramgamasamadhisutra*, p.116.
233 Bachelard, *Poetics of Reverie*, p.5.
234 See Lamotte, *Suramgamasamadhisutra*, p.150.
235 Rilke, *Letters on Cézanne*, p.3.
236 Lamotte, *Suramgamasamadhisutra*, p.192.
237 Lamotte, *Suramgamasamadhisutra*, p.193.

Chapter 10

238 Pablo Neruda, 'Keeping still', trans. Dan Bellm, *Literary Imagination* 8:3 (autumn 2006), p.512.
239 Shantideva, *Bodhicharyavatara*, chapter 5, verse 40, p.37.
240 *Complete Works of Sangharakshita*, vol.15, p.81.
241 *Complete Works of Sangharakshita*, vol.15, p.83.
242 Bachelard, *Poetics of Reverie*, p.5.
243 The classic source is the *Satipatthana Sutta, Majjhima Nikaya* 10.
244 This is a slight modification of a model created by my teacher Sangharakshita: mindfulness of things, of self, of people, and of reality. See *Complete Works of Sangharakshita*, vol.1, p.570–8.
245 Weil, *Gravity and Grace*, p.117.
246 Weil, *Gravity and Grace*, p.132.
247 Rainer Maria Rilke, 'Go to the limits of your longing', in *Rilke's Book of Hours: Love Poems to God*, Riverhead, 2005, trans. Anita Barrows and Joanna Macy, book I, p.59.
248 Bhikkhu Ñāṇamoli and Bhikkhu Bodhi, *The Middle Length Discourses of the Buddha*, p.149.
249 Bhikkhu Ñāṇamoli and Bhikkhu Bodhi, *The Middle Length Discourses of the Buddha*, p.146.

250 *Dhammapada*, verse 29, in *Complete Works of Sangharakshita*, vol.15, p.12.
251 Emmanuel Levinas, *Entre Nous: Thinking-of-the-Other*, A&C Black, 2006, pp.145–6.
252 *Vinaya Pitaka* 1:6. See Horner, *The Book of the Discipline*, p.9.
253 Shantideva, *Bodhicharyavatara*, chapter 5, verses 19–20, p.35.
254 *Dhammapada*, verse 36, in *Complete Works of Sangharakshita*, vol.15, p.13.
255 *Bashō: The Complete Haiku*, p.231.
256 *Treasury of the True Dharma Eye: Zen Master Dōgen's Shobo Genzo*, ed. Kazuaki Tanahashi, Wisdom Publications, 2012, p.29.
257 From Mary Oliver, 'When death comes', in *Devotions*, p.285.
258 Edmund Husserl, *The Phenomenology of Internal Time-Consciousness*, Indiana University Press, 1964, p.51.
259 Edmund Husserl, *On the Phenomenology of the Consciousness of Internal Time*, trans. John Barnett Brough, Kluwer Academic Publishers, 1991, p.65.
260 *Complete Works of Sangharakshita*, vol.13, p.428.
261 Jorge Luis Borges, *In Praise of Darkness*, trans. Norman Thomas di Giovanni, Dutton, 1974, p.31.
262 Rudolf Bultmann, *Jesus and the Word*, available at https://www.religion-online.org/book-chapter/chapter-2-the-teaching-of-jesus-the-coming-of-the-kingdom-of-god/, accessed on 28 January 2026 (original emphasis).
263 Gaston Bachelard, *The Intuition of the Instant*, Northwestern University Press, 2013, p.28.

Chapter 11

264 Walter Benjamin, *Reflections: Essays, Aphorisms, Autobiographical Writings*, Schocken Books, 1986, p.6.
265 Jean-Louis Chrétien, *The Unforgettable and the Unhoped For*, Fordham University Press, 2002, p.58.
266 See Anālayo, *Satipatthana: The Direct Path to Realization*, Windhorse Publications, 2003, p.47.
267 This theme is explored in Charles Dickens' story 'The haunted man'. Sangharakshita comments on the moral implications of memory in *Complete Works of Sangharakshita*, vol.15, pp.85–7.

He points out that, without memory, we 'disintegrate as moral beings' (p.86).

268 From Michael Donaghy, *Conjure*, Picador, 2000, p.6.

269 See https://interlude.hk/feel-key-b-minor/, accessed on 28 January 2026.

270 Donaghy, *Conjure*, p.9.

271 From his Nobel Lecture, delivered on 11 December 1986, available at https://www.nobelprize.org/prizes/peace/1986/wiesel/lecture/, accessed on 28 January 2026.

272 Elie Wiesel, 'A god who remembers', available at https://www.npr.org/2008/04/07/89357808/a-god-who-remembers, accessed on 28 January 2026.

273 Wiesel, 'A god who remembers'.

274 Cited in Chrétien, *The Unforgettable and the Unhoped For*, p.45 (emphasis added).

275 Friedrich Hölderlin, 'As on a holiday', trans. James Mitchell, available at https://holderlinpoems.com/poems/as_on_a_holiday1.html, accessed on 28 January 2026.

276 Chrétien, *The Unforgettable and the Unhoped For*, p.45 (emphasis added).

277 Bachelard, *Poetics of Reverie*, p.20.

278 Bachelard, *Poetics of Reverie*, p.104.

279 Bachelard, *Poetics of Reverie*, p.104.

280 Bachelard, *Poetics of Reverie*, p.105.

281 Cited in Chrétien, *The Unforgettable and the Unhoped For*, p.62.

282 Jean-Luc Marion, 'The hermeneutics of revelation', in Richard Kearney, *Debates in Continental Philosophy*, Fordham University Press, 2004, pp.15–32 (18).

283 Buddhaghosa, *Visuddhimagga*, pp.185–290.

284 Novalis, *Philosophical Writings*, State University of New York, 1997, p.31.

285 See Ashvaghosa, *Life of the Buddha*, trans. Patrick Olivelle, New York University Press and the JJC Foundation, 2008.

286 Ratnaguna and Sraddhapa, *Great Faith Great Wisdom*, pp.301–32.

287 Friedrich Wilhelm Nietzsche, *Unfashionable Observations*, vol.2, Stanford University Press, p.89.

288 Jorge Luis Borges, *Ficciones*, Grove Press, 1962, pp.107–15.
289 Borges, *Ficciones*, p.115.
290 Chrétien, *The Unforgettable and the Unhoped For*, p.60.
291 *Olympian* 2, in Frank Nisetich, *Pindar's Victory Songs*, Johns Hopkins University Press, 1980, p.88.
292 Hannah Arendt, *The Human Condition*, University of Chicago Press, 1958, pp.238–42.
293 Fernando Pessoa, *The Book of Disquiet*, Serpent's Tail, 2011, fragment 244.
294 Philippians 3:13.
295 e.e. cummings, 'Humanity I love you', in *100 Selected Poems*, Grove Atlantic, 2014, p.18.
296 Emmanuel Levinas, *Otherwise than Being or Beyond Essence*, Duquesne University Press, Pittsburgh, 1998, p.97.
297 Levinas, *Otherwise than Being or Beyond Essence*, p.13.
298 Jean-Luc Marion, *In the Self's Place: The Approach of Saint Augustine*, Stanford University Press, 2012, unpaginated e-book.
299 Marion, *In the Self's Place*, unpaginated e-book (emphasis added).
300 *Complete Works of Sangharakshita*, vol.20, p.85.
301 Chrétien, *The Unforgettable and the Unhoped For*, p.78.
302 Chrétien, *The Unforgettable and the Unhoped For*, p.86.
303 Chrétien, *The Unforgettable and the Unhoped For*, p.81.
304 Chrétien, *The Unforgettable and the Unhoped For*, p.90 (emphasis added).
305 John Hollander, 'Yellow', in *Spectral Emanations: Selected Poetry*, Knopf, 1997, unpaginated e-book.

Chapter 12

306 *The Blue Cliff Record*, p.66.
307 Mark J. McInroy, 'Origen of Alexandria', in *The Spiritual Senses Perceiving God in Western Christianity*, ed. Paul L. Gavrilyuk and Sarah Coakley, Cambridge University Press, 2012, pp.20–35 (23).

308 St Augustine, *Confessions*, trans. Henry Chadwick, Oxford University Press, 1991, p.183.
309 Gregory Palamas, *The Triads*, Paulist Press, 1983, p.106.
310 Cited in Vladimir Lossky, *The Mystical Theology of the Eastern Church*, Lutterworth Press, 1991, p.224.
311 Alexandros Chouliaris, *The Anthropology of St Gregory Palamas: The Image of God, the Spiritual Senses, and the Human Body*, Brepols, 2020, p.141.
312 Cited in Hans Urs von Balthasar, *The Glory of the Lord: A Theological Aesthetics*, vol.1: *Seeing the Form*, Ignatius Press, 2009, p.396.
313 Balthasar, *The Glory of the Lord*, p.396.
314 Shantideva, *Bodhicharyavatara*, chapter 5, verses 2–3, p.34.
315 From Wallace Stevens, 'Sunday morning', in *The Collected Poems of Wallace Stevens*, Knopf, 1971, p.67.
316 Ratnaguna and Shraddhapa, *Great Faith Great Wisdom*, p.257.
317 *Pindar II*, trans. William H. Race, Loeb Classical Library, Harvard University Press, 1997, pp.174–5.
318 Cited in Richard Capobianco, 'Heidegger on Heraclitus: kosmos/world as Being itself', *Epoché* 20:2 (spring 2016), pp.465–76 (467).
319 Cited in *Heidegger and the Holy*, ed. Richard Capobianco, Roman & Littlefield, 2022, p.68 (emphasis added).
320 Capobianco, *Heidegger and the Holy*, p.75.
321 As translated in Richard Capobianco, *Heidegger's Way of Being*, University of Toronto Press, 2014, pp.28–9.
322 Cited in Capobianco, *Heidegger's Way of Being*, p.35 (emphasis added).
323 Capobianco, *Heidegger's Way of Being*, p.32 (emphasis added).
324 In his key essay 'Being-time' (*uji*), Dōgen writes: 'you enlighten the entire world with the sixteen-foot golden body [...] To fully actualize the golden body – to arouse the way-seeking mind, practice, attain enlightenment, and enter nirvana – is nothing but being, is nothing but time.' *The Moon in a Dewdrop: Writings of Zen Master Dōgen*, ed. Kazuaki Tanahashi, North Point Press, 1985, p.79.

325 *Notes on Essentials of Faith Alone*, in *Collected Works of Shinran*, pp.459–60.
326 *The Three Pure Land Sutras*, trans. Hisao Inagaki, Numata Center for Buddhist Translation and Research, 2003, p.28.
327 Adapted from Heidegger: 'Κόσμος [as φύσις] *Phýsis* shimmers ungraspably through everything.' Cited in Capobianco, *Heidegger's Way of Being*, p.65.

Index

Introductory Note

References such as '178–9' indicate (not necessarily continuous) discussion of a topic across a range of pages. Wherever possible in the case of topics with many references, these have either been divided into sub-topics or only the most significant discussions are listed. Because the entire work is about 'amazement' and the 'five spiritual faculties', the use of these terms (and certain others which occur constantly throughout the book) as an entry point has been minimised. Information will be found under the corresponding detailed topics.

WINDHORSE PUBLICATIONS

Windhorse Publications is a Buddhist charitable company based in the UK. Our books, which are distributed internationally, champion Buddhism, meditation, and mindfulness. They offer fresh interpretations of Buddhist teachings and their application to contemporary life, with subject matter and authors from across the Buddhist tradition, catering for a broad range of interest and experience. In addition to publishing titles exploring classic texts for modern audiences, we aspire to publish books that offer a Buddhist perspective on today's challenges, including social inequality, the environment and climate, gender, mental health, and more. Established in the 1970s to publish the writing of Urgyen Sangharakshita (1925–2018), the founder of the Triratna Buddhist Order, Windhorse Publications continues to be dedicated to preserving and keeping in print his impressive and influential body of work, making it accessible for future generations. As well as high-quality print and e-books, Windhorse Publications produces accompanying audio, podcast, video, and teaching resources.

Windhorse Publications
38 Newmarket Road
Cambridge CB5 8DT
info@windhorsepublications.com

For information on distribution and trade orders visit:
www.windhorsepublications.com/trade-resources/

THE TRIRATNA BUDDHIST COMMUNITY

Windhorse Publications is a part of the Triratna Buddhist Community, an international movement with centres in Europe, India, North and South America, and Australasia. At these centres, members of the Triratna Buddhist Order offer classes in meditation and Buddhism. Activities of the Triratna Community also include retreat centres, residential spiritual communities, ethical Right Livelihood businesses, and the Karuna Trust, a UK fundraising charity that supports social welfare projects in the slums and villages of India.

Through these and other activities, Triratna is developing a unique approach to Buddhism, not simply as a philosophy and a set of techniques, but as a creatively directed way of life for all people living in the conditions of the modern world.

If you would like more information about Triratna please visit thebuddhistcentre.com or write to:

London Buddhist Centre
51 Roman Road
London E2 0HU
UK
contact@lbc.org.uk

Aryaloka
14 Heartwood Circle
Newmarket NH 03857
USA
info@aryaloka.org

Sydney Buddhist Centre
24 Enmore Road
Sydney NSW 2042
Australia
info@sydneybuddhistcentre.org.au

www.ingramcontent.com/pod-product-compliance
Lightning Source LLC
La Vergne TN
LVHW011028160826
845780LV00026B/201
9781915342690